UNCLOS

Solutions for Managing the Maritime Global Commons

UNCLOS

Solutions for Managing the Maritime Global Commons

Edited by

Alok Bansal
Deeksha Goel
Siddharth Singh

INDIA FOUNDATION

PENTAGON PRESS LLP

UNCLOS: Solutions for Managing the Maritime Global Commons
Edited by Alok Bansal, Deeksha Goel, Siddharth Singh

First Published in 2021

ISBN 978-93-90095-22-3

Published by
PENTAGON PRESS LLP
206, Peacock Lane, Shahpur Jat
New Delhi-110049
Phones: 011-64706243, 26491568
Telefax: 011-26490600
email: rajan@pentagonpress.in
website: www.pentagonpress.in

Printed at Aegean Offset Printers, Greater Noida, U.P.

Contents

Foreword

Ram Madhav

Global commons are always a challenge to manage due to competing interests and Cold War style group politics. These challenges are increasingly becoming acute in areas like the great oceans and the cyberspace. The Cold War era competition in the outer space had led to fictitious concepts like the star-wars. Those were supposed to be real wars fought with hi-tech weaponry. Luckily, the outer space is a domain only a few countries could explore so far and hence remained less confrontational.

However, the most significant commons are the oceans around us. Almost every country in the world has stakes in the oceanic waters that surround our land mass. Oceans are the lifelines for many countries. Many countries owe their development and prosperity to the oceans around them. Generally speaking, countries with long coastlines have always prospered more through their oceanic trade and global engagement compared to countries that are landlocked. If you look at the list of the world's most prosperous group of nations—the Organisation for Economic Cooperation and Development (OECD) member states—majority of them are coastal states. They drafted their development stories through conquering sea lanes and international trade. While the former Union of Soviet Socialist Republic (USSR) had given access to several Eastern European nations to the Indo-Pacific through Vladivostok in the past, the European Union offers similar access to many landlocked states in Western Europe to the Atlantic today.

The last century was the century of the Pacific-Atlantic powers. Global power axis was situated in that region. Countries in Western Europe and North America were the real drivers of growth in the world. These powers, because of the economic and the consequent political clout they enjoyed, were able to influence global order in the last century. Global institutions were built by them after the First and Second World Wars to address, among other issues, the management of global commons like the ocean routes and outer space. The United Nations Organization (UNO), formed after the Second World War in 1945, was responsible in putting in place several legal frameworks and instruments for managing the affairs of these commons. The United Nations Convention on the Law of the Sea (UNCLOS) was one such instrument created through a long process of deliberations among the member countries over a period between 1972 and 1984. Finally, the convention became operational in 1994. It today has 168 signatories who ratified it including 167 states and the European Union.

The UNCLOS came into limelight recently due to a dispute between the People's Republic of China and the Republic of Philippines over an imaginary and unilateral maritime boundary called the Nine Dash Line. The Nine Dash Line, which became Ten Dash Line after the insertion of a new dash in the East China Sea to the east of Taiwan in 2013, is a maritime boundary line unilaterally declared by China in 1947. Incidentally, the Line is considered a historic maritime boundary both by China and Taiwan (Republic of China) today. The Philippines government had challenged the Chinese claims of historic waters and activities of land reclamation and island making – euphemistically called 'The Great Wall of Sand' – and the matter went up to the UNCLOS for arbitration. In its decision on 12 July 2016, the UNCLOS had ruled that China has no legal authority to use the Nine Dash Line as the maritime boundary and make historic claims over the East and South China Sea. Both China and Taiwan have rejected this arbitration verdict.

China continues to assert its claims over large parts of the South and East China Seas. It is building new islands, encroaching on the existing land formations and expanding them, and has even built military facilities like landing strips on some of the reclaimed territories causing serious anxiety and resentment among the neighboring maritime powers like

Vietnam, Japan, South Korea, Philippines, Malaysia and Indonesia. The more the protests, the more assertive China became, in not only rejecting UNCLOS jurisdiction, but also flexing its military muscle at powers that tried to challenge it in the region.

South China Sea has emerged as a key area of the global commons because of the new geo-strategic changes that are shaping the 21st Century. The new century saw the economic and political heft of the West diminishing and the rise of Asian powers like China and India. The Asian Tigers—Hong Kong, Singapore, Taiwan and Japan—which became strong economic powers towards the end of the last century, continue to be the important economic powerhouses. Several other countries in the region, like Vietnam, Indonesia and Malaysia, are also rising as important players, leading to the gradual shifting of the global power axis away from the Pacific-Atlantic to the Indo-Pacific region.

The rise of the Indo-Pacific, from the West Coast of America to the East Coast of Africa as the new global power corridor, with over 70 per cent of the global energy trade and 50 per cent of the container traffic passing through it, is the new geo-strategic reality of the 21st Century. It is this reality that is exacerbating tensions in the commons in this region, whether it is the Somali pirates in the Gulf of Aden or the Chinese politics in the South China Sea. Managing the global commons in this most happening region in this century is the challenge that the world powers are seized with today.

This challenge can be met only when the countries voluntarily respect institutions and conventions. Big countries like India have always upheld the rule of law and adhered to verdicts by arbitration tribunals. In one such verdict in 2016, after a six-year hearings and site visits, the arbitration tribunal under the UNCLOS had upheld the claims of Bangladesh and rejected India's contention. Both countries have accepted the verdict in a spirit of friendship. In another matter Myanmar and Bangladesh too agreed to abide by the tribunal order.

Unfortunately, that was not the case to be with all. The 2016 verdict of the arbitration tribunal against China is a case in point. When countries refuse to respect the mandate of institutions like the UNCLOS, there is no mechanism for redress. Instead, it leads to competition for dominance by various powers, which we witness today in the region. The Americans today have their aircraft carriers like INS Roosevelt stationed in the South China Sea area to assert their authority of free passage. Incidentally, even the Americans are not a signatory to the UNCLOS convention. The American Senate, which requires two third majority to ratify the Convention, has repeatedly refused to do so as it does not agree with certain clauses in the Convention. That makes the UNCLOS even more handicapped in addressing the challenge.

Countries like India and Australia, who have enormous stakes in the region and are signatories to the Convention, have called for 'free, open, inclusive and prosperous Indo-Pacific'. At the moment, it looks like a tall order given the growing tensions and conspicuous great power rivalry in the region. It raises the important question about the efficacy of institutions like the UNCLOS. In its 75th year, the UN itself has come under scrutiny over its continued relevance for the 21st century global geo-politics. In such a scenario, responsible countries in the region have to come together to think about the need for effective institutional mechanisms to manage the global commons, especially those like the Indo-Pacific which have emerged as the new global powerhouses.

India Foundation had organised an international conference at Port Blair from 04-06 October 2017 on the efficacy and future of the UNCLOS for the region in India's neighborhood and the need for creation of new institutions and instruments. This book is the culmination of the ideas that emanated during the conference, by way of presentations made by eminent scholars.

Acknowledgements

This book is an outcome of the **Conference on UNCLOS: Solutions for Managing the Maritime Global Commons** organised by the India Foundation at Port Blair in Andaman and Nicobar Islands. Although, the book is not a compilation of the proceedings, the seed for coming out with a book on the subject germinated from the conference. Most of the contributors of the book did take part in the conference. Hence the book owes a lot to the Conference, which was organised with an aim to start discussions and deliberations on the role of UNCLOS in defining the maritime global order. The Conference brought together practitioners, defence personnel, lawyers and academics from various parts of the world to brainstorm on the need to enhance human capital and institutional capacity to support the achievements of the objectives set forth in the declaration of UNCLOS and to effectively implement agreed upon commitments and solutions.

The book would not have come into existence without the support extended by the leadership of India Foundation led by Shri Ram Madhav, who also very generously agreed to write the Foreword for this book. I would also like to acknowledge the contribution of other members of India Foundation team, namely, Vice Admiral Shekhar Sinha, PVSM, AVSM, NM & Bar, Major General Dhruv C Katoch, Wg Cdr Vikas Kalyani, Guru Prakash, Raghav Pandey and Ngawang Gamtso Hardy, for their valuable assistance and participation in the conference.

I would like to acknowledge the whole-hearted support of the Government of Sri Lanka for the participation of Dr Harsha de Silva, Deputy Minister of Policy Planning & Economic Development. It would not be out of place to acknowledge our gratitude to Shri MJ Akbar, the then Minister of State for External Affairs of India for his participation. I would like to wholeheartedly thank the administration of the Union

Territory of Andaman and Nicobar Islands, led by Shri Jagdish Mukhi, the then Lieutenant Governor, without whose support the Conference would not have seen the light of the day. The conference also received full support from Andaman & Nicobar Command led by Vice Admiral Bimal Verma, AVSM, who actively participated in the conference along with officers from his command. The conference was also enriched by the participation of Vice Admiral Vinay Badhwar, AVSM, NM, the Chief Hydrographer to the Government of India.

I would also like to acknowledge the support received from the Ambassadors of Germany, Indonesia, Lao PDR, Malaysia, Philippines and Vietnam, who rescheduled their itinerary, to participate in the conference. The conference also received full support from the Embassies of Japan, Malaysia, Myanmar, Singapore and the United States, who deputed representatives to participate. It would not be out of place to highlight the support that the book has received from the Embassy of Japan in facilitating the participation of experts and scholars from Japan to share their perspective and enriching the Conference with their valuable contributions.

I am extremely grateful to all the eminent contributors, who despite their busy schedules, accommodated us and made extremely insightful submissions which form a chapter each in this book. No academic discussion is ever complete without the valuable contribution of the participants who enrich these discussions with their experiences and comments, I am thus grateful to all those who participated in the Conference to further refine the quality of discussions. It would not be out of place to acknowledge the immense contribution of Ms Varsha Gupta, who did an excellent job in organising the conference in a rather remote corner of India.

I would like to thank the publisher of this book Shri Rajan Arya, the proprietor of Pentagon Press LLP, who went out of his way to accommodate our numerous editing requests and provided us with his support of the highest order. Finally I would like to thank my co-editors Deeksha Goel and Siddharth Singh for literally burning the mid night oil to bring out this volume.

I do hope the readers enjoy reading the arguments in the book as much as we enjoyed working on them.

Alok Bansal

List of Contributors

Captain Alok Bansal is the Director of India Foundation. He is also an Adjunct Professor at New Delhi Institute of Management (NDIM) and Secretary General of Asian Eurasian Human Rights Forum (AEHRF). A former Naval Officer he served in Indian Navy for almost 32 years, where he commanded two warships. He was the Executive Director of the National Maritime Foundation (NMF) and South Asian institute for Strategic Affairs (SAISA), and has worked with the Institute for Defence Studies and Analyses (IDSA) and Centre for Land Warfare Studies (CLAWS) . He has authored two books titled *Balochistan in Turmoil: Pakistan at Cross Roads* and *Gilgit Baltistan and its Unending saga of Human Rights Violation.*

Dr. Aniruddha Rajput is a Member of the United Nations International Law Commission. He served as the Chairperson of the Drafting Committee of the International Law Commission at its 69th Session in 2017. His areas of research, writing and practice are international law, law of the sea, boundary disputes, international trade and investment law. He is a member of the Governing Council of the Indian Council of World Affairs (ICWA). He was a member of the Study Group constituted by the Law Commission of India to revise the Model Bilateral Investment Treaty and member of the 5th Haryana State Finance Commission.

Apurv Mishra is Senior Research Fellow at India Foundation. He is also the Editor-in-Chief at India Law Journal and an adjunct Faculty at Ashoka University. He teaches courses on law at several institutions including Gujarat National Law University, Gandhinagar, Vedica Scholars Programme and Plaksha University.

Professor (Dr.) Bimal N. Patel is currently the Vice-Chancellor of Rashtriya Raksha University and a Member, National Security Advisory Board of India. He was the Director of Gujarat National Law University, Gandhinagar from 2008 to 2019. He also served as a member of the 21st Law Commission of India. Professor Patel obtained his PhD in International Law and LLM from, Leiden University and another PhD in international law from Jaipur National University. He has extensively analysed and published works on the administrative, procedural and substantive jurisprudence of International Organisations, State Practice and International Law, Law of the Sea and Maritime Laws, Dispute Settlement – International and National Courts and Tribunals, ICJ, ITLOS and International Criminal Tribunal for former Yugoslavia (ICTY).

Vice Admiral Bimal Verma, AVSM served as the Commander-in-Chief of the only tri-services command of India, the Andaman and Nicobar Command (ANC) from 29 February 2016 to 1 December 2019. He was commissioned into the Indian Navy on 1 January 1980 and specialised in Communication and Electronic Warfare. He has commanded four warships, which included two amphibious warfare ships and two guided missile destroyers. As a flag officer, he served as Flag Officer Commanding Maharashtra and Gujarat Naval Area as well as Assistant Chief of Naval Staff for Information Warfare & Operations. Prior to taking over the command of ANC, he was the Chief of Staff at Eastern Naval Command where he coordinated the International Fleet Review 2016.

Professor C Raja Mohan is Director, Institute of South Asian Studies. He has been the Professor of South Asian Studies at Jawaharlal Nehru University, New Delhi, and at the S Rajaratnam School of International Studies (RSIS), Nanyang Technological University, Singapore. He has been associated with a number of think tanks in New Delhi, including the IDSA, the Centre for Policy Research (CPR) and the Observer Research Foundation (ORF). He was also the founding director of Carnegie India, New Delhi. Professor Mohan was the Henry Alfred Kissinger Chair in International Affairs at the United States Library of Congress, Washington DC, from 2009 to 2010. He served on India's National Security Advisory Board. He led the Indian Chapter of the Pugwash Conferences on Science and World Affairs from 1999 to 2006. His most recent books include, *Samudra Manthan: Sino-Indian Rivalry in the Indo-Pacific* and *Modi's World: Expanding India's Sphere of Influence.*

Deeksha Goel is currently working as a Senior Research Fellow at India Foundation. Her research interests include Geopolitics of the Indian Ocean Region (IOR) and Development Financing in the IOR. Deeksha graduated as an Engineer specialising in Electronics and Communication and has a MBA in Finance.

Dhruva Jaishankar is Director of the U.S. Initiative at the New Delhi-based Observer Research Foundation (ORF). He is also a Non-Resident Fellow with the Lowy Institute in Australia and is a regular contributor to the media, presently writing a monthly column for the Hindustan Times. Jaishankar was previously a Fellow in Foreign Policy Studies at Brookings India in New Delhi. From 2012 to 2016, he was a Transatlantic Fellow with the German Marshall Fund (GMF) in Washington DC. From 2009 to 2012, he was programme officer with GMF. Before that, he worked as a research assistant at the Brookings Institution in Washington. In 2015-2016, he was a Visiting Fellow at the RSIS, Singapore. Jaishankar holds a bachelor's degree in history and classics from Macalester College, and a master's degree in security studies from Georgetown University.

Professor Gudmundur Eiriksson is Professor of Law at Jindal Global Law School and Executive Director of its Centre for International Legal Studies. He served from 1974 to 1976 as a Law of the Sea Officer in the Office of the Secretary-General of the United Nations for the Law of the Sea and from 1977 to 2014 in the Ministry for Foreign Affairs of Iceland, as Assistant Legal Adviser, Legal Adviser and Ambassador of Iceland in Ottawa, Pretoria and New Delhi. He was a member of the United Nations International Law Commission from 1987 to 1996, a Judge at the ITLOS from 1996 to 2002 and a Judge ad hoc from 2016 to 2019. Professor Eiriksson holds an A.B. degree and a B.S. degree in Civil Engineering from Rutgers College, an LL.B. (Honours) degree from King's College London and an LL.M. degree from Columbia University.

Captain (Dr.) Gurpreet S Khurana is a missile warfare specialist of the Indian Navy commissioned in 1988, who has commanded two warships and authored three books and numerous research papers on geopolitical, strategic, naval and legal issues relating to Indo-Pacific region. He is accredited to be the first to use the term 'Indo-Pacific' in contemporary geopolitical discourse in his article published in January 2007. He compiled the Navy's Handbook on Law of Maritime Operations 2013, and has also made pioneering contribution to Indian Maritime Doctrine 2009. During 2014-19, as Executive Director of NMF, he was closely associated with the Government, National Security Council and Navy for policy-formulation on maritime safety and security, multilateral organisations and legal issues. He is presently serving at Eastern Naval Command, and heads Centre of Excellence on China Maritime Studies.

Hamsa Devineni is a practicing lawyer and a maritime lawyer by specialization. She holds a distinction in LLM (Admiralty and Maritime Laws) from Tulane University Law School in USA. She worked as a project officer of the Oceans Beyond Piracy (OBP) programme of the One Earth Future Foundation in USA, framing policies for the United Nations Contact Group on Piracy off the Coast of Somalia (UNCGPCS) and aiding in identifying and addressing global challenges faced due to world maritime piracy. She is a visiting fellow at the India Foundation and the NMF and also a visiting faculty at the National Academy of Legal Studies and Research (NALSAR), Hyderabad and Nalanda University. Hamsa writes on contemporary maritime legal issues and has also assisted in drafting of various maritime legislative bills in India.

Dr Harsha de Silva is a Member of Sri Lankan Parliament. He is an economist and a former minister. He has been the Non-Cabinet Minister of Economic Reforms and Public Distribution; State Minister of National Policies and Economic Affairs; and Deputy Minister of Foreign Affairs. He was educated at Royal College Colombo, earning a BS in Business Management from Truman State University in 1988. He completed his MA and PhD in Economics at the University of Missouri in 1993. He participated in an executive program on evaluating social programs at the Massachusetts Institute of Technology in 2006 as an Eisenhower Fellow.

Admiral Jayantha Perera, RWP, VSV, USP, was the 19th Commander of the Sri Lankan Navy (SLN). Educated at Thurstan College, Colombo, Perera enlisted in the Sri Lanka Navy on 23 August 1978. He commanded the SLN flagship SLNS Sayura from 2000 to 2003 and was the Flag officer commanding the naval fleet from 2006 to 2007 based at Trincomalee, simultaneously serving as Deputy Area Commander for the Eastern Command. He has commanded SLN's Southern and Western Commands and following a brief three-month stint as the navy's Director General

Services, was appointed as Director General Operations, a position he occupied until July 2013, when he was appointed Chief of Staff of the SLN. He was awarded the Rana Wickrama Padakkama the same year. He was appointed Commander of the Navy on 1 July 2014, and was promoted to the rank of Admiral on his retirement from duty on 9 July 2015.

M.J. Akbar is an Indian journalist and politician, who served as the Minister of State (MoS) for External Affairs until 17 October 2018. Mr Akbar is a Member of Parliament in the Rajya Sabha, and was inducted into the Union Council of Ministers by PM Narendra Modi on 5 July 2016. He is also a veteran Indian journalist and author of several books. He first served as an elected Member of Parliament between 1989 and 1991, and returned to public life in March 2014, when he joined the BJP and was appointed national spokesperson during the 2014 general elections. During his long career in journalism, he launched, as editor, India's first weekly political news periodicals in India including India Today, Headlines Today, The Telegraph, The Asian Age and Deccan Chronicle, among others. His latest book is titled *Gandhi's Hinduism: The Struggle against Jinnah's Islam.*

Myo Htike Tan Thein has more than 20 year experience in the field of human rights, political affairs and international relations; field of economic, social and cultural rights; and areas of peace and security, humanitarian principles and international law. Currently, Myo is a National Expert for UNDP Myanmar and other UN Agencies for the Peacebuilding and Disaster Reduction. Prior to that, Myo was a Senior Advisor for the Geneva-based International Commission of Jurists (ICJ). Before joining ICJ, Myo was a Programme Director at the Bayda Institute. Previously, Myo was a Campaign Director of the London based Burma Democratic Concern (BDC) since 2007 embarking on public campaigns and lobbying international governments to bring about democratic change in Burma while working in tandem with people inside Burma opposing the military dictatorship. Myo is a holder of B.Sc. (IC) from Myanmar and M.Sc. (Development Studies) from the UK.

Shakti Sinha is a Distinguished Fellow at the India Foundation and is currently serving as the Honorary Director of the Atal Bihari Vajpayee Institute of Policy Research and International Studies, MS University,

Vadodara. Mr Sinha was the former director of the Nehru Memorial Museum and Library (NMML) and was part of the Indian Administrative Service from the 1979 batch. He has served as a Joint Secretary in the Prime Minister's Office, as well as the Chief Secretary of Andaman &Nicobar Administration. He has authored a book *Vajpayee: The Years that Changed India*, based on his association with Prime Minister Atal Bihari Vajpayee.

Siddharth Singh has done his Masters in International Relations and M.Phil. in Indo-Pacific Studies from the School of International Studies, Jawaharlal Nehru University (JNU), New Delhi. His PhD research is on "Comparative Analysis of India and China's Maritime Diplomacy in Indo-Pacific Region". His area of research includes Geopolitics in the Indo-Pacific region, India's Maritime Diplomacy and India's engagements in Multilateral Institutions.

Sidharto Reza Suryodipuro is serving as Indonesia's Ambassador to India since 2017. Prior to that, he served as the Deputy Chief of Mission at the Embassy of Indonesia in Washington DC between 2014 and 2017. Prior to that, as Director for Intra-Regional Cooperation in Asia Pacific and Africa, Ministry of Foreign Affairs, he managed the policy development and implementation of Indonesia's participation in or engagement with regional organizations in Asia Pacific and Africa and the Indian and Pacific Oceans. He studied International Relations at Universitas Parahyangan in Bandung and US-China relations at the Naval Postgraduate School in Monterey (with distinction). He was awarded the Fulbright Scholarship in 2002.

Dr. Sreeradha Datta is Centre Head, Neighbourhood Studies and Senior Fellow, Vivekananda International Foundation, New Delhi. She has a PhD from Jawaharlal Nehru University, New Delhi and has been the director of Maulana Abul Kalam Azad Institute of Asian Studies, Kolkata, and a Fellow with IDSA. She has written six books and monographs on Bangladesh, South East Asia, Myanmar and the Northeast and over 130 articles in journals, edited volumes, newspapers and academic websites. Her latest book is titled *Act East Policy and India's Northeast*. She serves on the academic boards of several universities and think tanks and is a regular participant in Track II dialogues.

Tariq Karim is a retired Bangladeshi diplomat who has served extensively in, and dealt with, Bangladesh's relations with India and neighbours as High Commissioner to India (with personal rank and status of a State Minister of Bangladesh from 2009-14), Deputy High Commissioner (1984-88) and Additional Foreign Secretary for South Asia and SAARC (1995-97). He has been closely involved with formulating policies and galvanizing efforts to promote and foster regional cooperation. He has been Strategic Adviser to the World Bank's South Asia Water Initiative and Consultant to the World Bank's South Asian Regional Integration and Engagement program. He was also a visiting Distinguished Fellow at the Vivekananda International Foundation from 2014-2017. He is currently Senior Fellow at Independent University, Bangladesh advising the Vice Chancellor on setting up a Centre for Bay of Bengal Studies at the University.

Ton Sinh Thanh has been one of the senior diplomats of Vietnam. He earned his master's degree in International Relations from Carleton University, Canada; Bachelor's Degree from Hanoi Diplomatic Academy besides Advanced Diplomas in Diplomacy from Moscow Diplomatic Academy and Advanced Diplomas in Public Management and Political Sciences, Training from Ho Chi Minh National Academy of Politics and Public Administration. His diplomatic career started in 1990-91, as a Desk Officer, Department of Southeast Asia - South Pacific. He served the Ministry of Foreign Affairs, Vietnam, in various positions. He has been the Ambassador of Socialist Republic of Vietnam in India. Earlier he was Vietnam's Ambassador to Sri Lanka. Earlier he had served in various capacities in Vietnam Embassy in India and has a deep understanding of various aspects of India and Indo-Vietnam relations.

Dr Vijay Sakhuja is co-founder and Trustee, The Peninsula Foundation, Chennai; Distinguished Fellow, Center for Public Policy Research, Kochi; Distinguished Fellow, Defence Research and Study, Kochi; Visiting Senior Fellow, Cambodian Institute for Cooperation and Peace (CICP), Phnom Penh; Adjunct Faculty, School of Maritime, Air and Space Studies (SMASS), Rashtriya Raksha University, Gujarat; and is associated with Kalinga International Foundation, and ICWA. He has been Director, National Maritime Foundation, Director (Research), ICWA and has worked with IDSA, Institute of Southeast Asian Studies (ISEAS),

Singapore; Gujarat National Law University; Vivekananda International Foundation; Observer Research Foundation (ORF), United Service Institution of India (USI) and Centre for Airpower Studies (CAPS). A former naval officer, he specializes in Indo-Pacific affairs, 4th Industrial Revolution technologies, Arctic issues and Blue Economy. He has published over 40 books, edited volumes and monographs.

Vice Admiral Vinay Badhwar, AVSM, NM is the Chief hydrographer to the Government of India. An alumnus of National Defence Academy, he was commissioned in the Indian Navy on 01 July 1982. He specialised in Hydrography and has been an instructor at National Institute of Hydrography, Goa. He commanded three survey ships and has over 31 years of experience in hydrographic survey and an in-depth knowledge on hydrography, digital cartography and different aspects of international charting. He has been a pivotal member of the International Hydrographic Organisation's Capacity Building Sub-Committee, since its inception. In 2019, he was awarded Alexander Dalrymple Award by the UK Hydrographic Office, for his outstanding contribution to Indian hydrography and across the wider Indian Ocean region. He was acclaimed for unlocking the economic potential of marine geospatial data and further hydrographic science in the region.

Dr Yurika Ishii is Associate Professor at National Defense Academy of Japan, where she is in charge of law of the sea and public international law courses. Her areas of interest include general public international law, law of the sea and international/transnational criminal law. She achieved LLB from the University of Tokyo, Faculty of Law (Political Science Course), LLM from Cornell Law School (with Rotary Ambassador Scholarship), and PhD from the University of Tokyo, Graduate Schools for Laws and Politics with a thesis on international regulation of economic crimes, which was published as *International Regulation of Transnational Crimes* in 2017 and awarded 51st Adachi Mineichiro Award. She has been a faculty member of Gujarat National Law University, Ahmedabad, University of Basel and University of Turin, Italy; and a guest lecturer at International Maritime Law Institute, Malta.

List of Abbreviations

ACRS	Arms Control and Regional Security in the Middle East
ADIZ	Air Defence Identification Zones
ADMM Plus	ASEAN Defence Ministers' Meeting Plus
AIS	Automatic Identification System
AMF	ASEAN Maritime Forum
ANC	Andaman and Nicobar Command
APEC	Asia Pacific Economic Cooperation
ARF	ASEAN Regional Forum
ASEAN	Association of South-East Asian Nations
ASEM	Asia Europe Meeting
ASI	Archaeological Survey of India
BCHP Act	The Protection and Inspection of Buried Cultural Heritage Act
BIMSTEC	Bay of Bengal Initiative for Multi-Sectoral Technical and Economic Cooperation
BIOT	British Indian Ocean Territories
BRI	Belt and Road Initiative
CAFGUs	Citizen Armed Force Geographical Units
CBM	Confidence Building Measure
CCG	China Coast Guard
CCS	Convention on the Continental Shelf
CFCLR	Convention on Fishing and Conservation of the Living Resources of the High Seas
CFP	Common Fisheries Policy
CHS	Convention on High Seas
CINCAN	Commander-in-Chief of Andaman and Nicobar Command

CLCS	The Commission on the Limits of the Continental Shelf
CMM	Chinese Maritime Militia
CNOOC	China National Offshore Oil Corporation
COC	Code of Conduct
COLREG	International Regulation for Preventing Collisions at Sea
COMM	Council of Ministers' Meeting
CORPAT	Coordinated Patrol
CSI	Container Security Initiative
CSIS	Centre for Strategic and International Studies
CTS	Convention on Territorial Sea and Contiguous Zone
CUES	Code for Unplanned Encounters at Sea
DMAAs	Dangerous Military Activities
DOC	Declaration of Conduct of Parties in the South China Sea
EAS	East Asia Summit
ECS	East China Sea
EEZ	Exclusive Economic Zone
Eni	Ente Nazionale Idrocarburi (National Hydrocarbons Authority) an Italian oil & gas multinational corporation
EU	European Union
FON	Freedom of Navigation
FONOPS	Freedom of Navigation Operations
GDP	Gross Domestic Product
GNP	Gross National Product
HADR	Humanitarian Assistance and Disaster Relief
ICC	Inter-regional Coordination Centre
ICJ	International Court of Justice
ICS	International Code of Signals
IFC IOR	Information Fusion Centre - Indian Ocean Region
IFR	International Fleet Review
ILC	International Law Commission
ILO	International Labour Organisation
IMAC	Integrated Management and Analysis Centre
IMBL	International Maritime Boundary Line
IMO	International Maritime Organisation

INCSEAs	Incidents at Sea Agreements
IND-INDO Corpat	India Indonesia Coordinated Patrol
IONS	Indian Ocean Naval Symposium
IOR	Indian Ocean Region
IORA	Indian Ocean Rim Association
IOTC	Indian Ocean Tuna Commission
ISA	International Seabed Authority
ISPS	International Ship and Port Security Code
ITLOS	International Tribunal on Law of the Sea
IUU	Illicit Unreported Unregulated
IWG	IONS Working Group
JCBC	Joint Commission for Bilateral Cooperation
LBA	Land Boundary Agreement
LNG	Liquified Natural Gas
MALINDO	Indonesia Malaysia Guideline of 2001
MCBM	Maritime Confidence Building Measure
MCGS	Mauritius Coast Guard Ship
MDA	Maritime Domain Awareness
MoU	Memorandum of Understanding
MMCC	Multinational Maritime Coordinating Centre
MPA	Marine Protected Area
MSR	Maritime Scientific Research
MSS	Maritime Safety and Security
MSY	Maximum Sustainable Yield
MZI	Maritime Zone of India
NM	Nautical Mile
NOTAM	Notice to Airmen
NMF	National Maritime Foundation
NSR	Northern Sea Route
OBOR	One Belt One Road
ODC	Over Dimensional Cargo
ONGC	Oil and Natural Gas Corporation
OPSD	Optional Protocol of Signature concerning the Compulsory Settlement of Disputes
OPV	Offshore Patrol Vessel

PCA	Permanent Court of Arbitration
PCG	Philippines Coast Guard
PLAN	People's Liberation Army Navy (of China)
PMSCs	Private Maritime Security Companies
PRC	People's Republic of China
SAARC	South Asian Association of Regional Cooperation
SAGAR	Security and Growth for All in the Region
SAR	Search and Rescue
SCS	South China Sea
SEZ	Special Economic Zones
SLOCs	Sea Lines of Communication
SONG	Swatch of No Ground
SUA	Suppression of Unlawful Acts
TCF	Trillion Cubic Feet
TCG	Taiwanese Coast Guard
TECO	Taiwan Economic and Cultural Office
UAW	Underwater Archaeology Wing
UCH	Underwater Cultural Heritage
UNCC	United Nations Compulsory Conciliation
UNCLOS	United Nations Convention on the Law of the Sea
UNCTAD	United Nations Conference on Trade and Development
UN	United Nations
UNGA	United Nations General Assembly
UNSC	United Nations Security Council
US	United States (of America)
USSR	Union of Soviet Socialist Republic
WGMSS	Working Group on Maritime Safety and Security
WPNS	Western Pacific Naval Symposium
WTO	World Trade Organisation

1

Introduction

Alok Bansal and Siddharth Singh

With increasing human population and economic activities, the resources on the land are depleting fast and consequently, human beings are harnessing the oceans—its surfaces, its waters and its sub-soil—to draw more and more resources. At the same time, the forces of globalisation, even though under attack from various quarters, are increasing the inter-dependence between human populations, leading to a continuous upsurge in global commerce. Most of this commerce is taking place through the seas. Consequently, more and more human activities are taking place in the seas, more than at any time in human history. Unbridled human activities and exploitation of its resources could lead to chaos and confrontation at sea. It is therefore essential that while exploiting the oceans, the human race needs to adhere to certain norms so that order could be maintained and the resources of the seas could be harnessed optimally.

The laws that governed human exploitation of global commons have evolved with the passage of time. Consequently, the norms and rules that governed the utilisation of the seas have transformed with the passage of time, on account of technological development as well as the changing needs of mankind. The governance of ocean spaces and the resources therein are presently governed by the United Nations Convention on the Law of the Sea (UNCLOS). UNCLOS also referred to as the "Constitution of the Oceans", is a detailed instrument that has 320 Articles divided into 17 parts. Each of these parts deals with a cluster of related issues ranging from jurisdiction over ocean spaces to exploration and exploitation of marine resources to settlement of disputes and to more general provisions related to the administration of the Convention.

All the activities in the seas and oceans, along with the sustainable use of ocean resources and conservation of the oceans, must be carried out within the legal framework as established under the UNCLOS. The three important pillars that are embodied in the UNCLOS are social, economic and environmental. These pillars set the legal framework under UNCLOS for the sustainable development of the seas and oceans. UNCLOS also attempts to balance the obligation as well as the rights of coastal countries with other countries. It also protects the rights of special category countries like Landlocked States. It aims to settle all issues relating to the law of the sea through the codification and progressive development of international law. The Convention reflects a pragmatic reconciliation of interests, advances multilateralism and the rule of law by codifying a delicate balance of rights and duties, as well as by addressing matters of State and of regional and global concerns.

Under the UNCLOS, a coastal State is entitled to a territorial sea not exceeding 12 nautical miles measured from the baseline of the coastal State. Within its territorial sea, the coastal State exercises sovereignty, including over its resources. As per the provisions of the Convention, all ships of all countries have the right of innocent passage into the territorial water zone. Apart all ships have the right of "transit passage" through the straits which are used for international navigation and countries can regulate the navigation and transit passage which has borders with these straits. In the high seas and in the Exclusive Economic Zones (EEZs), all countries have the freedom of navigation along with landlocked countries.

Piracy, armed robbery on the high seas, illegal drug trafficking and terror attacks on maritime installations, hijackings, the smuggling of arms and hazardous wastes, smuggling of migrants and other human trafficking by sea, illicit traffic in narcotic drugs and psychotropic substances, illegal fishing and dumping of toxic wastes, illegal discharge of pollutants, and other violations of environmental laws threaten the maritime safety and security of human life in the oceans and seas.

Competing claims by States regarding ocean space and natural resources in the oceans, which often result in protracted maritime boundary disputes, can also lead to tensions between States.

UNCLOS provides a framework to regulate all activities on and in seas and oceans. Its sole objective is to strengthen the regional and global cooperation in oceans and seas to avoid any confusion related to the maritime domain and to avoid any conflict emanating from such conflicts in international waters. UNCLOS has set out a chart of duties and rights which coastal countries have in regard to their jurisdiction over the maritime zones as coded under the Convention framework.

As per the UN Charter, it is propagated that all countries in the world must settle their bilateral or multilateral disputes by adopting peaceful means through negotiations and dialogue. This principle is also echoed in the terms of rules and regulations as articulated and coded under the framework of UNCLOS to settle all maritime disputes through dispute settlement mechanisms as coded in the law. If two or more countries have disputes between them in the maritime domain, then UNCLOS provides four options as per the Convention framework which are as follows:

(a) Submission of the dispute to the International Tribunal for the Law of the Sea
(b) Adjudication by the International Court of Justice
(c) Submission to binding international arbitration procedures, or
(d) Submission to special arbitration tribunals with expertise in specific types of disputes.

All these procedures involve binding third-party settlement, in which an agent other than the parties directly involved renders a decision that the parties are committed in advance to respect. Unfortunately, some strong nations have in the past not only challenged the jurisdiction of various arbitration mechanisms, but have also refused to abide by their decisions.

As the Indo-Pacific region is going to be the hub of economic activity in the foreseeable future, consequently, the 21st century has seen the rise of many economic powers in the region, which is a contiguous oceanic space covering the Indian and the Pacific oceans. As a result, there have been attempts by some of the powerful countries to dominate the waters in their vicinity, which are essential lifelines for trade. This has resulted in increased friction in the maritime domain. In the last two decades, there have been numerous disputes, which have the potential to threaten the regional as well as global peace. The possibility of such a conflict threatening stability in the region as well as in the wider Indo-Pacific region in the future cannot be ruled out. Thus, the UNCLOS becomes much more relevant and important in terms of implementation and maintenance of rule-based international order in the Indo-Pacific region. Many claims and counter-claims have been made about 'sovereign rights' and the applicability of international law, UNCLOS, and the legitimacy of the July 2016 ruling by the Arbitral Tribunal set up under Annex VII of UNCLOS. It is essential for global peace that all states act maturely and abide by all international laws and decisions of tribunals.

The management of oceanic resources in the Bay of Bengal, wherein three countries, namely, India, Bangladesh and Myanmar, had conflicting claims, is a shining example of a rule-based international order at a time when the powerful and mighty are trying to ride roughshod over international institutions as well as weaker nations. It was a case where an extremely complex problem involving delimitation of maritime boundaries has been resolved by way of international arbitration. More significantly, the three countries, by rigidly adhering to the decisions of international arbitration, have presented before the world an ideal of how mature states need to resolve bilateral disputes. The fact that the three states, irrespective of their differential size and power, agreed to override their individual interests to abide by the decisions of different international tribunals set up to arbitrate, have shown to the global community how a rule-based order can be maintained at sea. In the process, they have also shown to the world that it is often important to sacrifice perceived national interests to maintain harmony and peace in the region.

It has also highlighted the need to find solutions to the problems that exist in sharing the global commons. When it comes to the maritime domain, the eventual solution must be in accordance with the provisions of the UNCLOS and must be implemented under its framework in a coherent manner to suit the local and regional requirements of the situation. The international community needs to focus on building and enhancing the capacity-building of coastal states. An effective cooperation mechanism under a coordinated and cooperative framework will be critical in this context. There is an urgent need to facilitate and strengthen such global debates, dialogues, consultative mechanisms as well as regional and global dialogues to strengthen the UNCLOS across the regions in the world. This book is intended to highlight these aspects and to reinforce the fact that when it comes to managing the Maritime Global Commons, solutions have to be found within the framework of UNCLOS.

The initial chapters in the book introduce the theme and highlight the evolution and relevance of UNCLOS. They amplify its political and strategic dimensions and give an Asian perspective regarding the governance of oceanic spaces and how UNCLOS is not only helping to govern the maritime global governance, but also in fostering mutual cooperation. The rest of the chapters have been divided so as to highlight the following four sub-themes:

(a) Enduring legitimacy of UNCLOS and its continuing relevance in the 21st century.
(b) Role of UNCLOS in facilitating peaceful settlements of disputes: A case study of harmonious maritime dispute resolution in the Bay of Bengal.
(c) Growing problems of non-compliance with UNCLOS: Analysing the imbroglio in the South China Sea.
(d) Maritime Security architecture in the Indo-Pacific region to maintain Freedom of Navigation under UNCLOS.

Renowned journalist, Parliamentarian and India's former Minister of State for External Affairs, Shri M. J. Akbar highlights the startling difference between perceiving India as the land south of the Himalayas or the land north of the ocean. He further argues that at long last India's strategic thinking has begun to coordinate the defence of the nation on its land borders, and the management of the seas to ensure that they remain a free passage for international trade and communication outside the domination of any power. He opines that as land resources stagnate or dwindle, the wealth of the seas, possibly far greater than the riches of the land, has become a target for the powerful.

The Chief Hydrographer to the Government of India, Vice Admiral Vinay Badhwar, in his chapter, writes about the evolution and relevance of UNCLOS and explains UNCLOS as a tool in the governance of shipping activities. He writes that there are many instances, in which coastal states and regional powers have chosen to openly contest, selectively interpret and discretely subvert key principles of UNCLOS and thus expecting a result completely on the basis of UNCLOS is not always likely. He, therefore, suggests that it may be more prudent that countries also opt for dispute settlement in maritime arrangements beyond the provisions of UNCLOS. The resolution of disputes with innovative ideas and bold initiatives is the need of the hour and the declaration of such willingness and initiatives will be the first step in this direction.

One of India's most acclaimed strategic thinkers and presently the director of the Institute of South Asian Studies at the National University of Singapore, Professor C. Raja Mohan, in his chapter, writes about the increasing inability of the UNCLOS to persuade China to abide by its rules and explains the unilateral steps that China has taken to change the territorial status quo in the South China Sea, adopted a more muscular approach to its disputes with Japan in the East China Sea and entered into a broader contestation with the USA on the interpretation of the UNCLOS on the rules governing freedom of military navigation in the Western Pacific. He argues that if the capacity to enforce rules is missing then it does not matter how good the principle is. Similarly, if it is merely about power without principles, then it lacks legitimacy, morality and accountability.

Noted economist, politician and former Sri Lankan minister of Economic Reforms and Public Distribution, Dr. Harsha De Silva, in his chapter, advocates for India to play a more proactive role in working with countries of the Indian Ocean Region (IOR) to strengthen UNCLOS and develop a rule-based order in the IOR. He suggests that the existence of many regional institutional initiatives like Indian Ocean Rim Association (IORA), Bay of Bengal Initiative for Multi-Sectoral Technical and Economic Cooperation (BIMSTEC), Indian Ocean Naval Symposium (IONS), Indian Ocean Tuna Commission (IOTC), etc., are of marked importance and opines for greater integration of the mandate of such regional institutions with that of UNCLOS.

India's former Commander-in-Chief of the Andaman and Nicobar Command (CINCAN), Vice Admiral Bimal Verma, in his chapter, highlights that maritime disputes have escalated to the point of disturbing the existing regional order especially in the Indo-Pacific and writes that the genesis of these disputes lies in the varied interpretation of the clauses of the Convention among the parties and signatories vis-à-vis the stakeholders' national interests. He argues that although mechanisms for settlement of disputes are available within the Convention itself, they have fallen short on several occasions in providing effective resolution of disputes as was observed in China's case. He opines that it is in India's national interest at the strategic level that Indo-Pacific is peaceful and prosperous on a sustainable basis and thus fully endorses the tenets of UNCLOS to govern maritime global commerce.

The next four chapters deal with the issue of the legitimacy of UNCLOS and its relevance in the 21st century. Shri Shakti Sinha, former Chief Secretary of Andaman and Nicobar Islands and Ms. Deeksha Goel, Senior Research Fellow, India Foundation, in "UNCLOS: A Framework for International Legal Governance" explain the framework for international legal governance and write that UNCLOS was the product of over four decades of scientific research and negotiations which ensured that the seas, which are a global common, are available and accessible to human society without discrimination, for growth. The authors argue that zero-sum games have been kept in check through the arbitration mechanisms and in future, it would be risky to jeopardise all these gains which is a likely outcome if countries act arbitrarily and unilaterally in violation of accepted norms and institutions. The authors suggest that the lessons of UNCLOS should not be forgotten because it is in the interest of all countries and societies to work within the UNCLOS framework.

Editor-in-Chief of *India Law Journal* and Senior Research Fellow, India Foundation, Shri Apurv Kumar Mishra, in his chapter, "A Constitutional Crisis for UNCLOS", writes about the behaviour of states, especially their compliance with international law and also explains the challenges to the UNCLOS regime, the implication of China's conduct after the Arbitral Award in the South China Sea and cites India's example of abiding by the outcome of the arbitral process and respecting international law in the Bay of Bengal. He argues that a rule-based global order cannot sustain without strict and universal adherence to international law.

The Vice-Chancellor of the Rashtriya Raksha University, Gandhinagar, and member of India's National Security Advisory Board, Prof. Bimal N. Patel, in his chapter, "Enduring legitimacy of UNCLOS and its continuing vitality", covers issues like managing ocean resources, maritime security, marine scientific research, marine environment and ocean law and policy, categorises prominent short-term, mid-term and long-term challenges and responses not only for India and the Indian Ocean Rim Association (IORA) but also for similarly situated states and multilateral institutions across the globe.

Ms. Hamsa Devineni, distinguished maritime lawyer and Visiting Fellow, India Foundation, in her chapter, "UNCLOS: Its Significance and Legitimacy in 21st Century", assesses the legitimacy of the United Nations Convention on the Law of the Sea (UNCLOS) and its relevance by examining its provisions with respect to their applicability to current maritime issues. She writes about the Bangladesh vs. Myanmar or the Bay of Bengal Delimitation Case, the Philippines vs. China Case and Timor-Leste vs. Australia Case and then outlines the lack of enforcement provisions. She argues that the ascendancy of the Indo-Pacific and the growing economic might of its littorals have led to a change in the balance of power that requires a formal structural change in the existing international legal framework.

The next four chapters deal with the successful model of harmonious settlement of maritime dispute in the Bay of Bengal. Veteran diplomat and Bangladesh's former High Commissioner to India, Tariq Karim, in his chapter, "Role of UNCLOS in facilitating Peaceful Settlements of Disputes—India-Bangladesh: A case of Harmonious Maritime Dispute Resolution", gives a Bangladeshi perspective in deciphering the role of UNCLOS in facilitating a peaceful settlement of the dispute between India and Bangladesh. He suggests that a cooperative political atmosphere has to be conducive for arriving at a culture of consensus acceptable to all, for the greater good of the many. He opines that the India-Bangladesh maritime dispute settlement award and its subsequent implementation could work as a role model for resolving all such contentious maritime disputes across the globe.

United Nations International Law Commission Member Dr. Aniruddha Rajput, in his chapter, "Bay of Bengal Maritime Delimitation Cases: Upholding the Rule of Law in International Relations", argues that disputes are an inevitable reality in an interconnected world and puts the onus of addressing the dispute on States, especially with respect to the use of the oceans and the regulation of their use through the United Nations Convention on the Law of the Sea (UNCLOS) that could result in disputes. He writes about the legal framework, land boundary terminus and explains the base points and delimitation of the territorial sea. He suggests that rising powers like India and China that intend to take a larger role in international relations and global institutions need to show their commitment towards international law and particularly the law of the sea. It is only if they lead the way that the rest can follow suit and make international law and particularly UNCLOS an effective instrument for stability in the future world order and value-based international relations

Former senior advisor with the International Commission of Jurists, Mr. Myo Htike Tan Thein, in his chapter, "Myanmar and Bangladesh: A Case of Harmonious Maritime Dispute Resolution under UNCLOS", writes about the harmonious maritime dispute resolution under UNCLOS between Myanmar and Bangladesh as a landmark judgement as it was the first time ITLOS ruled on a maritime boundary dispute. He further explains in his chapter the uniqueness of the verdict in creating a 'grey area', where rights over the sea bed were given to Bangladesh, while Myanmar retained rights over superjacent waters. Mr. Myo hopes that the Myanmar-Bangladesh maritime dispute resolution will become a template for the establishment of 'rule-based International Order' at sea and is replicated by other states.

Former director of Maulana Abul Kalam Azad Institute for Asian Studies (MAKAIAS), Dr. Sreeradha Datta, in her chapter, "Maritime Dispute Resolution in Bay of Bengal: Leading to Greater Benefits", essentially argues that the maritime dispute resolution without any serious acts of aggression between India and Bangladesh was possible for a number of reasons. In the first section of her chapter, she briefly examines the history and causes of the hostility in the Bay of Bengal. In the second section, she writes about the big picture of neighbourliness and peaceful cooperation that emerged as a stronger development to rally around, and hopefully, in South Asia, a cooperative framework will emerge as a stronger commitment over smaller individual gains.

The next four chapters deal with the imbroglio in the South China Sea and the problems of non-compliance with UNCLOS. In her chapter, "Maritime Confidence-Building Measures and the Code of Conduct at Sea", Dr. Yurika Ishii, Associate Professor at National Defence Academy of Japan, explains the concepts and content of a code of conduct, focusing upon its relationship with international law in the first part while, in the second part, she analyses the relevant state practices that are limited to a situation where military or government ships or aircraft confront each other beyond territorial seas and air. She argues that international law with regard to safety at sea is evolving, and the obligation of safe conduct at sea is now a positive rule and such developments have important implications for maritime safety and security at sea.

Former Director of National Maritime Foundation, Dr. Vijay Sakhuja in his chapter, "Growing problem of Non-compliance with UNCLOS: An Indian Perspective", writes about the problems of non-compliance with United Nations Convention on the Law of the Sea (UNCLOS) 1982 and lists a few case studies of compliance and non-compliance and analyses the Chinese refusal to participate in the contentious South China Sea island dispute. He also analyses China's decision to remain absent from the Permanent Court of Arbitration in The Hague, a mechanism convened under the compulsory dispute settlement provisions of the 1982 UNCLOS. In his chapter, Dr. Sakhuja raises the important question as to who would enforce international law and is non-compliance primarily a problem of enforcement.

Former Vietnamese Ambassador to India, Ton Sinh Thanh, in his chapter, "Challenges in Implementation of UNCLOS in South China Sea", argues that the South China Sea (SCS) is important not only to the littoral states but also to outside regional and global powers. He writes that the navigation, overflight, access to natural resources, trade, energy transport, stability and security in the SCS are essential not only to internal but also to external nations, especially the USA, Japan, South Korea, Australia, India, etc. He argues that the combined power of supportive political will and use of international legal institutions may provide a strong pull in the direction of stability through normative compliance which is the reason why ASEAN in general and Vietnam, in particular, welcome all external powers to have a constructive engagement, contributing to peace, stability and security in the SCS.

Former Judge at the International Tribunal for the Law of the Sea and Iceland's former ambassador to India, Professor Gudmundur Eiriksson, in his chapter, "UNCLOS and the Relationships between Law & Power and Power & Principle; Lessons (to be) learned from the *South China Sea Arbitration*", focuses on the relationships between law and power and between power and principle. His chapter presents these relationships in the context of the South China Sea Arbitration (Philippines vs. China) before an Arbitral Tribunal constituted under Annex VII to the United Nations Convention on the Law of the Sea (UNCLOS). He argues that power relations are an inherently relative phenomenon and says that the jury is still out on whether the rule of law remains relevant in the disputes in the South China Sea.

The last four chapters deal with Maritime Security architecture in the Indo-Pacific region. In his chapter, "Freedom of Navigation in the Indo-Pacific: A View from the Indian Ocean", former Executive Director of National Maritime Foundation, Dr. Gurpreet S. Khurana explains how Pacific-Asia and the Indian Ocean Region (IOR) are lately being seen as an integrated 'Indo-Pacific' maritime supra-region. He writes that the security environment in the two regions is vastly dissimilar. Hence, the emergent issues relating to Freedom of Navigation (FON) would also differ. His chapter examines FON in the entire Indo-Pacific and seeks to provide a prognosis and policy prescriptions specific to the IOR.

Former Commander of the Sri Lankan Navy, Admiral Jayantha Perera, in his chapter, "Maritime Security Architecture in Indo-Pacific under UNCLOS: A Sri Lankan Perspective", writes about evolving security architecture and partnerships in the Indo-Pacific region under UNCLOS that are centric to the Indian Ocean region. He argues that new architecture should allow cooperation and partnership, promote rule-based maritime activity, allow bilateral and multilateral cooperation, create space for the assistance of needy nations to be supported by advanced nations for capacity building in a transparent approach, enhance maritime Domain Awareness and, most importantly, should have voluntary consensus on refraining from planning or carrying out actions that hinder the security balance of the Indo-Pacific Region.

Indonesian Ambassador to India, Sidharto Reza Suryodipuro, in his chapter, "Contribution of UNCLOS in Evolving Maritime Security Architecture in Indo-Pacific: An Indonesian Perspective", argues that the strength of laws and norms within the UNCLOS regime cannot be taken for granted. The region must be vigilant against efforts to weaken them. He writes that China's actions in the South China Sea have weakened the UNCLOS regime. He opines that there will always be efforts to build upon or change UNCLOS and, therefore, an agreement must be made on the elements to be strengthened. He stresses on the fact that ASEAN and Indonesia must seek to ensure the support and interest of others in making the Southeast Asia maritime region open for all, in accordance with UNCLOS.

In his chapter, "Law and Power: Enforcing UNCLOS in the Indo-Pacific", Director, US Initiative, Observer Research Foundation, Mr. Dhruva Jaishankar argues that order and norms are important and are valuable but they matter little when confronted with determined force. The act of preserving international order requires not just the ability but also the willingness to defend it, including through military means. He writes that it is still possible for the international community, and particularly like-minded and democratic governments that believe in the rule of law, to successfully take a few important and outstanding steps which include strengthening the legal basis for UNCLOS, improving the moral standing by highlighting successful precedents, better coordinating and sharing information, and helping each other build capacities to implement UNCLOS by military and non-military means.

The book endeavours to generate debate and create international support for managing maritime global commons in accordance with the provisions of UNCLOS. It is hoped that all lingering maritime disputes are resolved amicably in the manner disputes in the Bay of Bengal were resolved. A rule-based international order in the seas will facilitate optimum utilisation of the sea and its resources for the good of mankind. It is therefore imperative that all countries, especially the major powers, pursue this agenda rather than their perceived narrow national goals.

2

Size and Reach, Land and Sea:
Two Dimensions of a Strategic Horizon

M J Akbar

The sheer size of the subcontinent's landmass has finessed from our general consciousness a pertinent fact: that India's shoreline extends to the vicinity of the Arabian Sea in the west and the Malacca straits in the east.[1]

This perception is compounded by the reality that the principal strategic threat is, and has been, through land. From the time of the Persian monarch Darius and the Greek-Macedonian conqueror Alexander, to use only the recorded annals, invaders have come through the passes of the Hindu Kush and across the Indus, through Punjab to Delhi or Agra. They brought infantry and cavalry. No one equipped a navy, until the Portuguese and the British turned up. Perhaps Indians were also lulled by the fact that the Portuguese momentum stalled very quickly; and while the British used guns to reinforce their merchant fleets, the long trek from Bengal to Punjab and Mysore between 1757 and the 1840s was through land. It was the army that made the British monarch emperor of India. More recently, the Pakistani invasion of 1947 and the Chinese aggression of 1962 were both conflicts over land.

The stakes were always high. During the age of empires, the rewards of success were considerable, for the wealth of India was at the command of the sword. The price of failure was devastating, for a dynasty's credibility did not survive defeat even when the victor was more interested in plunder than power. The collateral benefits of victory, on the other hand, could bring a century of power. The Delhi Sultanate was rejuvenated when India became the only power to repeatedly crush the seemingly-invincible Mongols, who made repeated attempts to conquer Delhi from the time of Chengiz Khan, who turned back from the Indus, till 1327. Kashmir became Mongol territory. But in 1305 Alauddin Khilji crushed the Mongols at the battle of Amroha, leaving 20,000 of them dead.[2] Shocked and incensed, Duwa, ruler of the Chagtai Khanate, sent another force the following year, which too was annihilated. Those who were not killed were brought to Delhi and sold into slavery.[3]

Conversely, the power structure of the Tughluqs disintegrated when Emir Taimur sacked Delhi and massacred its inhabitants in the winter of 1398.[4] It is said that Delhi took a century to recover from that unprecedented brutality.[5] Similarly, the credibility of the Mughals, already enfeebled, collapsed in 1739 when Nadir Shah ordered a massacre in the capital and carted off its treasures.[6] Delhi witnessed a third massacre, in 1857, when vengeful British forces punished civilians for the failure of an impotent ruling class.

Perhaps the persistent indifference to sea power with some minor exceptions like the Marathas apart; was encouraged by the inability of the Portuguese to build from their base in Goa. Vasco de Gama came in 1498, and by 1510 his successors had secured this colony for Portugal. But there they nested. Daman and Diu were only trading beachheads for the manufacture of Gujarat. Their occasional military provocations were easily subdued, while the assets accrued from trade far outweighed the liability of their indiscretions.

Man, islanders apart, has generally been more comfortable with land than water. Psychologically, sea represents distance, land has the feel of proximity. Overseas is somehow more intimidating than overland. Man has evolved into a land creature; the economy is land-based, whether industrial or agricultural; water is a hunting space for food or seasonal trade. Culture is land-centric. Laws have found solutions for land-disputes, but it was United Nations Conventions on the Law of the Seas (UNCLOS) that made for a significant treaty devised for the seas.

For Indians, in what may seem a paradox, the sea never represented hostility. There was no sea-phobia. After all, India is the only land which has an ocean named after it. But the sea was a resource for productive travel, not aggression. Indian ports were launch stations of trade, not war. It is often forgotten that there is no record of any serious naval military engagement in the Indian Ocean until the arrival of Europeans. This might be described as an inactive fact; nothing happened, so nothing was written. But the importance of this "inactive fact" must not be underestimated. Europeans turned the Indian Ocean into a war zone.

India's mercantile prowess in the first millennium of the Christian era, and the multi-faceted, economic, artistic, philosophical, linguistic and religious interaction with South East Asia is too well to bear repetition. One of the most fascinating museums is at Angkor Wat, site of some of the most glorious temples in the world. The Sanskrit stone inscriptions are a sure reminder of how much of the past has been forgotten. India was never invaded from the east until the European powers arrived, first to trade, then to influence, and then to dominate.[7]

Two thousand years ago, the spread of Indian merchandise went in both the directions, east and west. The Roman historian Pliny records that the maritime trade between India and Egypt, which became a Roman province after Julius Caesar's invasion, drained 50 million sesterces to India. The balance of trade was overwhelmingly in India's favour, thanks to the luxury goods that found their way into the markets of Rome.[8]

The romantic adventures of King Arthur's knights are familiar to many, but most of this many will be surprised with this passage from the chronicle written by Chretien de Troyes. In his account of the adventures of Sir Perceval, he mentions that the knight received *"a shirt and breeches of fine linen brought to him as well as hose dyed with brazilwood and a tunic of indigo silk that had been woven and made in India"*.[9] It was Indian silk that was sought as a prized possession.

Arab traders were in Gujarat, Kerala and Sri Lanka, and Indians in Arabia and Africa, from much before the Islamic era. Lankan Muslims are still known as the Moors; they learnt Tamil to negotiate with Indian businessmen across the narrow strait. No kingdom with its epicenter in Delhi became an empire until it had conquered Gujarat, for Gujarati ports were the major hubs for lucrative trade. It was not until the 18th century that an Indian fief gave voice to a serious threat from the sea. Alivardi Khan, the wise if wavering grandfather of the infantile Siraj-ud-Daulah, last effective nawab of Bengal, asked: *"It is not difficult to extinguish fire on land; but should the sea be in flames, who can put it out?"*[10]

The metaphor is powerful. But by 1756, when Aliverdi Khan died, it was too late. The sea was already in flames lit by British gunpowder. The Bay of Bengal was part of every map, and Portuguese pirate ships were raiding the province from 1520s, but no nawab of Bengal had an effective navy.

The difference between seeing India as the land south of the Himalaya or the land north of the ocean is startling. The first visage displays the size of India. The second opens eyes to the reach of India.

From the waters, India ranges from the circa 100-kilometre gap between the Andaman Islands and Aceh in Indonesia to the Arabian Sea. But the favourite Indian perspective, thus far, has been to look through blinkers. Ask a simple question: how far is Indonesia from India, and the traditional reaction is to treat this as some kind of trick question. The geographical fact is that the southern tip of India is not Kanyakumari in Tamil Nadu, but Indira Point in the Andaman and Nicobar Islands,[11] from where Singapore's lights might glow on the edge of a dark night. Sri Lanka is not the only island neighbour of India.

At long last India's strategic thinking has begun to coordinate the defence of the nation on its land borders, and the management of seas to ensure that they remain a free passage for international trade and communication, outside the domination of any power. The myopia of the past has ended. The acceptance of an Indo-Pacific sea space in international terminology and growing diplomatic usage is a powerful indicator of this change.

Obviously, this also means recognition of new challenges. Water is fluid, and must find an echo in fluid thinking. Seas have no stark boundaries, and artificial attempts to "expand" any national claim cannot become another form of neo-colonisation. Disputes need a mechanism for resolution, or they quietly find the energy to explode into a crisis.

There is growing consciousness of three crucial realities. As land resources stagnate or dwindle, the wealth of the seas—possibly far greater than the riches of land—has become a target for the powerful. The 21st Century is becoming a century of the seas, skies and space. The clash of dangerous competition is already echoing through cyberspace. Encroachment has begun above the limits of gravity: airlines with the technology to climb into space and return will cover the distance between one end of the globe to another in the time that it takes for a domestic flight. Knowledge is expanding at an exponential pace, and knowledge is the key to wealth; it will determine who will control the rapidly changing world. This century which will be radically resurrected by new ideas, capabilities and technologies, while the human mind takes a quantum leap across the limitations of inheritance, if any, or exploits its advantages where they are passed down. India is going to be a major player in the realm of new horizons.

But before too much of optimism enthrals takes over, the central question should collectively be addressed: can the seas, skies and space become a creative arena of shared space, or will they become victims of that nasty human inclination towards conflict and the avaricious desire for supremacy? If they cannot be made into shared spaces, they will inevitably turn into zones of conflict.

India is very clear about the better, or perhaps the only rational, option. There must be equity in the management of the skies, seas and space, the shared gifts of nature. India has accordingly strived to create a rule based management of the ocean space and resources. It has abided by its commitment to UNCLOS and has resolved almost all its maritime disputes with its neighbours.

NOTES

1. The International Hydrographic organization defines the Western Limit of Malacca Strait as the line joining Pedropunt, the northern most point of Sumatra (5°402N 95°262E) and Lem Voalan the Southern extremity of Goh Puket (Phromthep Cape on Phuket Island) in Siam (Thailand) (7°452N 98°182E). India and Thailand are considered the basin state, apart from Indonesia, Malaysia and Singapore.
2. Banarsi Prasad Saksena, "The Khaljis - Alauddin Khalji: The Last Mongol Invasions-Malwa and Rajasthan" in *Mohammad Habib and Khaliq Ahmad Nizami (ed.),* A Comprehensive History of India Volume five: The Delhi Sultanat (A.D. 1206-1526), (New Delhi: Indian History Council/People's Publishing House, 1970), pp. 392-393.

3. Ibid., pp. 393-395.
4. William Irvine, "Muhammadan India (A.D. 637-1803)" in Henry Frowde (ed.), *The Imperial Gazetteer of India: The Indian Empire Volume II*, (Oxford: Clarendon Press, 1909), p. 366.
5. Mohammad Habib, "Successors of Firuz Shah Tughluq" in *Mohammad Habib and Khaliq Ahmad Nizami* (ed.). A Comprehensive History of India Volume five: The Delhi Sultanat (A.D. 1206-1526), (New Delhi: Indian History Council/People's Publishing House, 1970), p. 627.
6. William Irvine, op. cit., p. 409.
7. Vasco da Gama arrived Calicut on 20 May 1498, Portuguese were followed by the Dutch, British French and the Danes.
8. H.G. Rawlinson, *Intercourse between India and the World: From Earliest Times to the Fall of Rome* (Cambridge: At the University Press, 1916), pp. 101-103.
9. Chretien de Troyes (translated by Burton Raffel), Perceval: The story of the Grail, (New Haven & London: Yale University Press, 1999), p. 51.
10. Robert Harvey, *Clive: The life and death of a British Emperor* (Thomas Dunne Books 2000).
11. Indira Point, earlier called Pygmalion Point, is located in Great Nicobar Island and is the southernmost point of India. It is about 135 km from Rondo Island the Northern most point of Indonesia.

3

UNCLOS:
Evolution and Relevance

Vinay Badhwar

From time immemorial, man has been exploring seas and oceans for sustenance. These water bodies constitute 70 per cent of the earth's surface and man's dependence on the sea for trade and resources could never and will never be ignored. The use of oceans, throughout history, has been inseparably linked to prosperity.

Availability of technology especially in the last few decades has rapidly advanced and opened up new avenues but not sufficiently enough to allow us to fully explore and exploit this 70 per cent of relatively unknown part of the earth. While there might not be a requirement of any additional resources now but sooner or later in the future, it has to happen based on the commercial viability of the economics of exploration and exploitation.

Brief History of UNCLOS

The United Nations Convention on the Laws of the Sea (UNCLOS) evolved from the struggle between various coastal states who attempted to expand their control over marine areas bordering their coastline. By the 18th century, it was well understood and therefore desired that the coastal states should have sovereignty over some part of the adjoining coastal seas and a three nautical mile stretch was generally considered acceptable for national jurisdiction beyond the coast line. Changes started after the Second World War when coastal states extended their claims to the seabed adjoining the water off their coast. Technological advancements in oil and gas exploration were the key enablers along with the exploitation of living resources i.e. fish stocks.

It was on the request of the international community that the United Nations International Law Commission considered undertaking the codification of existing laws relating to the oceans. This resulted in preparation of four draft conventions in 1949 which were finally adopted at the first UN Conference on the law of the sea or UNCLOS I in 1958.[1] These were also known as the 1958 Geneva Convention and had four conventions, namely, the Conventions on Territorial Sea and Contiguous Zone (CTS), the Convention on Fishing and Conservation of the Living Resources of the high seas (CFCLR), the Convention on the High Seas (CHS), and finally the Convention of the Continental Shelf (CCS). These conventions came into force between 30 September 1962 and 20 March 1966. The conventions were also accompanied by an Optional Protocol of the Signature on Compulsory Settlement of Disputes (OPSD), which came into force on 30 September 1962 along with the CHS.[2]

This was considered to be a definite step forward; however, this convention did not establish the maximum width of the territorial sea. The second UNCLOS conference or UNCLOS II, which was held in Geneva from 17 March to 26 April 1960, recognised that "development of international law affecting fishing may lead to changes in the practices and requirements of many States". It also recognised the need of the coastal states to expand fishing and fishing industries, in view of rising standards of living. However, the international community once again failed to reach a consensus on a uniform width for the territorial seas or on the norms for sovereign fishing rights, consequently decisions on these crucial issues were deferred to a later date.[3]

The third convention, UNCLOS III, which was convened in New York in 1973, continued till 1982 and finally the convention came in to force on 16 November 1994. UNCLOS provides an effective, comprehensive and overarching international legal framework for the oceans and seas. The scope of the convention is very broad and apart from defining the maritime zones it provides what has been termed as the constitution of the oceans covering the utilization of resources, shipping, marine research, exploitation of the Exclusive Economic Zone (EEZ) and continental shelf and the prevention and avoidance of marine pollution.[4] A brief and specific component has also been placed in UNCLOS III with the aim of responding to maritime threats.

UNCLOS sets up Institutions and balances the rights and obligations of states with the interest of the international community and it is supplemented by other conventions and protocols. In today's international security paradigm, the applicability of the UNCLOS framework with regard to maritime security is often in question. These questions arise because of the existing warfare between traditional state and state being replaced by inclusion of non-state actors, which pose threat to not only maritime security but also those protecting international commerce.

Climate Change and UNCLOS

The Arctic, in many ways a 'final frontier', which while theoretically covered by existing legal instrument, is largely a region prone to unprecedented legal, environment and political challenges.[5] Climate change is heating up the race for the Arctic as receding levels of ice caps are giving way to increased human activity and opening of new sea lanes. Apart from the new sea lanes, states bordering the Arctic Ocean are also seeking to develop offshore resources, which according to some estimates are around 22 per cent of the undiscovered oil and gas reserves of the globe. Inter-governmental bodies like the Arctic council, which have played a useful role in multilateral cooperation;, completely lack authority to resolve conflicting territorial claims. In addition, the UNCLOS has little specific relevance to the Arctic; however, those portions of UNCLOS which are applicable to the Arctic have enormous potential for shaping the future of interactions in the Arctic.[6]

As far as protection of the marine environment is concerned, states are obliged to ensure the protection and preservation of the marine ecosystem in each of their zones. States are also required to ensure that their activities do not prejudice the environment of other states and to ensure that they adopt such laws and regulations which facilitate the protection of their marine environment from pollution emanating from land and seabed-based activities in their national jurisdiction. The provisions of UNCLOS concerned with the preservation and protection of marine ecosystem are limited in scope and do not apply to warships or any other vessels which are owned or are being operated by a state and are deployed on government non-commercial service.[7] The onus of ensuring adoption of appropriate measures consistent with UNCLOS lies with the states.

UNCLOS as a Tool in Governance of Shipping Activities

The governance of shipping activities is an extremely complicated mosaic. UNCLOS along with other international agreements addressed specific elements of shipping and related issues like safety, pollution and liabilities. The International Maritime Organization (IMO), the International Labour Organization (ILO) and the International Chromatographic Organisation (ICO) have played a seminal role in the establishment of minimal basic standards in Governance of international shipping.

UNCLOS has struck a balance between powers of the coastal states, the flag States and the port states to ensure jurisdictional control over shipping. The jurisdictional status in internal waters and Straits used for International navigation remains controversial and could potentially lead to disputes in the future. With regard to safety of navigation, coastal states may designate dedicated sea lanes and formulate traffic separation schemes for foreign ships. However, the states must keep in mind recommendations of the IMO and any channels customarily used for international navigation.

As regard coastal states which are bordering straits which are traditionally used for international navigation exercise very limited powers over foreign ships as they have the right to transit passage. They do not have the right to suspend passage and can only adopt laws that govern ship-source pollution which is applicable to foreign ships. A ship exercising transit passage can do so in its normal mode. A submarine may remain submerged otherwise but when undertaking an innocent passage, it must navigate on the surface and show its flag. UNCLOS, therefore, does not deal with the extent of international navigation required to transform such waters into straits used for international navigation. There has thus been a plethora of national opinions on the difference in application of straits used for international navigation regime.[8] Agreeing and fixing maritime boundaries involves the use of Geology, Oceanography, Technology, Hydrography, money, law, history, politics and diplomacy.

Today there are numerous ongoing disputes over maritime boundaries. Of more than 500 potential maritime disputes of the world, less than half have agreed to creating an environment of uncertainty and potential for disputes with respect to others. In some extreme cases, the conflicting parties have resorted to various levels of violence to assert their perceived rights. However, there have been cases where cooperation has prevailed over conflict. Cooperation has worked because of changing international environments or legal regimes and more specifically based on the bilateral relations between the disputing parties. However, in the context of the international environment, three factors exist:

Firstly, economic interests dominate and are often the driving factor in maritime boundary disputes with military concerns also being present frequently. As economic developments enable the expansion of military capabilities and reach, efforts to cooperate may take a back seat, but ultimately economic investment and activities require peaceful environment.

Secondly, in some cases international legal institutions can help facilitate cooperation. Despite UNCLOS being the most important legal document for dispute resolution, it does not provide specific requirements for resolving overlapping claims leaving it up to the parties to decide. The convention merely stipulates that the division of the sea-beds should be on equitable basis, international courts also favour this approach. In some situations, UNCLOS has even made it more difficult to come to an agreed resolution. By focusing on such technical issues as baselines, navigational regimes and EEZ, the UNCLOS has also created new areas of disputes that limit its effectiveness. It thus has an escalatory feature also because it forces countries to maximise their claims. On the other hand, in some cases, parties to a conflict consider appealing to the international courts as detrimental to their common interests and attempt to resolve issues mutually.

Finally, the UNCLOS requires and encourages good bilateral relations between states. Regional groupings of states also have a role to play. Such organisations are generally conceived for mutual economic cooperation and can facilitate positive outcomes. Trade between countries has also played a role in containing if not resolving disputes. Economic interdependence has repeatedly prevented disputes from escalating into conflicts.

The Convention has had some clear achievements while being coupled with ambiguities with specific reference to hydrographic surveying and the UNCLOS framework. As far as EEZ are concerned, the sovereign rights of exploitation, exploration, management and conservation of natural resources rests with the coastal states[9]. Research vessels that have claimed to be conducting military surveys have been warned to move out of the EEZ in some coastal states. In these circumstances, occurrences of incidents leading to disputes between parties over rights and duties in the EEZ cannot be ruled out. These disputes can be traced back to the ambiguities in the EEZ regime and the variety of interpretation and implementation. The convention lacks in its definition of key terms like marine scientific research, and survey activities such as hydrographic and military surveys[10].

The convention was formulated more than three and a half decades ago in a very different geopolitical and technological environment than what exists today. Though attempts were made to conduct research to propose some guidelines to clarify EEZ regime and address the issues of rights and duties as a confidence-building measure, they do not have a legal status and are rather viewed as broad principles of common understanding. Such guidelines represent a consensus among participants only without a legal status and incidents continue to occur which is a major source of tension and disputes. Moreover, a coastal state in the EEZ can erect offshore installations to impede movements of warships and submarines. UNCLOS is silent on navy's conducting exercise and weapon tests in EEZ of other states. This has resulted in some states claiming that other states cannot carry out military activities in or around their EEZ's without their consent. Unlike high seas, no provisions exist for reserving EEZ's for peaceful purposes.

The complex rules and norms of the convention have played a crucial role in maintaining a global common free from biased policies. It has provided a reference for multitude of contentious issues which could flare up disputes and conflicts and prevent them. However, there are many instances in which coastal states and regional powers have chosen to openly contest, selectively interpret and discretely subvert key principles. Further expecting a result completely on the basis of UNCLOS is always unlikely. In addition, even a settlement by arbitration requires both parties to accept the conditions of the convention before going for arbitration. Therefore, considering the prevailing global environment, it would be more prudent that countries also opt for dispute settlement in maritime arrangements beyond the provisions of UNCLOS. The resolution of the disputes with innovative ideas and bold initiatives is the need of the hour and the declaration of such willingness and initiatives will be a first step in this direction. The success of such ideas may result in confidence and boldness to deal with other outstanding issues between the states. In the contemporary geopolitical maritime conduct, the rising number and diversity of excessive claims is overwhelming. There are some 80 states whose borders have the potential to be expanded under article 76 of UNCLOS. A global framework like UNCLOS is an exceptional achievement in International Affairs. However, advocates and opponents of UNCLOS do acknowledge that the terms of the convention may not be possible to negotiate today.

NOTES

1. The first United Nations Conference on the Laws of the Sea was convened by United Nations General Assembly Resolution 1105 (XI) of 21 February 1957 from 24 February to 27 April 1958.
2. Tullio Treves, "1958 Geneva Conventions on the Law of the Sea", *Audiovisual Library of International Law,* 29 April 1958, available at https://legal.un.org/avl/ha/gclos/gclos.html (Accessed on 10 September 2017).
3. Second United Nations Conference on the Law of the Sea, Geneva, 17 March – 26 April 1960, "Law of The Sea and The UN Conventions", *Pence Law Library Guides,* available at https://wcl.american.libguides.com/c.php?g=563260&p=3877789 (Accessed on 15 September 2017).
4. Codification Division, Office of Legal Affairs, UN, "Second United Nations Conference on the Law of the Sea", available at https://legal.un.org/diplomaticconferences/1960_los/ (Accessed on 20 September 2017).
5. Lincoln P. Bloomfield, "The Arctic: Last Unmanaged Frontier", *Foreign Affairs,* Vol. 60, No. 1 (Fall 1981).

6. Kristen Bartenstein, 'The Arctic Exception' in the Laws of the Sea Convention: A contribution to Safer Navigation in the Northwest Passage? *Ocean Development & International Law*, Vol. 42, No. 1 (2011), pp. 22-53.
7. Arctic Council, "Law of the Sea as Reflected in UNCLOS: The Overarching Legal Framework" *AMSA Report 2009*, available at http://www.arctis-search.com/Law+of+the+Sea+as+Reflected+in+UNCLOS (Accessed on 20 October 2018).
8. Ibid.
9. United Nations Convention on the Law of the Sea, "UNCLOS Main Document", *UNCLOS Official*, available at https://www.un.org/depts/los/convention_agreements/texts/unclos/unclos_e.pdf
10. Sam Bateman, "Solving the 'Wicked Problems' of Maritime Security: Are Regional Forums up to the Task?" *Contemporary Southeast Asia*, Vol. 33, No. 1 (2011), pp. 1–28.

4

Governing the Seas:
Power of the Law and the Law of Power

C. Raja Mohan

Introduction

One of the widely acknowledged features of the current times is the rise of Asia. Just a few decades ago in the 1960s, the prospects for Asia, burdened by large population, food shortages, and presumed absence of the cultural will for modernisation, were considered dim. However, within a short span of few years, the developmental story of Asia found a new script. It started with the four Asian tigers (South Korea, Taiwan, Hong Kong, and Singapore) led by Japan and the United States, which emerged as the new centres of economic growth in Asia. Their growth path found emulation in the South East Asia. People's Republic of China (PRC), under Deng Xiaoping embarked on a bold strategy of reform and opening up at the end of 1970s, which resulted in a stunning four decades of extremely high growth rates. The rise of Asia gained further momentum when India opened up its economy at the turn of the 1990s. Joining the party after the collapse of the Soviet model, were the Indo-Chinese states of Vietnam, Cambodia and Laos. Myanmar was the last large nation in Asia to turn to economic reforms.

As Asia began to emerge as a trading region and contribute to global growth in a significant manner, the sea lines of communication within Asia and between Asia and the rest of the world began to acquire even greater importance. As a result Asia's hunger for resources, the livestock as well as energy and mineral riches of the oceans began to gain enormous significance. The rise and integration of Asia, unfortunately, also led to the intensification of territorial disputes, especially in the maritime domain. Deng's China was eager and willing to seek peace on its land frontiers. It took special efforts to either resolve its long-standing land boundary disputes with its neighbours or agreed to freeze them for the time being. However, by the end of the first decade of the 21st century, a newly assertive China was taking a muscular approach to its past territorial claims, both on land as well as on sea. While the land boundary issues with India were dealt within a bilateral political framework, Asia hoped that China would abide by the rules laid down by the United Nations Convention on the Law of the Sea (UNCLOS) that opened for signature in December 1982 and came into force in November 1994. This chapter is not about the legal intricacies of UNCLOS that came out of prolonged negotiations and complex compromises among the negotiating parties. The focus of the chapter is on the increasing inability of the UNCLOS to persuade China to abide by its rules. China has taken unilateral steps to change the territorial status quo in the South China Sea, a more muscular approach to its disputes with Japan in the East China Sea and broader contestation with the United States on the interpretation of the UNCLOS on the rules governing freedom of military navigation in the Western Pacific. The Philippines took the dispute over the South China Sea islands to the Permanent Court of Arbitration (PCA) in The Hague. The PCA rejected Chinese claims on all issues raised by the dispute.[1] Beijing, however, refused to accept the jurisdiction of the PCA and rejected the ruling, by citing its historical claims to the waters.[2] That brings up the question of the relationship between power and international law, as the issues raised are not only of concern to the neighbours of China but also to all other states in Asia and the world.

Law and Power

No one can deny the power of law and norms in shaping international societies, for that matter any society. There can be no coherent societies, without norms of some kind. Yet, there is no escaping the fact that the laws of power matter equally in the world. No decision-maker in any capital can simply assume all countries will follow international law in a consistent manner. The power of laws and the law of power are not the same thing. While the power of laws provides a basis on which we can live together, the laws of power have their own impact. Power shapes how laws are crafted and the laws negotiated do indeed reflect the distribution of power within the international system. Power is also critical in defining how laws are implemented. Today most scholars and practitioners of statecraft agree that the tectonic plates of power distribution are moving again. The rise of China has altered the balance not only between Beijing and the West, but also within Asia. The changing balance of power has triggered the renewal of great power rivalry that had seemed to ebb after the end of the Cold War and the contestation between the great powers is most intense in Asia and its waters.

Distribution of power within the international system is not the only factor that contributes to the making and enforcement of international law. Technological change is an equally important factor in persuading nations to rethink old laws and devise new ones to meet the conditions created by advances in science and technology. New technologies allow the exploration of new frontiers, and demand the drafting of new laws. For example, the transformation of shipbuilding and navigation helped open up the maritime space and create economic links between distant entities. As seafaring moved beyond coastal shipping to the high seas, new conventions had to be developed for the management of the maritime commons. Subsequently, as outer space became amenable to man, nations began to focus on creating laws for outer space. Similarly, now that the computing power and telecommunication have merged to usher in a digital revolution, there is an intense effort to define rules of the road for cyberspace. The opening up of new frontiers generated soaring hopes that nations will learn to avoid conflict within them and treat the new domains as global commons. But there is no escaping the conflict. In all these domains there has been unending tension between power and principle, might and right, and between collective good and interest of individual great powers.

There have been multiple tensions playing out in the South China Sea during last few years. In its legal battle with China, the Philippines, won the argument comprehensively in the permanent vote of arbitration, but lost in the realm of power. What is more sobering is the fact that a newly elected President of the Philippines who took charge amidst an impressive legal victory decided it is not worth fighting with China on this issue and hoped a reasonable deal with Beijing could be secured at the bilateral level through political means.[3] Power, then, has a way of skirting the law and seeks acquiescence from the weaker party.

Lawfare

In thinking about international law, one ought to note how different it is from the nature of domestic law. Unlike in the domestic sphere, there is no constitution that lays down the law in the international sphere, even though the scope of norms of international law has dramatically expanded in the last century. There is also no central authority or a world government to enforce those laws. It is neither easy to implement the norms that states have negotiated or signed, nor is it feasible to generate a consensus on how to interpret existing laws. In the domestic sphere, the courts adjudicate disputes and the state his monopoly over the use of force facilitates the enforcement of the judicial decisions. For all its legal advances in the last century and more, the international society remains a collection of states that do not pay obeisance to a higher authority. Anarchy, in a basic sense, continues to prevail in the world of international politics, especially in the domain of security, where states tend to guard their rights zealously.

The role of power in shaping laws is quite evident from the evolution of the laws governing maritime spaces. In 1603, the Dutch East India Company captured a Portuguese ship, *Santa Catarina,* laden with goods from China and Japan as it was transiting through the Malacca Straits. They looted the ship and sold the goods in the European markets, for big profits. For the Dutch East India Company, this was a good turn of events. However, among the shareholders, was a small group of religious people, the Mennonites, who felt that looting and profiteering from the sale of stolen goods, was not moral. So the Dutch East India Company hired Hugo Grotius (now referred to as the Father of International Law) and asked him to make a public case to justify their deeds. He created the argument that the sea belonged to everyone and was not closed by monopolies of countries. Thus the idea of an open sea was developed in a long pamphlet by Grotius for the Dutch East India Company. This later became the basis for the International Law of the Sea. The incident also tells the story of rising and falling powers wherein Dutch capitalism prevailed over Portuguese mercantilism. The Dutch in turn paved the way for Britain and the United States that have since dominated the making of international law in the last few centuries.[4]

Norms do not come on their own, but from the contestation for power. It is the dominant powers that tend to set the rules. And as new powers emerge, they want to rewrite or reinterpret the existing rules. China's own approach to international law comes from its claim that many extant rules have been made by the Western powers that had humiliated China in the past and dominated the seas. The Chinese unsurprisingly question the very legitimacy of the current arguments in favour of rules-based maritime order. Beijing claims that the 'rules-based order' is a means of denying China its legitimate space and rights as it becomes a great power. Chinese publicists claim that they are not obliged to respect 'Western rules' which they did not make and demand that they have a say in the making of new rules. Thanks to their power accretion, China is now in a position to not just make rules but increasingly enforce them in the waters adjacent to it.

The idea of 'lawfare'—the use of law as a weapon of conflict has become quite central to contemporary Chinese statecraft and diplomacy. Amidst China's rise and the relative decline of the US and the growing power imbalance between Beijing and Asian neighbours, international law and norms have become hostage to the shifting power dynamics. This is not about abstract theories but actually translation of the widening power differential into concrete outcomes on the ground. The last few years have seen China's capability and will to create new facts on the ground that others have no option but to live with. In debating and interpreting UNCLOS, the countries of the Indo-Pacific have to continuous attention to question of power and how shifts in its distribution for the law of seas.

Power and Law in the Indo-Pacific

The economic future as well as the prosperity of India depends entirely on having a good order at sea, as India has become a trading nation and security of its Sea Lines of Communications (SLOCs) is critical for the well-being of its people. China's dependence on sea is even more, given its new position as the world's second largest economy and the foremost trading nation. Japan and Korea have historically been the first countries to build modern capitalism that has been dependent on the sea. Asian prosperity today depends on the waters of the Indo-Pacific. Just as the seas have become vital for India and its neighbours, there is breakdown in the legal order governing the seas thanks to the maritime ambition and assertion of a newly risen China. The big question that the region will continue to engage with is the relationship between international law and power.

As highlighted earlier, the question of power is central, however, it cannot ignore the importance of law and norms in the construction of a stable and peaceful maritime order. The challenge for the global community is to find ways to produce the power balance that facilities the widest possible adherence to international law. Ever since the Second World War, the US has underwritten the framework for a stable balance of power in the Pacific and Indian Oceans. Today a rising China is contesting that framework, and this contest, which has sharpened in recent years, will have a powerful impact on the maritime environment of the Indo-Pacific.

As Chinese military power expands, it has the capacity to threaten the American forward military presence that has been sitting on the so-called first island chain that includes Japan, Philippines, Taiwan and the ASEAN. There is now a breakdown of not just the power balance but also the legal system. The new rules of governance for the seas are likely to emerge not on the basis of the first principles of international law, but on the nature of the power distribution between the two great powers and the kind of political accommodation that they might arrive at.

This could pose a serious problem for other countries in the region. If the Americans and the Chinese come to terms on a new set of rules, will these suit others? How would these two powers respond if there is contestation? Not all countries in Asia are small—India has one billion people, Indonesia has about 250 million, while the Philippines and Vietnam have about 100 million. Therefore it is necessary to ensure that the interests are maintained in a stable and legal order. Where does that leave the rest of the Indo-Pacific?

Security Cooperation among Middle Powers

While the argument between the Americans and the Chinese continue, other Asian countries must move decisively towards resolving their bilateral disputes and resolve them peacefully. It has been clearly demonstrated in case of Bay of Bengal. In settling the maritime territorial disputes between India and Bangladesh, Bangladesh and Myanmar as well as between India and other South East Asian neighbours, an important template of peaceful resolution has been established. A lot of credit should go to Bangladesh for taking its maritime disputes with Myanmar and India for international arbitration. The credit is also due to Myanmar and India for accepting the international awards. The Indian government's decision was indeed a political one. The argument that won in Delhi under the Prime Minister Narendra Modi's government was that Bangladesh is an important neighbour and partner and an early resolution of the maritime dispute would serve India's long term interests. Delhi rightly avoided the temptation to contest the judgement, since it was tilted in favour of Dhaka.[5]

A second important imperative is the need to pool the power resources of the middle powers in the Indo-Pacific. None of the middle powers may be strong enough to produce balance and stability in the seas or hope to replace the US and a rising China. But nations like India, Indonesia, Australia and Vietnam possess enough capabilities to deter aggression by enhancing security cooperation amongst them in the Indo-Pacific.

The third element, of course, is about capacity building in small and vulnerable states. Many tiny islands in the Indian Ocean or the Indo-Pacific possess vast expanses of Exclusive Economic Zones (EEZ), but do not have the resources to patrol them, let alone manage them. India has been providing hydrographic service to a large number of countries in the region by carrying out surveys, or supplying equipment or creating shared maritime domain awareness. The scarce resources can be pooled in to help smaller countries acquire maritime capabilities, so that they do not become simple victims of unilateral policies by the dominant powers.

The fourth element is about sub-regional cooperation. While the UNCLOS may have provided a good framework of rules, it is important to turn the Bay of Bengal into a cooperative zone. The South China Sea will remain disputed for a long time, but India and Bangladesh along with Myanmar, Sri Lanka, Indonesia and Thailand could get together to make this a zone of peaceful cooperation. They could work towards pooling resources and constructing a whole new framework for regional engagements.

The Sri Lankan leaders often speak about their country's maritime identity. Sri Lanka is not just a South Asian country, but also an Indian Ocean country. Colombo has repeatedly emphasised that the Bay of Bengal is a zone of historic expansive cooperation that existed in the past. The political challenge today is to revive some of those forms of cooperation across the waters and this will involve expanding connectivity, of creating links between South Asia and Southeast Asia, of turning the Bay of Bengal into a bridge between different parts of the world. Translating this vision will certainly not be easy and will require a lot of purposeful political and diplomatic effort.

In the end, there is a huge need for reimagining the future of our neighbouring seas, including the Bay of Bengal and other sub-regions of the Indo-Pacific. As the largest country in the Indian Ocean littoral, India has a special responsibility in this regard. One-way forward is to turn the Andaman and Nicobar islands to an open platform, which is accessible to all of the neighbours and create a structure of Regional Corporation in the Bay of Bengal. Transforming the Andaman and Nicobar islands will itself provide the basis for constructing a very different order.

A final thought in conclusion about the tension between law and power. Can the two co-exist? Both are needed because law without power is impotent. If the capacity to enforce rules is missing, it does not matter how good the principle is. Similarly, if it is merely about power without principles, then it lacks legitimacy, morality and accountability. What produces the right mix of power and principle is a stable balance of power system in the region that works in tandem with a rules-based order.

NOTES

1. "Award" PCA Case No. 2013-19: in the Matter of the South China Sea Arbitration before an Arbitral Tribunal constituted under Annex VII to the 1982 United Nations Convention on the Law of the Sea between the Republic of the Philippines and the People's Republic of China, *The Hague: Permanent Court of Arbitration (PCA)*, 12 July 2016, pp. 471-477.
2. Atul Aneja, "China rejects Hague tribunal ruling as 'null and void'", *The Hindu*, 12 July 2016.
3. Renato Cruz de Castro, "The Duterte Administration's appeasement policy on China and the crisis in the Philippine–US alliance", *Philippine Political Science Journal*, (December 2017), pp. 8-9.
4. Prashanth Parameswaran, "The One Moment in Singapore's History You Should Know About', *The Diplomat*, 03 March 2015.
5. Mercedes Page, "India's approach to maritime disputes: lessons for Beijing in the South China Sea?", *The Strategist*, Australian Strategic Policy Institute, 25 November 2015.

5

Global Ocean Governance:
An Asian Perspective

Harsha de Silva

Oceans throw open a plethora of opportunities for both the growth and prosperity of a country as well as the region and beyond. Being surrounded by the Indian Ocean, Sri Lanka too has accepted this fact and thus envisions playing a greater role by becoming a hub of maritime activities in the Indian Ocean Region in the coming decade.

An interesting statistics from the World Bank shows that coastal areas within hundred kilometres of the oceans account for an estimated 61 per cent of the world's total Gross National Product (GNP).[1] The fact is also consistent with the colonial history of the world with heightened economic activities taking place around coastal areas because of trading among nations. This trade traditionally consisted of shipping and logistics services to states. With time, the form of this overseas trade has changed and now includes a greater number of services in its ambit. In present times, ports and Special Economic Zones (SEZs), connected to global production networks and accompanying ecosystems consisting of verticals like finance, legal, real estate and accounting, are becoming centres of unprecedented wealth creation. China's model of investments in ports and related infrastructure provides ample evidence. With the impetus being laid on a blue economy and the vast potential to exploit the economic opportunities that lie beneath and on the ocean surface, the share of littoral countries in global GNP is expected to surpass the current 61 per cent.

In the past, the rules of the sea were written by those Powers which traditionally dominated the region and exploited its economic potential to generate wealth elsewhere. In a post-colonial Asia, economic activity moved away but with changing global dynamics the global balance of power has also started to shift.

Asia is fast emerging as the centre of wealth creation led by India and China. The Gross Domestic Product (GDP) of Asia is rising rapidly and is reflected in countries like Bangladesh, Vietnam, Myanmar and even Sri Lanka,[2] where economic transformation is almost palpable. Cities in these countries and others in Pakistan are transforming from sleepy old towns to megacities. Such transformations signify that trade both within the region and beyond are expanding by leaps and bounds, guided by the rules of the World Trade Organisation (WTO) and numerous other bilateral and multilateral trade agreements.

With increased opportunities of employment and an equitable access to wealth, per capita incomes are rising. There has been an upward trend in the consumption pattern of billions of people as they are graduating from their existing classes. To sustain this transformation, governments are partnering with private investors to build infrastructure leading to employment generation and a sustainable economy.

The dip in global trade in the recent past rests on the pillar of a world recovering from financial crisis. The rise of protectionist policies in some European capitals and in the United States of America, though a worrying trend, is evidenced to be temporary. Any slowdown in European or Western trade is only expected to have a minimal impact on Asian powers owing to the enormous unprecedented potential that lies in Asian waters; however, this has been limited by narrow political ideologies of a few. Thus, in order for trade to flourish in Asia, ensuring peace and security within its waters is of paramount importance while still working with multiple stakeholders and global partners.

The United Nations Convention on the Law of the Sea (UNCLOS) came into existence in 1982[3] when the bipolar world was engulfed in a power battle between capitalism and communism led by the USA and the Soviet Union, respectively. It is remarkable and highly commendable that global leaders were able to agree on a common set of laws to govern the seas when the global environment was marred by a demanding political power play. In present times, it is incumbent upon the global community to further strengthen this Convention to ensure a rule of law in the oceans. The 21st century belongs to the seas and UNCLOS provides a specific pathway to achieve that.

As the world is witnessing a shift in the global power balance, oceans are becoming critically important to several global and regional players, a fact that is also evident by the American primacy being challenged by China. In the larger context of things, the USA and China are not the only two players; the emergence of Russia as a global naval power cannot be ruled out as yet and also perhaps that of Japan and Australia. China with its ambitious One Belt One Road (OBOR) initiative is exploring new horizons in the Indian Ocean Region including in the south of Sri Lanka in Hambantota.

Chinese investment in Sri Lanka's Hambantota port is purely an economic investment with absolutely no military involvement.[4] Extraordinary measures have been put in place by the Government of Sri Lanka to ensure the realisation of the joint venture between Sri Lanka and China as a commercial transaction. In fact, Sri Lanka has considerably influenced the port business as well as port services there. Naval operations are being shifted from Galle to Hambantota. Steps are also being taken to ensure that no new disputes are created in the region owing to Sri Lanka's strategy of leveraging the vast potential of the Indian Ocean which belongs to Sri Lanka as a sovereign nation.

From Sri Lanka's vantage point, there is a need for India to play a more proactive role in working with its friends in the region to strengthen UNCLOS and develop a rule-based order in the Indian Ocean. The existence of many regional institutional initiatives like Indian Ocean Rim Association (IORA), Bay of Bengal Initiative for Multi-Sectoral Technical and Economic Cooperation (BIMSTEC), Indian Ocean Naval Symposium (IONS) and the Indian Ocean Tuna Commission (IOTC) is of marked importance and calls for greater integration of their mandate with that of UNCLOS.

Several simmering conflicts are seen amongst the waters of Asia-Pacific where application of UNCLOS has been ineffective. The disputes in South China Sea have had a heavy impact on regional bilateral relations and are also impacting China's relations with the Association of Southeast Asian Nations (ASEAN). Continuing conflicts highlight the gaps that exist in UNCLOS and the need for the international community to revisit the statutes to keep the relevance of the institution alive in line with the present times.

Sri Lanka is hopeful of a peaceful settlement of the South China Sea dispute through dialogue while upholding the rule of law in interstate affairs. The resolution of the India-Bangladesh Maritime dispute by means of peaceful negotiations through international arbitration at the Permanent Court of Arbitration under the terms of UNCLOS 2014 is a tribute to those who have struggled for the implementation of the Convention. The peaceful resolution of the dispute rests on India's strong political leadership and graceful acceptance of the verdict of the Permanent Court of Arbitration. Bilateral understanding and acceptance of institutional rulings lays the ethos of an ideal order of dealing with interstate conflicts.

The world is grappling with an increase in sea piracy, human smuggling and drug trafficking in high seas where provisions of UNCLOS have not been able to sufficiently mitigate threats. Pirates operating from Somalia started hijacking transit and commercial ships in 2005[5] with such incidents escalating in 2010. The global community took a series of measures including naval cooperation and deploying security personnel on merchant vessels. This move gave birth to a new debate around the privatisation of maritime security; however, such strategies have worked well in reducing the rate of piracy and associated crime.

The major powers have consistently relied on customary international law and the provisions of UNCLOS to justify their military activities. Article 58 of UNCLOS provides that in the Exclusive Economic Zones, all states, whether coastal or landlocked, enjoy the freedom of navigation and overflight and other international lawful uses of the sea, subject to relevant provisions of the Convention.[6] However, the dilemma lies in devising a mechanism to distinguish between regular and nonproliferating activities and activities aimed at information collection and surveillance measures which give a strategic upper hand to certain countries. UNCLOS has thus fallen short on its enforceable measures and provisions insisting on state sovereignty.

An issue that has impacted the successful implementation of UNCLOS is that not all major stakeholders are parties to the Convention. The USA, for example, is the most prominent state whose name is absent from the list of 168 countries that have ratified the Convention.[7] Another reason for UNCLOS and other ocean regulations not achieving their full potential is the lack of coordination between international and national organisations responsible for oceans. Strengthening national legislations of the countries that are party to the Convention providing adequate financial, technical and human capital to the signatories and proactive cooperation and coordination between stakeholders is of vital importance.

Nevertheless, UNCLOS has had its success stories too. The amicable resolution of the dispute on the definition of the border between Singapore and Indonesia is a case in point.[8] It is against the backdrop of these contemporary developments of a multi-polar world that Sri Lanka believes in initiating a dialogue with the objective of developing an Indian Ocean code of conduct on freedom of navigation.

Sri Lanka is willing to initiate explanatory talks on a stable legal order for freedom of navigation in the waters of the Indian Ocean. The outcomes of such talks could be looked at in the form of an agreement on issues of navigation, seabed mining, hydrographic survey and fisheries, amongst others. However, in order to initiate any such dialogue, it is of paramount importance for the littoral nations to build a consensus based on the norms of an existing mechanism.

The Indian Ocean Rim Association (IORA) can thus be utilised to ensure dialogue between all coastal states, Permanent Members of the Security Council and major maritime users. Indian Ocean littoral states must reach an agreement on the measures required to supplement such an effort to ensure freedom of navigation in the Indian Ocean. At the same time, the IORA should also welcome initiatives being proposed by neighbours aimed at creating better understanding around cooperation of navies of the region. The proposed institution is by no means an alternate to UNCLOS but is envisaged as a supporting legal framework based on the basic tenets of UNCLOS.

NOTES

1. "The World Bank and The Ocean: A healthy and productive ocean to help reduce poverty", from World Bank website https://www.worldbank.org/content/dam/Worldbank/World%20Bank%20and%20the%20ocean.pdf (Accessed on 28 July 2020).
2. World Bank Data on *"GDP per capita growth (annual %)"*, available at https://data.worldbank.org/indicator/NY.GDP.PCAP.KD.ZG (Accessed on 10 October 2020).
3. Final Act of the United Nations Convention on the Laws of the Sea.
4. "Hambantota port not a military base for foreign countries: Sri Lanka", *The Economic Times*, 01 September 2017 (Accessed on 11 October 2020).
5. World Bank, *"The Pirates of Somalia: Ending the threat, rebuilding a nation"* (World Bank Group, 2013), available at https://openknowledge.worldbank.org/handle/10986/16518 (Accessed on 28 July 2020).
6. *"United Nations' Convention on the Laws of the Sea"* Article 58, p. 44, available at https://www.un.org/depts/los/convention_agreements/texts/unclos/unclos_e.pdf (Accessed on 28 July 2020).
7. *"Chronological lists of ratifications of, accessions and successions to the Convention and the related Agreements"*, Division for Ocean Affairs and Laws of the Sea, United Nations, available at https://www.un.org/depts/los/reference_files/chronological_lists_of_ratifications.htm (Accessed on 11 October 2020).
8. "No. 54672 - Treaty between the Republic of Singapore and the Republic of Indonesia relating to the delimitation of the territorial seas of the two countries in the eastern part of the Strait of Singapore (with maps)", recorded with Secretariat of the United Nations on 25 September 2017, available at https://treaties.un.org/doc/Publication/UNTS/No%20Volume/54672/Part/I-54672-08000002804cce54.pdf (Accessed on 11 October 2020).

6

Role of UNCLOS in Governing Global Maritime Commerce and Fostering Cooperation in the Indo-Pacific Region

Bimal Verma

In the contemporary geopolitical context, the term "Indo-Pacific" is a relatively new one with its first usage dating back to more than a decade ago in Indian academic writings.[1] Indo-Pacific is much more than merely a term describing the union of the Indian and Pacific Oceans. It represents a concept and a vision. It represents the growing maritime security linkage between the two oceans since the turn of the 21st Century; and therefore, it envisions an adherence by all countries to the established norms and rules of conduct in this 'maritime underbelly' of Asia to ensure the 'rise of Asia' fructifies *sans* insecurities, for the ultimate prosperity of all regional countries and its stakeholders.[2] This was reinforced by Japanese Prime Minister Shinzo Abe during his August 2007 address to the Indian Parliament in New Delhi, where he said,

> *The Pacific and the Indian Oceans are now bringing about a dynamic coupling as seas of freedom and of prosperity.... By Japan and India coming together, this "broader Asia" will evolve into an immense network spanning the entirety of the Pacific Ocean,...Open and transparent, this network will allow people, goods, capital, and knowledge to flow freely...as maritime states, both India and Japan have vital interests in the security of sea lanes.*[3]

Of late, the term 'Indo-Pacific' has entered into common parlance amongst the watchers of the region. It was also referred to in the joint statement issued by the Prime Minister of India Narendra Modi and the President of the United States (US) Donald Trump on 26 June 2017, when the former visited Washington D.C. at the invitation of the US President. The objectives highlighted in the joint statement included "combating terrorist threats, promoting stability across the Indo-Pacific region, increasing free and fair trade, and strengthening energy linkages." The two sides also "expressed confidence that, together, the United States and India will provide strong leadership to address global challenges and build prosperity for their citizens in the decades to come".[4]

Notwithstanding the aforesaid "Indian-connections", New Delhi took more than a decade to internalise the "Indo-Pacific" concept. During his address at the *Shangri La Dialogue* held at Singapore in June 2018, the Indian Prime Minister Narendra Modi stated,

> *India's vision for the Indo-Pacific Region is...a positive one. And, it has many elements... We believe that our common prosperity and security require us to evolve, through dialogue, a common rules-based order for the region.... These rules and norms should be based on the consent of all, not on the power of the few. This must be based on faith in dialogue, and not dependence on force. It also means that when nations make international commitments, they must uphold them. This is the foundation of India's faith in multilateralism and regionalism; and, of our principled commitment to rule of law.*[5]

The United Nations Convention on the Law of the Sea, 1982 (UNCLOS) forms the very basis of the rules of governance of global maritime commons that is critical for economic development and prosperity in the predominantly maritime-configured Indo-Pacific region. It codified the rules for jurisdiction of national maritime spaces, of the areas beyond national jurisdiction (albeit, to an extent), and freedom of navigation, thereby striking a historic balance between *Mare Liberum* (free sea) and *Mare Clausum* (closed sea),[6] which later translated into the balance among national security concerns, global economic transactions, and more lately, the imperatives of preservation of the marine environment.

This extensive UNCLOS document articulating the laws of the sea in the form of a "Constitution of Oceans" is a result of more than three decades of hard work and fortitude of jurists and diplomats worldwide spanning three conferences (UNCLOS-I, -II and -III). The UNCLOS is also a codification of customary international law and provides a framework for maintenance of good order at sea, and is thus accepted as a legally binding instrument for the 168 States (including India)[7] and the European Union that are party to the UNCLOS. The assent of the other 14 signatories pending their ratification unarguably highlights the widespread acceptance of UNCLOS by the international community. However, ratification of the Convention in no way guarantees consensus in views on its implementation. This represents the foremost challenge for fructifying the Indo-Pacific vision.

During the past decade and a half, maritime disputes have escalated to the point of disturbing the existing regional order especially in the Indo-Pacific. The genesis of these disputes lies in the varied interpretation of the Convention among the parties and signatories vis-à-vis the stakeholders' national interests. The key contentions today arise when State parties differ in interpreting 'historic' claims, which is aggravated by their propensity to avoid subjecting these disputes to the due process compulsory settlement under international law. While mechanisms for such settlement are available within the Convention itself, on several occasions, major powers have interpreted the law in a manner to make it ineffective and impotent in providing effective resolution of the disputes.

The recent legal case between China and the Philippines is the most conspicuous in the Indo-Pacific. In January 2013, the Philippines initiated an international arbitration case against China under Part XV, Section 2 on "Compulsory Procedures Entailing Binding Decisions" and Annex VII ("Arbitration") to the UNCLOS.[8] The case concerned the prevailing maritime disputes in the South China Sea, and broadly concerned the role of historic rights relating to the "nine-dash line", its maritime entitlements therein, the status of maritime features and the lawfulness of certain actions by China, upon which, the Philippines alleged that China had violated the Convention. China adopted a position of non-acceptance and non-participation in the proceedings of the Permanent Court of Arbitration (PCA), and eventually, rejected its verdict declared in July 2016.[9] It even refused to participate in the proceedings of arbitration and eventually expressed its unwillingness to comply with its rulings. When a superior power loses an international dispute and we have seen this in the past in several occasions there is no effective enforcement mechanism. History indicates that despite having a seemingly legal binding effect among parties, rules can be trifled with by parties that wield enormous power in international relations.[10]

However, UNCLOS has had its success stories too. The cases in point are the settlements of the long outstanding maritime body delimitations in the Bay of Bengal between Bangladesh and Myanmar by the International Tribunal on Law of the Sea (ITLOS) in March 2012,[11] and between India and Bangladesh by the PCA in July 2014.[12] Notably, all three parties willingly embraced the verdict of the concerned international courts. This amply showcases the political will of New Delhi of using its growing comprehensive power in a constructive manner, and that of India's immediate maritime neighbours to embrace the spirit of SAGAR, meaning 'Ocean' in Hindi language, and an acronym for 'Security and Growth for All in the Region'. The concept was enunciated by the Indian Prime Minister Narendra Modi at Port Louis, Mauritius, during the commissioning ceremony of Mauritius Coast Guard Ship (MCGS) *Barracuda*, an Indian-built Offshore Patrol Vessel (OPV) in 2015.[13]

It is well known that the US was an active participant of the UNCLOS-III deliberations and may even be considered as being among the chief architects of UNCLOS, 1982. It signed the Treaty in 1982, but never ratified it to become a State party. The reservation of Washington D.C. is primarily based on its concerns with respect to Part XI of UNCLOS with regard to deep-seabed mining and the mandate of International Seabed Authority (ISA).[14] Though the US wholeheartedly conforms to the provisions laid down by UNCLOS. It also regularly conducts operational challenges to the different interpretations made by various countries through the freedom of navigation programme, which commenced in 1979. As stated in the U.S. Oceans Policy (1983), the United States "will exercise and assert its rights, freedoms, and uses of the sea on a worldwide basis in a manner that is consistent with the balance of interests" reflected in the Law of the Sea Convention.[15]

A few of the more regular instances involve the Freedom of

Navigation Operations (FONOPS) by the US Navy in the South China Sea against Chinese maritime claims.[16] The instances of US FONOPS in the Straits of Hormuz against the Iranian claims is also on the rise, in response to the growing threat that Tehran poses to merchant shipping in the Gulf.[17] Notably, in October 2016, the US Navy also undertook FONOPS in the Strait of Bab al-Mandeb against the Houthi rebels of Yemen. The US also routinely conducts operations against the real interpretations on the EEZ's of coastal States. Since 2013, when China declared an Air Defence Identification Zones (ADIZ) in the East China Sea (ECS) overlapping with the ADIZ of Japan and South Korea, the US also conducted bomber flight operations overflying the ECS as a measure of military assertion of the freedom of overflight.[18]

The maritime environment has undergone significant changes since then. Various maritime security initiatives have come into force such as the International Convention on Maritime Search and Rescue (SAR) 1979,[19] the Convention for Suppression of Unlawful Acts against the Safety of Maritime Navigation (SUA), 1988,[20] the International Ship and Port Security Code (ISPS) 2004,[21] the Container Security Initiative (CSI) 2005;[22] and these are only a few. These have given rise to certain state practices, which are at various points related to the UNCLOS as the 'umbrella' Convention. Yet, challenges remain, more generically, in the growing need for States to achieve convergence in their interpretation of UNCLOS against competing geopolitical imperatives. More specifically, there is the quest for answers to the vexing questions, *inter alia*, how can one distinguish between the UNCLOS provision of Maritime Scientific Research (MSR) and military surveys, and what is the legal basis for promulgation of security zones like ADIZ.

Going by the history of UNCLOS it took almost a decade for decision makers to finalise the convention in its present existing form, thus, the time is now opportune for the regional organisations to amplify and interpret its provisions in a manner that is acceptable to all regional and extra-regional stakeholders. India is fully committed to peace and stability in its neighbourhood, a commitment which India has shown in its outreach to its neighbours in building strong relations and partnerships. The growing relevance of the of Indian Ocean Naval Symposium (IONS), the fledging Information Fusion Centre - Indian

Ocean Region (IFC-IOR) established near New Delhi, and the success of the International Fleet Review (IFR) conducted by India in 2016, all stand testimony to the increasing role being played by Indian Navy as the 'net security provider' in the IOR and beyond, and the key facilitator for cooperative security in the region.

Launched in India in February 2008 at the initiative of the Indian Navy,[23] the IONS functions with the help of a series of biennial meetings and other activities among the navies (other maritime forces), which are littoral to the Indian Ocean. It provides a forum to increase maritime security cooperation, providing a forum for discussion of regional maritime issues and promote friendly relationships among the member nations. The IONS is presently collaborating through three IONS Working Groups (IWG), viz., Maritime Security (including anti-piracy), Information Exchange and Interoperability, and Humanitarian Assistance and Disaster Relief (HADR). Within the ambit of IONS, the Indian Navy is developing a draft Code for Unplanned Encounters at Sea (CUES), modelled on the lines of the arrangement developed by the Western Pacific Naval Symposium (WPNS) in 2014,[24] an effort that is being spearheaded by the National Maritime Foundation (NMF), New Delhi. This gives rise to the encouraging prospects of linking up the WPNS to the IONS for enhanced synergy among navies of the Indo-Pacific. Notably, as an Indian Ocean littoral, India is privileged to be an observer at the WPNS, and is committed to enable such synergy.

In response to the Mumbai terror attack of November 2008, India bolstered its coastal security apparatus *inter alia* through enhanced national measures to enhance Maritime Domain Awareness (MDA). These measures included the establishment of the *Integrated Management and Analyses Centre* (IMAC) in November 2014[25], which was upgraded to the Information Fusion Centre for Indian Ocean Region (IFC-IOR) in December 2018.[26] The IFC-IOR is drawing permanent naval liaison officers from a host of littoral and stakeholder navies, which has provided a major boost to India's role in cooperative security in the Indo-Pacific region.

In February 2016, India conducted the International Fleet Review (IFR) at Visakhapatnam, 15 years after it conducted the first IFR in January 2001 at Mumbai. These congregations are held to foster closer ties amongst participating countries and emphasis on building friendship across the seas. Whereas IFR-2001 had involved the participation of foreign warships from 29 countries, the number of countries grew to 50 countries during IFR-16.[27] This clearly indicates India's growing international eminence and stature, as also its increasing relevance as a 'net security provider' in the domain of maritime security in the Indo-Pacific region. On similar lines, India's only integrated Military Theatre Command—the Andaman and Nicobar Command (ANC)—has been conducting the *'Milan'* (meaning 'meeting' in Hindi language) series of exercises at Port Blair involving navies of the littoral countries. The effort commenced in 1995, and has since grown in the last edition of March 2018 to the participation of 16 countries,[28] with eight countries sending 11 warships.[29]

It is in India's larger national interest that the largely maritime-configured Indo-Pacific region maintains the established good order at sea and remains peaceful and prosperous on a sustainable basis. This would make it essential for the regional countries and stakeholders to adhere to the existing maritime-legal order and established norms of conduct in the global maritime common. As international law evolves and refines itself from within, India would, therefore, continue to endorse the tenets of the UNCLOS, which is the only recourse that the region has to seek the Indo-Pacific vision.

NOTES

1. In the contemporary geopolitical context, the term 'Indo-Pacific' was first used in January 2007. Gurpreet S Khurana, "Security of Sea Lines: Prospects for India-Japan Cooperation", *Strategic Analysis*, Vol. 31, No. 1 (January 2007), pp. 139–153.
2. Gurpreet S Khurana. "The 'Indo-Pacific' Idea: Origins, Conceptualizations and the Way Ahead", *Journal of Indian Ocean Rim Studies*, Vol. 2, No. 2 (October-December 2019), pp. 58-76.
3. Confluence of the Two Seas", Speech by H.E. Mr. Shinzo Abe, Prime Minister of Japan at the Parliament of the Republic of India, 22 August 2007, Japan *Ministry of Foreign Affairs* (MOFA), available at https://www.mofa.go.jp/region/asia-paci/pmv0708/speech-2.html (Accessed on 27 August 2020).
4. "United States and India: Prosperity Through Partnership", Joint Statement, Ministry of External Affairs (Government of India) Press Release, 27 June 2017, available at https://mea.gov.in/bilateral-documents.htm?dtl/28560/United_States_and_India_Prosperity_Through_Partnership (Accessed on 27 August 2020).
5. Prime Minister's Keynote Address at Shangri La Dialogue, Ministry of External Affairs

(MEA), Government of India, 01 June 2018, available at https://www.mea.gov.in/Speeches-Statements.htm?dtl/29943/Prime+Ministers+Keynote+Address+at+Shangri+La+Dialogue+June+01+2018 (Accessed on 27 August 2020)

6. *Mare Liberum* (Latin for 'Free Sea') was a principle propounded by Dutch jurist and philosopher Hugo Grotius in 1609, which implied that sea was international territory and all nations were free to use it for seafaring trade. It was directed towards Portugal's policy of *Mare Clausum*, leading to its claim of monopoly on trade with the East Indies.
7. Cambodia is the latest State to have ratified UNCLOS in January 2020.
8. The South China Sea Arbitration (The Republic of Philippines vs. The People's Republic of China), Permanent Court of Arbitration (PCA), *The Hague*, available at https://pca-cpa.org/en/cases/7/
9. "The Tribunal's Award in the 'South China Sea Arbitration' initiated by the Philippines is Null and Void", Chinese Society of International Law, *People's Daily Online*, 13 June 2016, available at http://www.globaltimes.cn/content/988029.shtml (Accessed on 27 August 2020)
10. For a geopolitical analysis of China-Philippines case, see Hamsa Devineni and Gurpreet S Khurana, "China and the South China Sea Arbitration: Analyses in the Indo-Pacific Context", *National Maritime Foundation* (NMF), New Delhi, 28 December 2018, available at http://www.maritimeindia.org/View%20Profile/636815534849570738.pdf
11. 'Dispute concerning Delimitation of the Maritime Boundary between Bangladesh and Myanmar in the Bay of Bengal', Case No. 16, Judgment of 14 March 2012, International Tribunal on Law of the Sea (ITLOS), available at https://www.itlos.org/fileadmin/itlos/documents/cases/case_no_16/published/C16-J-14_mar_12.pdf
12. Bay of Bengal Maritime Boundary Arbitration (Bangladesh V. India) Award, Permanent Court of Arbitration, *The Hague*, 7 July 2014, available at www.pca-cpa.org/showpage.asp?pag_id=1376
13. Text of the PM's remarks on the Commissioning of Coast Ship Barracuda, Prime Minister's Office (PMO), 12 March 2015, available at https://www.pmindia.gov.in/en/news_updates/text-of-the-pms-remarks-on-the-commissioning-of-coast-ship-barracuda/ Also see, "Mr Modi's Ocean View". *The Hindu*, 17 March 2015. https://www.thehindu.com/opinion/editorial/mr-modis-ocean-view/article7000182.ece
14. "Agreement relating to the Implementation of Part XI of the United Nations Convention on the Law of the Sea of 10 December 1982", *Division for Ocean Affairs and the Law of the Sea, United Nations*, 02 September 2016, available at https://documents-dds-ny.un.org/doc/UNDOC/GEN/N94/332/98/PDF/N9433298.pdf?OpenElement (Accessed on 27 August 2020)
15. U.S. Department of Defense Freedom of Navigation (FON) Program, *Dept of Defense*, 28 February 2017, available at https://policy.defense.gov/Portals/11/DoD%20FON%20Program%20Summary%2016.pdf?ver=2017-03-03-141350-380 (Accessed on 27 August 2020)
16. Geoff Ziezulewicz and Shawn Snow, "Navy conducts year's first FONOP in South China Sea", *Navy Times*, 28 January 2020, available at https://www.navytimes.com/news/your-navy/2020/01/28/navy-conducts-years-first-fonop-in-south-china-sea/
17. Farzin Nadimi, "Clarifying Freedom of Navigation in the Gulf", *The Washington Institute*, Policy Analysis, Policy Watch 3154, 24 July 2019.
18. Zachary Keck, "US Bombers Challenge China's Air Defense Identification Zone", *The Diplomat*, 27 November 2013.
19. "International Convention on Maritime Search and Rescue (SAR)", International

Maritime Organisation (IMO), available at http://www.imo.org/en/About/Conventions/ListOfConventions/Pages/International-Convention-on-Maritime-Search-and-Rescue-(SAR).aspx (Accessed on 27 August 2020).

20. "Convention for the Suppression of Unlawful Acts Against the Safety of Maritime Navigation, Protocol for the Suppression of Unlawful Acts Against the Safety of Fixed Platforms Located on the Continental Shelf", International Maritime Organisation (IMO), available at http://www.imo.org/en/About/Conventions/ListOfConventions/Pages/SUA-Treaties.aspx (Accessed on 27 August 2020).
21. Having entered into force under SOLAS chapter XI-2, on 01 July 2004, the ISPS Code has since formed the basis for a comprehensive mandatory security regime for international shipping. See, "The International Ship and Port Facility (ISPS) Code", International Maritime Organisation (IMO), available at http://www.imo.org/en/OurWork/Security/Guide_to_Maritime_Security/Pages/SOLAS-XI-2%20ISPS%20Code.aspx
22. "CSI: Container Security Initiative" from the Official website of the Department of Homeland Security, available at https://www.cbp.gov/border-security/ports-entry/cargo-security/csi/csi-brief (Accessed on 27 August 2020)
23. Gurpreet S Khurana, "Indian Ocean Naval Symposium (IONS): Where from...Whither-Bound?", *Institute for Defence Studies and Analyses IDSA Comment*, 22 February 2008.
24. "Member nations of Western Pacific Naval Symposium in China agree to maritime code of conduct", *ABC News*, 22 April 2014, available at https://www.abc.net.au/news/2014-04-22/an-asia-pacific-nations-agree-to-maritime-accord/5405104 (Accessed on 27 August 2020). For text of CUES document, see, "Document: Code for Unplanned Encounters at Sea", *USNI News*, 22 August 2016, available at https://news.usni.org/2014/06/17/document-conduct-unplanned-encounters-sea (Accessed on 27 August 2020)
25. "Raksha Mantri Shri Manohar Parrikar Inaugurates IMAC, a Navy-CG Joint Operations Centre", Indian Navy website, available at https://www.indiannavy.nic.in/content/raksha-mantri-shri-manohar-parrikar-inaugurates-imac-navy-cg-joint-operations-centre (Accessed on 27 August 2020)
26. "Raksha Mantri Inaugurates Information Fusion Centre – Indian Ocean Region (IFC-IOR)", Ministry of Defence (Government of India) Press Release, 22 December 2018, available at https://pib.gov.in/Pressreleaseshare.aspx?PRID=1557074 (Accessed on 27 August 2020).
27. "International Fleet Review – 2016", Indian Navy website, available at https://www.indiannavy.nic.in/content/international-fleet-review-2016-1 (Accessed on 27 August 2020).
28. These countries are Australia, Malaysia, Seychelles, Mauritius, Myanmar, Oman, New Zealand, Vietnam, Tanzania, Sri Lanka, Singapore, Thailand, Bangladesh, Kenya, Indonesia and Cambodia.
29. "Sixteen Countries Participate in Milan-2018 at Port Blair", *United News of India*, 08 March 2018, available at http://www.uniindia.com/sixteen-countries-participate-in-milan-2018-at-port-blair/states/news/1161366.html#:~:text=Navy%20delegates%20from%20sixteen%20countries,participated%20in%20the%20international %20event (Accessed on 27 August 2020).

Legitimacy of UNCLOS and Relevance in 21st century

7

UNCLOS:
A Framework for International Legal Governance

Shakti Sinha and Deeksha Goel

With the flux in global power equations in the first quarter of the 21st century, the world is at the crossroads of major changes. In times like these, where the very notions of globalisation have been challenged, the reliance on global value chains has shown frailties and countries are contemplating a more inward-looking approach to economic development and growth, the role of seas has become all the more important. Historians, naval experts and leaders like K.M. Panikkar have all predicted the rise of a maritime power in the 21st century along the shores of the Indian Ocean. In times like these, when global super-powers are relying on control of, or at least access to, the seas for everything from transportation of basics like crude oil to the most sophisticated technology transfer, an unsaid contest of controlling the unruly waters has emerged as potentially a major flash point.

In this context, it becomes inevitable that the global community relies on conventions and institutions like the United Nations Convention on the Law of the Sea (UNCLOS) to ensure a fair, free and equitable access to common resources of humanity while ensuring a balanced approach towards protection of marine ecosystems. The UNCLOS, which was adopted in 1982 and came into force in 1994, is the most comprehensive document, which codifies international law and ocean governance. It would not be wrong to call it the Constitution of the Sea.

Evolution of International Maritime Law

The origins of the Law of the Sea date back to the beginning of the European colonisation of America (New World), Africa and of access to India. Portugal, which initiated what it called the Age of Discovery in the mid-15 century (CE), and Spain were in competition to seize and control territories and sea-routes, particularly of the New World, which they saw as part of the Asian landmass providing access to India, the islands of the Indies and China. They then decided to come to an agreement on who had the monopoly of colonisation where, and signed the Treaty of Tordesillas in 1494. This was the first delineation of maritime rights, and can be said to mark the beginning of international maritime law, though of course, the motivation was territorial control. A red North-South line was drawn in the Western Atlantic, 100 leagues west of Cape Verde Islands[1] off the West Coast of Africa, leaving Spain to do what it pleased on the western side of the line, and Portugal was allotted the eastern side. Later the line was shifted further to the west, allowing Portugal to colonise the eastern coast of Brazil. No other European power had started its colonial initiatives and the local inhabitants did not count for the protagonists.[2] Portugal and Spain also got the Pope (Alexander VI) to bless this 'unholy' division, the violation of which invited the punishment of excommunication.[3]

Later the schism in the Church and the rise of Protestant maritime powers of The Netherlands and England, as well as of Catholic France challenged this preventive duopoly and made the oceans the site of disputation of legal authority of passage, exploitation and control. The development of mercantilism and a body of laws governing contracts and liability in The Netherlands set the stage for laying down the basis of international law of the sea, whose principles are encoded in UNCLOS. The Dutch legal theorist, Hugo Grotius, wrote the *Mare Liberum* (The Free Sea) in 1608, specifically to deal with the attack on a Portuguese ship in the East Indies by a Dutch privateer. However, its principles of the free seas that challenged the Tordesillas' monopoly, lies at the core of international maritime law, even as the detailing has evolved over centuries.[4]

Initiation of UNCLOS Process

With the overt dependence on oceans and the need for peaceful co-existence, attempts were made repeatedly to codify the laws of the sea to ensure safe passage, sustainable exploitation of resources and strengthening of trade and commerce while retaining essential and graded national sovereignty over coastal waters. The League of Nations' Hague Conference was held in 1930 to codify the laws on (a) Nationality, (b) Territorial Waters, and (c) States' responsibility towards damage done to foreigners when in their waters.[5]

The Conference was to establish a framework for delimiting the breadth of territorial water under the jurisdiction of a country along with points of measurement for delimitation, the extent to which a coastal state can exercise authority in these waters to prevent exploitation and strengthening peace and security and the right to safe passage of foreign vessels when sailing through international waters.[6] Though the need to ensure freedom of navigation and the right to secure the adjacent waters in the best interest of the respective nation was recognised, the participating delegations failed to reach a consensus on defining the parameters to ascertain the breadth of territorial waters. While countries like the USA voted in favour of a 3 nautical miles out limit from the low water mark, the Scandinavian countries of Norway and Sweden were adamant on 4 nautical miles width of territorial waters, whereas some others wanted it up to 6 miles, while Greece was prepared for only 2 nautical miles width, if the others agreed.[7]

On the issue of the need to demarcate a contiguous zone, the USA supported the concept of certain rights and control in the waters adjoining territorial seas, but not a defined contiguous zone. Besides ambiguity on the need to demark contiguous zones and the respective governing laws, there were differences on governance of adjacent islands and units of islands, defining the marine space between two islands. Despite having faced a stalemate in not being able to firm up a consensus on territorial waters, the Hague Conference is seen as a landmark event in the evolution of what was to become UNCLOS in 1982. Although, the limit of the territorial waters was not defined, it adopted a resolution defining its nature, which stated that the "territory of a coastal state includes also the air space above the territorial sea, as well as the bed of the sea, and the subsoil." This formed the basis for subsequent conventions. The Hague Conference placed on the table the priorities and peculiarities of each of the coastal states with respect to their geographies and national needs.[8]

First Conference on the Laws of the Sea (1956)

As early as on 21 November 1947, the United Nations General Assembly (UNGA) vide Resolution Number 174 (II) established the International Law Commission (ILC) with the objective of the promotion of the progressive development of international law and its codification.[9] It was at the 8th session of the ILC in Geneva in 1956 that the Commission presented a report which was also their final report pertaining to the laws of the sea.

The final report of 1956 was preceded by intense efforts to develop a body of law pertaining to a regime of the high seas and territorial waters based on usage, customs and national interests. In fact, the need for such codification of laws was brought out in the first session of the Commission in 1949.[10] In the second session in 1950, it was decided to restrict the scope of codification to specific aspects of the high seas. Being mindful of the dangers of an overly ambitious agenda, the commission decided to only cover those aspects which were not being catered to by any of the existing organs of the United Nations (UN) or other specialised agencies. The scope was further brought down to eliminate all technical subjects which did not suit the nature of study and the ones which did not require consideration.[11]

It was at the third session in 1951 that the Commission decided to go public with its first draft which dealt with continental shelves, conservation of resources of the sea, sedentary fishing and contiguous zone.[12] The draft was put up for other national governments to share their views. By the time of the fourth session, views, comments and concerns were received from all concerned governments and discussions were deferred to the fifth session in 1953. However, during this time deliberations were initiated on the subject of territorial waters and states and governments were called upon to submit their practices along with special considerations, if any.[13]

At the fifth session in 1953, re-examination of the continental shelf, fishery resources and contiguous zones took place. Based on the rapporteur's reports and governments' inputs certain unexplored areas of the high seas and territorial waters were also included. The sixth session in 1954 concluded with the adoption of a number of articles with respect to territorial waters, which were then left open for observations.

At the seventh session in 1955, a draft of the report on the High Seas was adopted and left open for views from national governments and concerned international organisations. In dealing with the chapter on Conservation of Living Resources, organisations represented by observers at the International Technical Conference on the Conservation of Living Resources of the Sea were also consulted.

Thus, after a long process of deliberations and consultations with multiple stakeholders, a final two-volume report on Territorial Sea and High Waters was submitted by the Commission at its eighth session in 1956. This led, in a short while, to the conclusion of four treaties in 1958. Based on the report of the ILC and its recommendation of having an International Conference with all stakeholders to further the scope of the first report from just legal governance of the sea to a more inclusive convention covering all aspects—technical, biological, economic and political—the first International Conference of UNCLOS was held in Geneva in 1958. The following four conventions of UNCLOS were adopted:

(a) On Territorial Seas and Contiguous Zones that came into force on 10 September 1964.[14]

(b) On the High Seas that came into force on 30 September 1962.[15]

(c) On Fishing and Conservation of Living Resources of the High Seas that came into force on 20 March 1966.[16]

(d) Continental Shelf that came into force on 10 June 1964.[17]

UNCLOS-I was just the first, though very important step, in the long journey towards arriving at consensus in these difficult and unchartered waters. The 1956 ILC report also provided the skeleton structure of the UNCLOS which was finally adopted as a convention in 1982 and continues to govern oceanic space.[18]

A second conference on UNCLOS was held in 1960 to decide the extent of the territorial sea and fishery limits which could not be agreed upon in 1958. However, the second conference too was unsuccessful in taking any substantive decisions on these two fronts and thus concluded with no new agreements.[19]

The third conference on UNCLOS was then held between 1973 and 1982 in 11 sessions and is considered to be a landmark event for it was at this conference that UNCLOS was adopted in its present state and form.[20]

The final resolution was adopted on April 30, 1982[21] and opened up for signatures on 10 December 1982. On the first day itself, the Convention was signed by a record 119 countries representing all regions of the world[22] from North to South and East to West, not just island or coastal states but also land-locked nations. The new Convention replaced the four conventions adopted after the first conference in 1958 and was based on the following resolutions:

> ***Resolution I:*** *Establishment of the Preparatory Commission for the International Sea Bed Authority and for the International Tribunal for the Law of the Sea (ITLOS)*
>
> ***Resolution II:*** *Governing Preparatory Investment in Pioneer Activities relating to Polymetallic Nodules.*
>
> ***Resolution III:*** *Relating to territories whose people have not obtained either full independence or some other self-governing status recognised by the United Nations or territories under colonial domination.*
>
> ***Resolution IV:*** *Relating to national liberation movements.*[23]

Speaking during the adoption of the resolution, the then President of the UNLCOS, Mr. Tommy Koh, who was Singapore's Permanent Representative to the United Nations, elaborated on the major themes of the convention.[24] First, the UNLCOS was the most comprehensive treaty that deals with all aspects of uses of the resources of the seas and oceans while accommodating the views of all the stakeholders involved. Second, the convention forms an integral package and has to be followed as a whole, states or parties could not choose to follow one part while negating the other except for where it provides for such relaxations. Third, UNCLOS was not just a codification exercise of existing international law or customary legal practices. With the introduction of a regime of transit passage through straits and a regime of archipelagic lanes passage, the convention had established new concepts and practices. Fourth, with the establishment of authorities like the International Sea Bed Authority, the convention has been given enough teeth to deal with any infringement or claims of excessive ownership by any member state over marine resources which were the common heritage of humanity and lay outside the territorial jurisdiction of the party concerned.

Significance of UNCLOS

UNCLOS was the first major multilateral convention to be ratified in the field of Ocean Governance. This Constitution of the Oceans is the most comprehensive document that deals with delimitation of maritime boundaries, oceanic governance and marine life protection.

Since its adoption in 1982 and until date, the UNCLOS has maintained its mandate of promoting international peace and security by replacing conflicting claims of coastal states and standardising territorial waters in contiguous zones, exclusive economic zones and continental shelves. The convention is also aligned with Sustainable Development Goal No. 14 of "Life below water: Conserve and sustainably use oceans, seas and marine resources for sustainable development" by promoting marine scientific research while ensuring the protection of the marine environment."[25]

Resolution I of UNCLOS called for the establishment of the International Seabed Authority (ISA) and ITLOS. The International Sea Bed Authority with its headquarters in Jamaica came into existence in 1994.[26] The Authority is mandated to regulate all activities including exploration, exploitation and extraction of mineral resources in the deep-sea beds while preserving marine life and their habitat. The Authority fulfils its obligations under Articles 143 and 144 of UNCLOS[27] by promoting marine scientific research and enhancing capacity building in deep sea research and technology.

Similarly, ITLOS also came into existence with the adoption of UNCLOS in 1994 and is one of the mechanisms for state parties to settle disputes arising out of interpretation and application of the Convention. Apart from the establishment of ITLOS, the Convention also provides for the establishment of the International Court of Justice (ICJ); an arbitral tribunal in accordance with Annexure VII to the 1982 Convention and a special arbitral tribunal in accordance with Annexure VIII of the Convention.[28] State parties are free to choose the mechanism they want to adopt for dispute resolution.

Increasing Relevance of UNCLOS

The American political scientist, Graham Allison, has drawn attention to the potential of a major conflict when an existing hegemon is challenged by a rising challenger. In his book, *Destined for War,*[29] which built on his earlier works, Allison drew inspiration from the work of the ancient Greek historian and general, Thucydides, who in his *History of the Peloponnesian War*, described how the established power, Sparta, felt challenged by the rise of Greece leading to a devastating conflict. Allison's study of 16 cases showed that in 12 of them, it led to war. The relative decline of USA, specifically, and the West in general, has been interpreted in China and Russia as an indication of inevitability. This trend accelerated with the global financial crisis of 2008-09 and the general retrenchment from the world by successive US Presidents, Obama and Trump. The latter's avowal of global leadership, and even withdrawal from international institutions that the USA itself established and championed, and the widening domestic divide has apparently convinced the leadership of the Chinese Communist Party that the time has come for them to jettison Deng Xiaoping's famous 24-character slogan of 'hide your capability, bide your time...and never seek leadership.'[30]

Xi Jinping, the General Secretary of the Chinese Communist Party since 2012 has changed course quite dramatically, though the first signs of China revaluating its position in the global firmament goes back to a decade before him. Xi's Belt and Road Initiative (BRI), the establishment of new institutions like the New Development Bank, Asian Infrastructure Investment Bank, etc., and the aggressive island-building programme in the South China Sea demonstrated China's determined efforts to change the rules of the game. Later, in violation of Xi's commitment to Obama,[31] China went ahead and militarised the newly-created islands in the South China Sea.[32] It also rejected the award of the Permanent Tribunal on the Law of the Sea in the case brought by the Philippines, even though China is a contracting party to UNCLOS. This exposes the fragility of international law when a major power decides to violate it.

China's behaviour was in contrast to India's which accepted the Tribunal's award in the India-Bangladesh maritime boundary dispute despite the fact that the Tribunal's award was largely perceived to be against India.

Recent Chinese moves in Ladakh, Hong Kong, Taiwan, the South China Sea and deterioration in its relations with Australia, Canada, Europe, besides the USA and India, is pushing the world dangerously close to conflict, which may arise accidentally or unintentionally. The heightened tension in the South China Sea particularly in the Taiwan Straits and the determination of the USA and others to prevent China from effectively converting this large body of international waters into a Chinese lake and China's recent firing of two anti-ship missiles in protest against the operations of US planes off Taiwan,[33] even though it was in international waters, indicates the uncertainties that the global order faces, due to disregard for settled international law.

Developing countries have justified criticism of the world order that was constructed at the end of World War II. International institutions were skewed against their interests, perpetuated by lack of adequate representation. Some of it, are China's claiming its seat in the UN Security Council replacing Taiwan, the change in the International Monetary Fund's quotas to better reflect the changed economic realities, etc. Critically, as the work of the Canadian-American scholar Steven Pinker has shown, the world is actually a much safer place than it was before.[34] Levels of violence are at their lowest level ever, with health and quality of life at their best.[35] All this has come within the framework of the extant global institutions and rules. These have not been static but changes have generally come about through negotiations and compromises. UNCLOS was the product of over four decades of hard work, scientific research and negotiations. It has ensured that the Sea, which is a global common, is available and accessible to human society without discrimination for growth. Zero-sum games have been kept in check through its arbitration mechanisms. It would be risky to jeopardise all these gains, a likely outcome if countries act arbitrarily and unilaterally, in violation of accepted norms and institutions.

The lessons of UNCLOS should not be forgotten, for it is in the interest of all countries and societies to work within its framework, else we all sink together.

NOTES

1. Officially known as the Republic of Cabo Verde.
2. "Jun 7, 1494 CE: Treaty of Tordesillas", available at https://www.nationalgeographic.org/thisday/jun7/treaty-tordesillas/#:~:text=On%20 June%207%2C%201494%2C%20the, Americas%20between%20the%20two%20superpowers (Accessed on 06 September 2020).
3. Stephen R. Brown, "Treaty of Tordesillas: The 1494 Decision Still Influencing Today's World", *The History Reader*, 12 April 2012, available at https://www.thehistoryreader.com/world-history/treaty-tordesillas-1494-decision-still-influencing-todays-world/ (Accessed on 03 September 2020).
4. Ibid.
5. Hunter Miller, "The Hague Codification Conference", *The American Journal of International Law*, Vol. 24, No. 4 (Oct. 1930), pp. 674-675.
6. Ibid., pp. 686-688.
7. Ibid., also see Terasaki Naomichi Hiro, "The Regime of Islands in International Convention (Part I)", available at https://www.spf.org/islandstudies/transfer/research/docs/a00010r.pdf (Accessed on 07 September 2020).
8. Hunter Miller, op. cit., pp. 688-689.
9. "Statute of the International Law Commission, 1947," United Nations, 2005, p. 2.
10. Report of the International Law Commission on the work of its first session, 12 April 1949, Official Records of the General Assembly Document - A/CN.4/13 and Corr. 1-3, pp. 278, available at https://legal.un.org/ilc/documentation/english/reports/a_cn4_13.pdf (Accessed on 06 September 2020).
11. "Law of the Sea", *Documents of the eighth session including the report of the Commission to the General Assembly*, Yearbook of the International Law Commission 1956, Vol. II, (New York: United Nations, 1957), p. 254 (Accessed on 31 August 2020).
12. Ibid.
13. Ibid.
14. "No. 7477- Convention on the Territorial Sea and the Contiguous Zone: Done at Geneva, on 29 April 1958", *Treaty Series: Treaties and international agreements registered or filed and recorded with the Secretariat of the United Nations*, Vol. 516 (New York: United Nations, 1966), p. 206 (Accessed on 17 September 2020).
15. "No. 6465- Convention on the High Seas: Done at Geneva, on 29 April 1958", *Treaty Series: Treaties and International Agreements registered or filed and recorded with the Secretariat of the United Nations*, Vol. 450 (New York: United Nations, 1964), p. 82 (Accessed on 17 September 2020).
16. "No. 8164- Convention on Fishing and Conservation of the Living Resources of the High Seas: Done at Geneva, on 29 April 1958", *Treaty Series: Treaties and International Agreements registered or filed and recorded with the Secretariat of the United Nations*, Vol. 559 (New York: United Nations, 1966), p. 285 (Accessed on 17 September 2020).
17. "No. 7302-Convention on the Continental Shelf: Done at Geneva on 29 April, 1958", *Treaty Series: Treaties and International Agreements registered or filed and recorded with the Secretariat of the United Nations*, Vol. 499 (New York: United Nations, 1964), p. 311. (Accessed on 17 September 2020).
18. *The official records of the First United Nations Conference on the Laws of the Sea*, Summary, record of meetings and annexes (Geneva: United Nations Publications, 1958) (Accessed on 17 September 2020).

19. *The official records of the Second United Nations Convention on the Laws of the Sea*, Summary Records of Plenary Meetings and of Meetings of the Committee of the Whole, Annexes and Final Act (Geneva: United Nations Publications, 1960) (Accessed on 17 September 2020).
20. *Third United Nations Conference on the Laws of the Sea*, Summary Records of Plenary Meetings recorded in A/CONF.62/SR.1 to A/CONF.62/SR.51 (Geneva: United Nations Publications, 2009) (Accessed on 21 September 2020).
21. Final Act of the 3rd United Nations Conference on the Laws of the Sea, p. 12.
22. "A Constitution for the Ocean", Remarks by Tommy Koh, President of the Third UNCLOS, available at https://www.un.org/Depts/los/convention_agreements/texts/koh_english.pdf (Accessed on 31 August 2020).
23. Final Act of the Third United Nations Conference on the Laws of the Sea, p. 168, available at https://www.un.org/depts/los/convention_agreements/texts/final_act_eng.pdf on 6 September 2020 (Accessed on 31 August 2020).
24. "A Constitution for the Ocean", Remarks by Tommy Koh, President of the Third UNCLOS, available at https://www.un.org/Depts/los/convention_agreements/texts/koh_english.pdf (Accessed on 31 August 2020).
25. "Goal 14: Conserve and sustainably use the oceans, seas and marine resources", available at https://www.un.org/sustainabledevelopment/oceans/ (Accessed on 21 September 2020).
26. "International Seabed Authority", available at https://www.isa.org.jm/about-isa (Accessed on 31 August 2020).
27. United Nations Convention on the Laws of the Sea, adopted in 1982 (Accessed on 17 September 2020).
28. Ibid.
29. Allison Graham, *Destined for War: Can America and China escape the Thucydides' Trap?* (Boston: Houghton Mifflin Harcourt, 2017).
30. Congressional Record, Vol. 164, No. 11, pp. H541-H547, available at https://www.congress.gov/crec/2018/01/18/modified/CREC-2018-01-18-pt1-PgH541-2.htm (Accessed on 31 August 2020).
31. Remarks by President Obama and President Xi of the People's Republic of China in Joint Press Conference in 2015, available at https://obamawhitehouse.archives.gov/the-press-office/2015/09/25/remarks-president-obama-and-president-xi-peoples-republic-china-joint (Accessed on 17 September 2020).
32. Steven Stashwick, "China's South China Sea Militarisation has peaked" Foreign Policy 2019, available at https://foreignpolicy.com/2019/08/19/chinas-south-china-sea-militarization-has-peaked/ (Accessed on 17 September 2020).
33. Kristin Huang, "Chinese military fires 'aircraft-carrier killer' missile into South China Sea in 'warning to the United States'," *South China Morning Post*, 2020, available at https://www.scmp.com/news/china/military/article/3098972/chinese-military-launches-two-missiles-south-china-sea-warning (Accessed on 17 September 2020).
34. Pinker Steven, *Enlightenment Now: The Case for Reason, Science, Humanism, and Progress* (New York: Viking Press, 2018).
35. Ibid., pp. 324-478.

8

A Constitutional Crisis for UNCLOS

Apurv Kumar Mishra

At the dawn of Indian independence, when the process of drafting the Indian Constitution was complete, its chief architect Dr. B.R. Ambedkar was asked to deliver his final speech in the Constituent Assembly. He spoke on the larger question of whether the Indian Constitution was good enough to serve the interests of a complex nation like India and noted:

> *"...however good a Constitution may be, it is sure to turn out bad because those who are called to work it, happen to be a bad lot. However bad a Constitution may be, it may turn out to be good if those who are called to work it, happen to be a good lot."*[1]

The 1982 United Nations Convention on the Law of the Sea (UNCLOS) is popularly referred to as the "Constitution of the Oceans" and stands out as a shining symbol of order and cooperation in the anarchical world of international relations. However, Dr. Ambedkar's remark is a timely reminder that UNCLOS, like all other constitutions, is merely words on a piece of paper unless stakeholders put continuous efforts to make it work.

We must begin by first acknowledging that UNCLOS has had remarkable success as an international treaty. Nearly 167 countries and the European Union (EU) are parties to UNCLOS and to a large extent, its provisions now have the status of customary international law as a result of uniform and general state practice. By way of illustration, even though the United States of America (USA) signed UNCLOS only in 1994 and has still not ratified the Convention, it has been committed to abiding by its principles since inception through policy statements and conduct. Further evidence of its success is the fact that new categories of disputes are being settled through the binding decisions of dispute settlement mechanisms under UNCLOS. For example, issues relating to detention of ships and marine pollution cases are increasingly being decided through UNCLOS mechanisms.

Constitution of the Oceans

The phrase "Constitution of the Oceans" was notably used by Tommy Koh of Singapore who was the President of the 3rd UN Conference on Law of the Seas that finalised UNCLOS.[2] There are several aspects of UNCLOS, which are constitutional in nature. Firstly, it is a comprehensive outline of rights and duties of all parties involved; secondly, it prescribes a binding and (almost) compulsory mode of governance and dispute settlement; finally, it codifies certain cherished values of the community. On each of these three criteria, UNCLOS provides considerable evidence of its constitutional character.

It is important to note that UNCLOS was negotiated and finalised by overwhelming participation of the entire international community at the height of the Cold War. This is because UNCLOS put an end to the legal disorder which reigned before its adoption[3] and every nation stood to benefit by it.

Underlying the idea of UNCLOS as the "Constitution of the Oceans", in fact, any constitution, is the belief that the rule of law is a pre-requisite for peace and prosperity of the community. What does it mean to insist on the rule of law in governance of the world's oceans? As Judge Jin-Hyun Paik (President of ITLOS) explains, "It means justice can be done for all states, big or small, strong or weak, developed or developing"[4] This is often the case under UNCLOS where smaller and less powerful countries regularly file and win cases against bigger and more powerful countries.[5]

A second aspect of the rule of law is self-restraint and predictability in the conduct of states. Former Prime Minister of Japan, Shinzo Abe, in his keynote address at the Shangri-La Dialogue 2014 succinctly summarised this aspect of rule of law under the UNCLOS regime:

> *"Now, when we say "the rule of law at sea"—what exactly do we mean in concrete terms? If we take the fundamental spirit that we have infused into international law over the ages and reformulate it into three principles, we find the rule of law at sea is actually a matter of common sense. The first principle is that states shall make and clarify their claims based on international law. The second is that states shall not use force or coercion in trying to drive their claims. The third principle is that states shall seek to settle disputes by peaceful means".*[6]

Challenges to UNCLOS

UNCLOS came into force in 1994 after Guyana became the 60th country to ratify it. This was a uniquely unipolar moment in modern history when no other country had the military prowess or technological capabilities of the USA to police the oceans and harness its resources. A lot of water has flown under the proverbial bridge since then. We live in a multipolar world with the rise of several non-Western great powers in Asia. While the USA still remains the pre-eminent military force in the world, other countries like the People's Republic of China (PRC) have greatly expanded their power projection capabilities. Technologies to harness biotic and abiotic resources in the ocean have also greatly advanced since and are now available with several developing nations. Goods over USD 19 trillion are now exported globally[7] of which around 80 per cent (by volume) are conducted through sea.[8] These changed circumstances have posed new challenges for the UNCLOS regime.

In October 2019, an UNCLOS Conference was organised at the International Tribunal for the Law of the Sea (ITLOS) Headquarters in Hamburg by Indiana University's Hamilton Lugar School of Global and International Studies, Universität Hamburg and the International Foundation for the Law of the Sea on the theme *'How healthy is the ocean's constitution? 25 Years of the United Nations Convention on the Law of the Sea'*.[9] The conference highlighted the following key challenges facing UNCLOS in the 21st century:

1. Peaceful settlement of disputes arising under UNCLOS
2. Global warming and ocean acidification
3. Maritime terror
4. Illegal and unreported fishing
5. Technological development on ocean governance
6. Land and ocean use reaching threatening levels for marine environment
7. Negotiations on conserving biodiversity in areas beyond national jurisdiction

Of these, the first, peaceful settlement of disputes, poses an existential challenge because it undermines the legitimacy of the entire regime and disinclines states to cooperate within the UNCLOS framework to solve any of the other six challenges that are considerable in their own regard.

At first instance, this sounds uncontroversial and hardly an existential challenge because nations have a fundamental obligation to settle disputes peacefully under Article 2(3) of the UN Charter[10] read with Article 33. States are accordingly bound by the dispute settlement mechanisms of the treaties they are governed by. However, the actions of the People's Republic of China (PRC) before and after the 2016 judgment of an Arbitral Tribunal constituted under Article 287, Annex VII of UNCLOS under the aegis of the Permanent Court of Arbitration (PCA) in *Philippines vs. China*[11] have created an existential crisis for UNCLOS and raised serious questions about its continuing relevance as the foundational text to resolve maritime disputes between countries and safeguard the world's oceans.

South China Sea case

By way of a quick recap, the Philippines initiated arbitration proceedings under UNCLOS after the PRC seized Scarborough Shoal in 2012 which fell within its EEZ. In a unanimous decision, the tribunal comprehensively ruled against the PRC on all moot points in the case. Firstly, it clarified that its decision was only limited to interpretation of UNCLOS principles and not in any way deciding claims of sovereignty. This had been PRC's rationale for rejecting its jurisdiction and not participating in the proceedings.

Most importantly, it declared that PRC's so-called Nine Dash Line and all claims arising from it had no basis in international law. It further clarified the definition of "island" under UNCLOS and confirmed that all attempts by the PRC to change the facts on the ground by constructing artificial structures had no legal standing since they were built on rocks, low tide elevations or submerged banks which have limited or no maritime entitlements. Next, it held the PRC guilty of violating the Philippines's sovereign rights by exploring for oil in its Exclusive Economic Zone (EEZ). This has important implications for other claimant states like Vietnam in whose EEZ, the PRC has been conducting similar operations. The arbitral tribunal also held that the PRC's reclamation spree caused extensive ecological damage to the marine environment.

Implication of PRC's Conduct after Arbitral Award

The Great Powers have a complicated track record on their compliance with decisions of international tribunals.[12] A day before the 12 July 2016 decision of the PCA, Harvard Professor Graham Allison wrote an article in *The Diplomat* magazine with a provocative title, *"Of Course China, Like All Great Powers, Will Ignore an International Legal Verdict"*.[13] The truth is, the Great Powers face tremendous pressure to showcase their credentials as a responsible actor in the international system and always find a way to satisfy the claims of their opposite party as long as they get a plausible face-saver.[14]

After the USA lost the International Court of Justice (ICJ) case to Nicaragua,[15] it predictably responded by questioning the legitimacy of the ICJ to decide the dispute and refused to abide by its ruling. However, by 1992, it agreed to pay a sizable compensation (classified as "aid") to Nicaragua and its conduct caused sizable reputational damage to the USA that persists even today. Similarly, after Russia lost the *Arctic Sunrise* case[16] to the Netherlands in 2015, it yet again questioned the jurisdiction of ITLOS and PCA to decide various elements of the dispute. But it eventually released the detained crew members and agreed to pay a reasonable compensation to the Netherlands, albeit on pretext of complying with their domestic law and not because it was forced by the decisions of international tribunals.

Finally, as Professor Erik Voeten explains in his *Washington Post* article,[17] decisions of international tribunals may also provide "focal points"[18] to anchor future negotiations if the ruling clearly favours one party to the dispute. Indeed, there was a view in some sections of the international community that despite its immediate and loud denouncement of the PCA decision, the judgment had the effect of toning down the PRC's actions and nudging it a peaceful solution to the dispute. There was a temporary pause in its artificial island building spree and there were several attempts to conduct joint expeditions with other claimant states to explore marine resources in the area.

However, the belligerent tone and actions of the PRC in recent times makes it clear that it has no intention of respecting the decision of the PCA. It has continued the militarisation of its artificial structures in South China Sea (SCS), conducts aggressive patrolling and has begun enforcing its domestic laws in the disputed territory. Therefore, unwarranted aggression by the PRC has escalated the situation in SCS from a dispute to a full-fledged crisis. In 2020, there have been several examples of PRC's "bullying behaviour". It has provoked confrontations with Indonesia over Natuna Islands (January 2020), prevented the Philippines from exploration in West Philippines Sea (February 2020), sunk and detained Vietnamese fishing vessels (April 2020) and engaged in a standoff with Malaysia over its oil and natural gas operations (May 2020).

Taking note of the PRC's unusual aggression in the middle of the pandemic, former Chief Justice of the Philippines Supreme Court, Antonio Carpio, who played a key role in the PCA case, warned that UNCLOS will collapse if the PRC continues to encroach on the exclusive economic zones of countries in the South China Sea (SCS), including the Philippines.[19]

> *"If China can seize the exclusive economic zones of five coastal states in the South China Sea that would mean UNCLOS will collapse...UNCLOS will no longer serve as the constitutional law for the oceans and seas of our planet and all other coastal states, the small coastal states, will be at the mercy of their bigger neighbours who will just seize their exclusive economic zone."*

Further, the international community must understand that the PRC's ambition for maritime *lebensraum* does not end with SCS. Instead, their eventual goal is to dominate the Pacific waters through control of a

"Second Island Chain"[20] which includes the islands of Micronesia, Guam, Saipan and Okinawa. This makes the PCA ruling a litmus test of the international community's resolve to protect cherished values like a rule-based global order, free and open seas and principles of common heritage of mankind under UNCLOS. If the world acquiesces to China's unlawful claims, despite a clear ruling, it will further embolden the PRC to continue its disruptive behaviour and the prospects of a long-term peace in the Indian Ocean Region will become very bleak.

Image Source: Wall Street Journal (see note 20)

The PRC's conduct and the international community's diffidence in enforcing its compliance are already creating a template for other belligerent actors to emulate its illegal behaviour and further erode the UNCLOS regime. Turkey, for example, has begun extensive exploration of oil and gas inside Cyprus's EEZ in the Eastern Mediterranean Sea and has announced similar plans in the EEZ around Greek islands in Aegean Sea.[21] In February 2019, the Turkish navy conducted its largest ever exercise called *Mavi Vatan* (Blue Homeland) to buttress its claims to sovereignty over large parts of the Black Sea, Aegean Sea and

Mediterranean Sea. Several analysts claim this is a Turkish version of the infamous Nine Dash Line.[22]

Contrast with India

Almost in parallel to the *Philippines vs. China* case at the PCA, another maritime dispute between India and Bangladesh was being heard by the tribunal on delimitation of their respective maritime boundaries in the Bay of Bengal.[23] The contrast in response between the foreign ministries of India and the PRC to the respective judgments is striking. The official spokesperson of India's Ministry of External Affairs issued a statement on the day of the arbitral award saying,[24]

> *"...We respect the verdict of the Tribunal and are in the process of studying the award and its full implications. We believe that the settlement of the maritime boundary will further enhance mutual understanding and goodwill between India and Bangladesh by bringing to closure a long pending issue."*

The Ministry of Foreign Affairs of the PRC similarly issued a statement on the day of the 2016 arbitral award saying,[25]

> *"The Ministry of Foreign Affairs of the People's Republic of China solemnly declares that the award is null and void and has no binding force. China neither accepts nor recognizes it. China's territorial sovereignty and maritime rights and interests in the South China Sea shall under no circumstances be affected by those awards. China opposes and will never accept any claim or action based on those awards."*

India's insistence on abiding by the outcome of the arbitral process and respecting international law even though over 19,000 sq. km. of area in the Bay of Bengal was awarded to Bangladesh is a shining example of respecting the rule of law and conduct befitting a responsible great power. India's then Minister of State for External Affairs, Gen. V.K. Singh highlighted this contrasting approach in a speech at the 5th East Asia Summit Foreign Ministers' Meeting in Kuala Lumpur in August 2015 noting,[26]

> *"In a world of inter-dependence and globalisation, there is no option but to follow international laws and norms. India supports freedom of navigation in international waters, including the South China Sea,*

> *the right of passage and overflight, unimpeded commerce and access to resources in accordance with principles of international law, including the 1982 UN Convention on the Law of the Sea. Territorial disputes must be settled through peaceful means, as was done by India and Bangladesh recently using the mechanisms provided under UNCLOS [emphasis added]. India hopes that all parties to the disputes in the South China Sea will abide by the guidelines on the implementation of the Declaration on the Conduct of Parties in the South China Sea."*

Conclusion

An oft-repeated phrase used to describe democratic constitutions around the world is that they are "living documents" which is to say that their key provisions are deliberately kept ambiguous so that they may be reinterpreted to suit the needs of future generations. Our own national experience in India indicates radical reinterpretations of constitutional provisions after the sustained attacks on constitutional values during the Emergency of 1975 to preserve democracy in our society. Constitutions can remain relevant only to the extent they are successful in restraining the behaviour of powerful actors. Faced with an existential crisis during the Emergency, the Indian Constitution was re-imagined to create the basic structure doctrine to limit executive power and institute a collegium system for appointments in the higher judiciary to preserve judicial independence.

UNCLOS faces its own 1975 moment because of the PRC's actions in SCS. If the international community does not impose deterring costs on PRC's belligerence and seeks its strict compliance with the PCA decision, we risk a slide back to an unstable and combustible global maritime disorder. Further, it erodes the legitimacy of UNCLOS to enforce its other provisions relating to protection of marine environment, maritime delimitation exercises and sustainable exploitation of deep-sea resources.

Finally, the behaviour of states, especially their compliance with international law, is shaped by their expectations concerning the future behaviour of others. Important conversations are currently underway to negotiate a treaty to conserve marine bio-diversity in areas beyond national jurisdiction. There are similar discussions being undertaken on each of the six challenges to the UNCLOS regime outlined above. These discussions are at risk because parties do not see the value of imposing self-restrictions if stronger states are allowed to get away with blatantly illegal actions.

To this end, it is encouraging to note that all stakeholders have begun a concerted effort to impress the weight of world opinion on the PRC. On 13 July 2020, the US Secretary of State, Mike Pompeo, issued a statement expressly aligning the USA's views with the PCA ruling,[27] a welcome change from its earlier position of not taking any view on the substantive merits of any side's claims in the dispute. Even at the UN, the USA has joined four ASEAN nations—Malaysia, Indonesia, the Philippines and Vietnam—who have each sent circular notes to Secretary General António Guterres over the last one year opposing the PRC's unlawful claims in SCS.[28] These are important steps towards mobilising international opinion against the PRC's aggression. Similarly, after years of uneven response by its member nations, ASEAN presented a united front and issued a joint statement at the end of its 36th Summit in June 2020 "reaffirming the importance of upholding international law, including the 1982 UNCLOS"[29] in SCS.

There needs to be sustained diplomatic pressure on the PRC to respect the PCA decision by all peace-loving nations (not just claimant states in SCS) across all international fora, similar to the sustained campaign in support of Nicaragua[30] to force the USA to abide by the ICJ ruling in the 1986 case.[31] The PRC must suffer prohibitive reputational costs and international isolation in case it remains obtuse and refuses to mend its ways. A rule-based global order cannot sustain without strict and universal adherence to international law.

NOTES

1. Vasant Moon, *Dr. Babasaheb Ambedkar Writings and Speeches, Vol. 13*, (New Delhi: Dr. Ambedkar Foundation Ministry of Social Justice & Empowerment, Govt. of India, 2014), p. 1210, available at https://www.mea.gov.in/Images/attach/amb/Volume_13.pdf (Accessed on 24 September 2020).
2. Tommy Koh, *A Constitution for the Oceans*, Remarks of the President of the Third United Nations Conference on the Law of the Sea at the Conference at Montego Bay (December 1982).
3. Judge Shunji Yanai of ITLOS, *The Rule of Law in the Seas of Asia: Navigational Chart for*

the Peace and Stability, Keynote Speech at International Symposium on The Law of the Sea (12-13 February 2015).

4. Judge Jin-Hyun Paik, President ITLOS, Keynote Address at *UNCLOS Conference: How healthy is the ocean's constitution?* (Hamburg, 17 October 2019), available at https://www.itlos.org/fileadmin/itlos/documents/statements_of_president/paik/UNCLOS_25_171019_ en.pdf (Accessed on 24 September 2020).
5. See, for example, *Chagos Marine Protected Area Arbitration, Mauritius vs. United Kingdom* ICGJ 486 (PCA 2015), a 2015 decision of Permanent Court of Arbitration.
6. 13th IISS Asian Security Summit, *The Shangri-La Dialogue—Keynote Address by Shinzo Abe, Prime Minister, Japan*, 30 May 2014, available at https://www.mofa.go.jp/fp/nsp/page4e_000086.html (Accessed on 24 September 2020).
7. International Merchandise Trade, *"UNCTAD Handbook of Statistics 2019"*, available at https://unctad.org/en/PublicationChapters/tdstat44_FS01_en.pdf (Accessed on 24 September 2020).
8. United Nations Conference on Trade and Development, *Review of Maritime Transport 2018*, available at https://unctad.org/en/pages/PublicationWebflyer.aspx?publicationid=2245 (Accessed on 24 September 2020).
9. UNCLOS Conference, *How healthy is the ocean's constitution? 25 Years of the United Nations Convention on the Law of the Sea*, available at https://hls.indiana.edu/unclos/index.html (Accessed on 24 September 2020).
10. Article 2 (3) of UN Charter: All members shall settle their international disputes by peaceful means in such a manner that international peace and security, and justice, are not endangered.
11. PCA Case No. 2013-19.
12. Richard Javad Heydarian, "Can China Really Ignore International Law?" *The National Interest*, 01 August 2016, available at https://nationalinterest.org/feature/can-china-really-ignore-international-law-17211 (Accessed on 24 September 2020).
13. Graham Allison, "Of Course China, Like All Great Powers, Will Ignore an International Legal Verdict", *The Diplomat*, 11 July 2016, available at https://thediplomat.com/2016/07/of-course-china-like-all-great-powers-will-ignore-an-international-legal-verdict/ (Accessed on 24 September 2020).
14. Antonio T. Carpio, "Do great powers comply with arbitral rulings?" 16 January 2020, available at https://opinion.inquirer.net/126630/do-great-powers-comply-with-arbitral-rulings (Accessed on 24 September 2020).
15. *Nicaragua vs. United States* 1986 I.C.J. 14 (Accessed on 24 September 2020).
16. *The Arctic Sunrise Arbitration (Netherlands vs. Russia)*, PCA Case No. 2014-02 (Accessed on 24 September 2020).
17. Erik Voeten, "Why the South China Sea ruling matters", *Washington Post*, 13 July 2016, available at https://www.washingtonpost.com/news/monkey-cage/wp/2016/07/12/why-the-south-china-sea-ruling-matters/ (Accessed on 24 September 2020).
18. Paul Huth, Sarah Croco & Benjamin Appel, "Does International Law Promote the Peaceful Settlement of International Disputes? Evidence from the Study of Territorial Conflicts since 1945", *American Political Science Review*, Vol. 105, No. 2 (2011), pp. 415-436.
19. Jeffrey Damicog, "Carpio warns of UNCLOS collapse due to China", *Manila Bulletin*, 10 September 2020, available at https://mb.com.ph/2020/09/10/carpio-warns-of-unclos-collapse-due-to-china/ (Accessed on 24 September 2020).
20 Trae Sebastian, Can the United States Defend Its Allies in East Asia? *Berkeley Political*

Review, 26 November 2019, available at https://bpr.berkeley.edu/2019/11/26/can-the-united-states-defend-its-allies-in-east-asia/ (Accessed on 24 September 2020).
21. Panagiotis Kouparanis, "Turkey's maritime claims in the Mediterranean Sea raise thorny legal questions", *Deutsche Welle*, 21 July 2020, available at https://www.dw.com/en/turkeys-maritime-claims-in-the-mediterranean-sea-raise-thorny-legal-questions/a-54256300 (Accessed on 24 September 2020).
22. Friso Dubbelboer, "UNLCOS Under Pressure: Law of the Jungle or Law of the Sea", *Clingendael Spectator*, 28 July 2020, available at https://spectator.clingendael.org/nl/publicatie/unclos-under-pressure-law-jungle-or-law-sea (Accessed on 24 September 2020)
23. Bay of Bengal Maritime Boundary Arbitration (Bangladesh vs. India), Permanent Court of Arbitration, 07 July 2014.
24. Official Spokesperson's response to a question on the award of the Tribunal on the Maritime Boundary Arbitration between India and Bangladesh, 08 July 2014, available at https://mea.gov.in/outoging-visit-detail.htm?23575/Official+Spokespersons+ response+ to+ a+question+on+the+award+of+the+Tribunal+on+the+ Maritime + Boundary+ Arbitration+between+India+and+Bangladesh (Accessed on 24 September 2020).
25. Statement of the Ministry of Foreign Affairs of the People's Republic of China on the Award of 12 July 2016 of the Arbitral Tribunal in the South China Sea Arbitration Established at the Request of the Republic of the Philippines, 12 July 2016, available at https://www.fmprc.gov.cn/nanhai/eng/snhwtlcwj_1/t1379492.htm (Accessed on 24 September 2020).
26. Remarks by Minister of State for External Affairs at the 5th East Asia Summit Foreign Ministers' Meeting, Kuala Lumpur, 06 August 2015, available at http://mea.gov.in/aseanindia/Speeches-Statements.htm?dtl/22589/Remarks+by+Minister+of+State+for+ External+Affairs+at+the+5th+East+Asia+Summit+Foreign+Ministers+ Meeting+Kuala+ Lumpur (Accessed on 24 September 2020).
27. Michael R. Pompeo (Secretary of State), U.S. Position on Maritime Claims in the South China Sea, *Press Statement*, 13 July 2020, available at https://www.state.gov/u-s-position-on-maritime-claims-in-the-south-china-sea/ (Accessed on 24 September 2020).
28. Text of Letter from Ambassador Kelly Craft, the United States Representative to the United Nations to Secretary-General of the United Nations regarding Note Verbale No. CML/14/201, available at https://usun.usmission.gov/wp-content/uploads/sites/296/200602_KDC_ChinasUnlawful.pdf (Accessed on 24 September 2020).
29. Chairman's Statement of the 36th ASEAN Summit, 26 June 2020, Cohesive and Responsive ASEAN, available at https://asean.org/storage/2020/06/Chairman-Statement-of-the-36th-ASEAN-Summit-FINAL.pdf (Accessed on 24 September 2020).
30. Antonio T. Carpio, Why the UNGA Matters, *Inquirer.net*, 03 September 2020, available at https://opinion.inquirer.net/133261/why-the-unga-matters (Accessed on 24 September 2020).
31. Supra note 12.

9

Enduring Legitimacy of UNCLOS and its Continuing Vitality

Bimal N. Patel

Nearly 26 years have passed since the United Nations Convention on the Law of the Sea (UNCLOS) came into force. From 16 November 1994, when it was enforced, till today; the policies and practices of 167 states and the European Union, as far as ocean governance is concerned, have been influenced by UNCLOS. In the last two decades, the Convention, which is also called the Constitution of the Ocean[1], and a political document instead of a truly multilateral treaty, has thrown open several issues and challenges. In most cases, unfortunately, one could not find the answer in the Convention; hence, state practices have remained the major source of analysis and understanding. The question arises whether those issues and challenges hardly envisaged could have a critical impact to the extent that the Convention may break down or, like the UN Charter, can the interpretation of the Convention by the courts and tribunals and commitment and faith of the international community allow it to survive for decades to come? This chapter covers issues like managing ocean resources, maritime security, marine scientific research, marine environment and ocean law and policy, categorises prominent short-term, mid-term and long-term challenges and responses not only for India and the Indian Ocean Rim Association (IORA) but also for similarly situated states and multilateral institutions across the globe.

The conference at the Law of the Sea Institute in the University of Berkeley in 2014 where 25 specialists and experts of the law of the sea gathered to discuss the major law and policy issues for 20 years to structure UNCLOS, culminated in one of the latest scholarships, namely, *Ocean Law and Policy: 20 Years under UNCLOS*, edited by Carlos Esposito, James Kraska, Harry Scheiber and Moon-Sang Kwow. A similar conference was organised by the same institute 35 years ago also before UNCLOS became reality.

Living Resources: Fisheries and Food Security

The Law of the Sea Institute, in 1985, had some interesting discussions in the sense that some of the contributors of the 1985 conference were optimist about the establishment of 200-mile fishing zones and the vesting of sovereign rights and management powers in a single unified entity, the coastal state, away from the global commons, on the ground that it would resolve many of the over-exploitation issues stemming from the insuperable common property approach that had plagued the management of fisheries for much of the 20th century. The questions are—can IORA or BIMSTEC follow the European Common Fisheries Policy (CFP) model and what are the pros and cons as far as CFP implementation within the UNCLOS is concerned.

The maritime states of BIMSTEC, for example, can have CFP, which can seek to manage fish stocks in an integrated manner, irrespective of the maritime boundaries of the member states, traditionally on the basis of maximum sustainable yield and more recently by using new normative principles including the ecosystems-based approach and the precautionary principle. Let's be reminded that the European CFP based on a traditional approach has not been successful and 88 per cent of EU fish stocks have been fished beyond the 2009 maximum sustainable yield (MSY). As Prof. Long states, the European common fishery policy remains a most controversial one.[2] Although controversial, the CFP has been subjected to periodic review in 1992, 2002 and 2009 through to 2013 undergoing review and reforms; thus, IORA/BIMSTEC nations too can initiate and let the policy be reviewed on a regular basis instead of sticking to a hard-law treaty approach. A study may be called upon to understand how the EU law influenced the possibilities for strengthening governance structures and stakeholder involvement in fishery regulation and management under a reformed CFP like socio-economic project.

We have to see the impact of how the EU's reform based on right-based fishery management system as a means to allocate individual fishing rights to fishermen, fishing vessels, enterprises, cooperatives or fishing communities can work in IORA. The EU has focussed on involving the industry more closely—responsibilities and rights. Industry can be given more responsibility through self-management. Result-based management could be a move in this direction, instead of establishing rules about how to fish. The rules can focus on the outcome and the more detailed implementation decisions would be left to industry. Result-based management would relieve both industry and policy makers from part of the burden of detailed management of technical issues. In the Indian context, this can really work well. It would have to be linked to a reversal of the burden of proof; it would be up to industry to demonstrate that it operates responsibly in return for access to fishing. This would contribute to better management by making the policy considerably simple and removing the current incentives for providing false or incomplete information.

The EU Parliament recommended that the responsibilities for developing and implementing fisheries management plans should be devolved to member states and regional bodies.[3] In order to achieve this objective, the Parliament called for the abandonment of the traditional top-down approach to fisheries management and its replacement with a bottom-up decision-making process under the reformed CFP.

The IORA countries can adopt the EU model whereby the EU Parliament supported the codification of a requirement for mandatory environmental impact assessment prior to EU vessels gaining access to new fisheries. The environmental impact assessment has improved the quality, accountability and legitimacy of environmental and planning decisions in both the EU and the member-states. Furthermore, the assessment of the environment impacts of fisheries is fully consistent with the provisions on the controlling and monitoring of pollution under UNCLOS.

Is the much fought-over regime of the Exclusive Economic Zones

(EEZ), a major achievement of the developing coastal states, under threat from certain countries? The IORA records on delivering sustainable fisheries are a cause of significant concern.[4] The IORA countries are actually said to be considered as facing a fisheries crisis. One way could be to improve governance by managing fish stocks as ecological units and through the application of new normative tools including the precautionary principle and ecosystem-based management. IORA countries can gradually evolve a culture of compliance and cooperation among all operators and fishers. The Common Fisheries Policy of the European Union has been seen as reformatory but IORA countries can have much less to learn from this area.

As India and several IORA countries move towards the goal of achieving food security and factors such as sea protein as an important source of protein and promotion of food security-related blue economy industry will be required and India on its own or together with its immediate Indian Ocean Region (IOR) neighbours can use the potential to strengthen the effective role and defined responsibilities of industry in the management and conservation of living resources. Currently, states pursue a unilateral policy.

Underwater Cultural Heritage Convention 2001

Another important issue is the Underwater Cultural Heritage (UCH), a subject that though remains in the margins of important forums, is critically important as it has past, present and future importance in the overall governance of the law of the sea. India is yet to sign and then ratify the 2001 Underwater Cultural Heritage Convention of the UNESCO. Although the reasons may be not completely known, one could expect that maritime jurisdiction and issues of sunken ships in and around Indian waters may be one of the important factors for non-membership of the Convention. India can develop both administrative and legal arrangements to respond to changing international and national environments concerned with the UCH. As India has maritime boundaries with seven states, it needs to initiate cooperation to prevent future conflicts over UCH. None of the seven states having maritime boundaries with India have signed or ratified the Convention. In the absence of India's accession, some guidelines can be developed based on the experience of South Korea to ensure protection of the UCH.[5] Although South Korea has not acceded and is unlikely to accede in the future, there are suggestions to improve the existing BCHP Act (The Protection and Inspection of Buried Cultural Heritage). For example, a new provision on reporting and notification can be inserted into the Act in a way that stipulates separate reporting notification procedures for UCH located in the Exclusive Economic Zone, Contiguous Zone and on the seabed or outside territorial waters. This would keep key issues at a minimum level of explicitness and at the same time state that remaining issues, which are not critical, will be consistent with Convention provisions and the UNCLOS.

India has a rich underwater cultural heritage, however, but in the absence of domestic laws and also lack of ratification of the UNESCO 2001 Convention, it can start preparing its views as to how to deal with concepts of warships and other government ships and military aircraft found underwater, the scope of temporal limits and ownership of and jurisdiction of UCH. Establishment of the Underwater Archaeology Wing (UAW) in the Archaeological Survey of India (ASI) in 2001 marked a major step towards the development of the subject—the Ancient Monuments and Archaeological Sites and Remains Act, 1958, and the Antiquities and Art Treasures Act, 1972. There is no agreement for cooperation with other countries in this domain. India can initiate cooperation with other countries in the Indian Ocean region. For example, India can develop, in collaboration with South Korea, the standardisation of recovery criteria and the specification of procedures and measures to prevent illicit recovery or exports.

Was marine archaeology considered as marine scientific research during the negotiations? Modern underwater technology, particularly the use of remote sensing equipment and different unmanned submersible vehicles, permits the gathering of massive information from the bottom of the seas, which may be directly transformed in a tradable commodity. While pure research does not simply direct economic revenue, applied research is primarily focused on future and foreseeable commercial activities. The information gathered by modern underwater technology, when directed at an archaeological target (for example, a shipwreck) is likely not characterised as pure marine scientific research.

This has a significant impact as to how India implements the UNCLOS. Activities directed at UCH in the EEZ or on the continental shelf may then be subject to the coastal state's discretion, depending on the nature and purpose of that activity. Coastal states, in order to protect UCH located in their EEZ on their continental shelf, have the discretion to grant or withhold any permit to those actors. Furthermore, the regime of MSR grants research rights only to states, not private actors. Private companies such as treasure hunters are not inherently entitled to be granted such permits. Perhaps the basic criteria to be used when protecting UCH in the EEZ is the interest of the international community as a whole. UCH, as any other cultural heritage, must be generally protected.

Maritime Security Threats

The 2008 UN Secretary-General's Report has identified seven specific maritime security threats—piracy, terrorism, illicit trafficking in arms and weapons of mass destruction, narcotic drugs, smuggling and trafficking in persons, IUU fishing and damage to the marine environment. The analysis of the threats and state practice mainly focussing on the legislative framework among the IORA countries have shown that there exists a low level of critical awareness among policy makers about the scope and size of each of the maritime security challenges. The development of a legal and juridical framework ranges from a very robust to weak system. IORA states also need to identify and systematically assess the impact of each of these threats on their varied levels of political and economic development including the future growth potential.

Civil Disobedience in the Maritime Domain

Although piracy may have receded, there are other threats or challenges such as how to address aggressive civil disobedience about appropriate boundaries between two bodies of international law—international human rights norms that reflect the rights of all people to exercise free expression and the principles of good order, safety and security at sea embodied in the international law of the sea.[6] The laws that govern protests on land and at sea are different. In the last 10 years, the Mox Plant, *Arctic Sunrise* case and Whaling case are all too vivid reminders as to how NGOs and like-minded institutions could pose challenges, yet also offer certain opportunities to state institutions to reconcile conflicting interests. The efforts to address civil disobedience on land unfold within clear boundaries of sovereignty and jurisdiction, and they typically involve the timely intervention of law-and-order authorities to separate protesters from other citizens in order to preserve public safety and order, while also protecting the right of free expression to make demands on the polity. In contrast, civil disobedience at sea occurs under conditions and areas of authority shared by more than one state, so competence to prescribe and enforce rules are shared. Such situations can lead to violence and case law is emerging at ITLOS.[7] This issue was hardly foreseen by the UNCLOS. India with vast coastlines and various water-bodies is likely to face civil disobediencc instances. In the process, the government and maritime law enforcement authorities will have to deal with the issues of shared authority, overlapping jurisdiction, and functional governance divided between flag states and coastal states.

Employment in Private Maritime Security Companies (PMSCs) has now become quite an established norm but they raise questions on liability for wrongful acts by PMSC on board ships, such as use of force, with regard to corporate civil liability for wrongful acts. PMSCs have been successful in suppressing piracy in the western Indian Ocean and are used in the Gulf of Guinea but they have their fair share of controversy. Flag state, coastal and port state jurisdiction are all in play against a background of and often in tension with basic UNCLOS provisions and a set of larger international law concepts. Moreover, even where carrying weapons on board and where the use of force is authorised by international law and guidelines, there remains the difficulty in harmonising human rights standards and penal regimes. Can victims of wrongful action seek both criminal and civil penalties?

States should strive to achieve legal harmonisation on the use of force by PMSCs and armed personnel, as well as treatment under national law of human rights abuses or violations, namely through the enactment of legislation on the liability of PMSCs and armed personnel on board. Meaningful cooperation between states' judicial and judiciary bodies on the enforcement of common standards is indispensable in avoiding a permissive environment for wrongful acts by companies of all kinds without adequate sanctioning and reparation. The Universal Declaration on Human Rights gives little support to the conclusion that PMSCs as non-state actors are subject to direct human rights obligations and provide protection against their conduct. In this case, human rights would only apply indirectly through states, seeing that only the latter are under obligation to protect individuals.

There is no legal framework binding PMSCs to human rights protection despite general recognition that their activities should be properly regulated and subjected to public international law. A national legislation survey by the United Nations concluded that there is a widely divergent level of regulation of PMSCs among states, and there is a need for an internationally legally binding instrument in order to ensure effective regulation. India should take the lead, as, even if piracy is reduced, the PMSCs are required. The rendering of military and security services by PMSCs and the presence of armed personnel on board ships shall continue to be a key element of maritime security as a result of their impressive levels of efficiency, taken with the fact that the overwhelming majority of the world's trade will continue to depend on maritime transportation. Likewise, the profitable and complex business that is criminality at sea makes it highly difficult for states to comprehensively tackle the different root causes.

Blue Economy

The development of a blue economy has become an economic and political imperative with maritime spatial planning as the essential dimension. There is a need to have a proper legal framework so that economic benefits are realised through the maritime sector. A blue economy is no more utopian or another development concept but a reality. The Law of the Sea, like almost all other faculties of international law, has remained Eurocentric or Euro/North American-centric. The above issues which are critical are also emanating from the state practice of these two regions and obviously, therefore, their state practice and views would prevail over other regions and states too. Therefore, in the larger interest of the universal norms of the law of the sea it is necessary that developing states play a more meaningful role.

NOTES

1. Any activity at sea is regulated partly or fully by the UNCLOS. It is widely held that all treaties, bilateral or multilateral, concluded after UNCLOS are compatible with the UNCLOS. Given the widely held perception that UNCLOS reflects customary international law in most respects, it is expected that even non state-parties will not act contrary to UNCLOS. Churchil, *OHLS*, p. 45.
2. Ronan Long, "Stakeholder Participation in the European Common Fisheries Policy: Shifting the Legal Paradigm toward Rights and Responsibilities", in Carlos Esposito, James Kraska, Harry Scheiber and Moon-Sang Kwon (ed.), *Ocean Law and Policy: Twenty Years Development under the UNCLOS Regime* (Leiden: Brill, 2016), pp. 11-67.
3. David Symes, "Regionalising the Common Fisheries Policy: Context, Content and Controversy", *Maritime Studies,* Vol. 11, art. 6 (2012), available at https://doi.org/10.1186/2212-9790-11-6. (Accessed on 25 September 2020).
4. See *supra* note Ronan Long.
5. Seoung Wook Park and Chang Soo Choe, "Protection and Management Policy of Underwater Cultural Heritage in Korea" in Carlos Esposito, James Kraska, Harry Scheiber and Moon-Sang Kwon (ed.), *Ocean Law and Policy: Twenty Years Development under the UNCLOS Regime,* (Leiden: Brill, 2016), pp. 148-162.
6. James Kraska, "The Laws of Civil Disobedience in the Maritime Domain", in Carlos Esposito, James Kraska, Harry Scheiber and Moon-Sang Kwon (ed.), *Ocean Law and Policy: Twenty Years Development under the UNCLOS Regime* (Leiden: Brill, 2016), pp. 163-202.
7. Ibid.

10

UNCLOS:
Its Significance and Legitimacy in 21st Century

Hamsa Devineni

Introduction

"Whoever rules the waves rules the world," said Sir Alfred Thayer Mahan, a revered American strategist, in the year 1890 in his book, *"The Influence of Sea Power Upon History"*[1]. This appears to be true even today! The growing strategic importance of the world's oceans and the race amongst States to acquire sovereign rights and territory over maritime spaces are underpinnings to most, if not all, of the global maritime challenges staring at us today.

The role of the sea has never before been as important as it is today.[2] Considering today's globalised and high-tech world, where data flows via fibre optic cables and satellites, most goods continue to be transported by sea, the world's oceans are equally important for all nations, both littoral and land-locked.[3] Whether they are manufactured products, construction material, food or fuel—most commodities still rely on traditional shipping through international sea-lanes to reach their markets.[4] The United Nations Conference on Trade and Development (UNCTAD) estimates that about 11 billion tons of cargo was moved by sea in 2018.[5] Additionally, the world's oceans contain huge quantities of underwater resources such as oil, gas, minerals and a rich marine biological diversity. Recent technological advancements and increased globalisation have led to the growth in maritime infrastructure and networks of undersea cables, which connect continents.[6] With these changing dynamics and the growing importance of the ocean space, the consequential risks and challenges, as we witness, are both vast and fragile.

The United Nations Convention on the Law of the Sea, 1958 (UNCLOS III), commonly regarded as the 'Constitution for the Oceans', hereinafter referred to in this paper as, 'the Convention', is the supreme law governing the maritime global commons. It is thus critical at this juncture to examine the legitimacy of the Convention and its relevance to address contemporary maritime challenges.

This paper seeks to assess the legitimacy of the Convention and its relevance by examining its provisions with respect to their applicability to current maritime issues. Most twenty-first century maritime challenges arise from the now strategically significant Indo-Pacific region, which among other water bodies also encompasses the South China Sea and the East China Sea. The South China Sea encompassing 3.5 million sq. km. of water surrounded by its littorals—China, Vietnam, Philippines, Malaysia, Brunei Darussalam and Indonesia—is a semi-enclosed maritime space that is of vital strategic importance and is also the most contested maritime space in the world. One third of the world's shipping passes through the South China Sea carrying more than $ 3 trillion in trade every year.[7] The water column and the seabed of the South China Sea are also crucial as they contain huge quantities of lucrative fish and oil and gas reserves. Additionally, China claims most of the South China Sea through its nine-dash-line, which encompasses 90 per cent of the waters comprising the South China Sea.[8] China unilaterally and on the basis of its historic rights claims its exclusive sovereign jurisdiction within the waters and features comprised within the nine-dash-line. A mix of all these factors has led to the South China Sea being the hotbed for many daunting maritime challenges today. This paper, therefore, examines a few important global maritime challenges, most of which may pertain to disputes arising from the South China Sea, although a few disputes outside this region have also been examined.

To better appreciate the legitimacy and relevance of UNCLOS in the

21st century, it would be pertinent to first understand the evolution and purpose of the Convention.

Origin and Development of the Law of the Sea

From the historical perspective, around the 17th century, to safeguard equal rights of participation of all nations in the East India spice trade, a Dutch legal scholar, Hugo Grotius, now regarded as the father of international law, for the first time, codified into international law the legal principle of 'res communis' which means the 'common right' of all nations to use the seas for the purposes of navigation and trade.[9]

In 1930, the League of Nations initiated the first conference in The Hague, "The Hague Conference for the Codification of International Law", to determine and codify the law of the sea. The Conference, which was attended by representatives from forty-seven governments, was unable to adopt a convention, due to the lack of an agreement on the question of the breadth of territorial waters and the problem of the contiguous zone.[10] The Conference, however, witnessed some measure of agreement regarding the legal status of the territorial waters, the right of innocent passage on the high seas, and the baseline for measuring the territorial waters.[11] In 1958, the United Nations (UN), the successor of the League of Nations, held its *"First United Nations Conference on Law of the Sea"*, to codify the Law of the Sea in Geneva. The conference having participants from 86 States, adopted four conventions, namely, The Convention on the Territorial Sea and the Contiguous Zone, the Convention on the Continental Shelf, The Convention on the High Seas, and The Convention on Fishing and the Conservation of the Living Resources of the High Seas, all of them, together referred to as UNCLOS I, 1958. To a certain extent, UNCLOS I codified customary international law and also established the regime of a continental shelf and contiguous zone. There was, however, no agreement between the States on the breadth of the territorial sea under the Convention on the Territorial Sea, 1958. The Second UN Conference on the Law of the Sea was held in Geneva in 1960 mainly, to settle the question of the 'breadth of the territorial sea', but failed due to irreconcilable differences among States.

The absence of an international agreement on the breadth of the territorial sea led to conflicts between the coastal States and distant fishing

States. For instance, vessels flying the flag of a State maintaining a 3-nm territorial sea were arrested by a coastal State claiming a 12-nm territorial sea, on the grounds of fishing without licence in its territorial waters.[12] Additionally, the Convention on the Continental Shelf of 1958 left room for varying interpretations in respect of the outer limits of the continental shelf. The disorder at sea was further aggravated in the 1970s by the unilateral claims of fishery zones or exclusive economic zones (EEZ) extending to 200 nm by many coastal States. Negotiations for determining new rules for the seas were necessitated because of the technological advances that were changing the relationships between societies and the sea in the post Second World War period.[13] Following nine years of consistent negotiations, with more than 160 nations participating, in 1982, the States finally reached a consensus about the text of the agreement, and the third UN Convention on the Law of the Sea (UNCLOS III) (hereinafter referred to as, 'The Convention') was adopted in 1994 after it was ratified by 60 States.

As per the preamble of the Convention, its purpose was to establish an international legal order for the seas and oceans in order to facilitate international communication, promote the peaceful uses of the seas and oceans, ensure the equitable and efficient utilisation of its resources and the protection and conservation of its living resources and marine environment.[14] The Convention has introduced several new regimes like straits used for international navigation, archipelagic waters, the 200-nm Exclusive Economic Zone, redefined the Continental Shelf within and beyond 200 nm, and also incorporated a compulsory dispute settlement mechanism for resolving disputes arising under the Convention. The compulsory dispute mechanism provisions are contained under Part XV of the Convention, under which four institutions are tasked with jurisdiction to resolve disputes arising under the Convention, namely, The International Tribunal for the Law of the Sea (ITLOS), the International Court of Justice (ICJ) and the Arbitral Tribunals constituted under Annexures VII and VIII of the Convention. The Convention also created an entirely new international maritime regime including the seabed, ocean floor and the subsoil of waters, beyond the limits of national jurisdiction which is termed as, 'The Area'. The Convention establishes that the Area and its resources are the common heritage of mankind.[15] Further, the Convention has created three new international institutions, The International Seabed Authority (ISA), The Commission on the Limits of the Continental Shelf (CLCS), and The International Tribunal for the Law of the Sea (ITLOS). The CLCS consisting of subject matter experts is entrusted with the task of examining and determining the Continental Shelf claims of the Coastal States beyond 200 nm. The outer-limits of the Continental Shelf of a Coastal State that are established in accordance with these recommendations by the CLCS would be final and binding under the Convention.[16] The ISA is tasked with the activities of exploration and exploitation of mineral resources from 'the Area' while the ITLOS is a specialised judicial institution under the Convention tasked with resolving disputes arising under the Convention. The Convention has also clarified in its Preamble that for those matters that are not covered under the Convention, the principles of general international law apply.[17]

The Convention, presently with a membership of 168 countries out of the world's 193 countries, is considered the most important international legal instrument of the 20th century following the Charter of the United Nations, 1945.[18] It is also now regarded as a codification of the customary international law relating to the law of the sea.[19]

Success of UNCLOS III

The Convention, i.e., UNCLOS III, may be termed as successful, insofar as the codification of international law pertaining to the law of the sea is concerned and thus it has contributed significantly towards development of the law of the sea. The International courts and tribunals established under the Convention under the dispute resolution mechanism have also made important contributions to the development of the law of the sea, both in the exercise of their advisory jurisdiction as well as through their decisions issued in the course of their dispute resolution. Till date, the ITLOS alone has adjudicated 27 cases and has also provided two advisory opinions addressing issues arising under the Convention.[20]

A few of the decisions of international institutions created by the Convention, which have significantly contributed to the development of the law of the sea, are as follows:

- **Advisory Opinion of the Seabed Disputes Chamber**

In 2010, the Council of the ISA, under the provisions of the Convention, requested the Seabed Disputes Chamber of ITLOS, constituted under the Convention, to render an advisory opinion with respect to the legal obligation and responsibilities of States with respect to sponsorship of activities in 'the Area'. After examining the written views expressed by fourteen State parties to the Convention, the ISA and four other international organisations, the Chamber delivered its advisory opinion in nine months.[21] The Chamber has taken into consideration larger aspects of the Convention, like protection of the marine environment while it clearly explains the nature and extent of the responsibilities and obligations of a sponsoring State with respect to conducting activities in the Area.[22] The opinion further held that amongst the many obligations of the Sponsoring State, the most important ones are the obligation to assist the ISA in the exercise of its control over activities in the Area, the obligation to apply a precautionary approach, the obligation to apply best environmental practices, and the obligation to conduct environmental assessments.[23] The ISA welcomed the opinion of the Chamber and adhered to the follow-up actions as per the opinion. This holistic and well-considered opinion of the Chamber has contributed to the development of the law of the sea in matters concerning 'the Area'.

- **Bangladesh vs. Myanmar or the Bay of Bengal Delimitation Case**

In December 2009, the first delimitation case was filed before the International Tribunal for the Law of the Sea (ITLOS) by Bangladesh concerning the delimitation of its maritime boundary with Myanmar in the Bay of Bengal.[24] The Tribunal rendered its judgment in 2012, whereby it delimited the territorial sea, the EEZ, and the continental shelf beyond 200 nm between Bangladesh and Myanmar. It is important here to recollect that the Convention has established CLCS to examine and make recommendations to States regarding their claims to continental shelf beyond 200 nm. In this case, the CLCS had decided to defer the consideration of the submissions of two States on the outer limits of the continental shelf beyond 200 nm, in the light of the maritime boundary dispute between Bangladesh and Myanmar.[25] Critics argued that ITLOS should not have decided claims over the continental shelf beyond 200 nm, as the outer limits of the continental shelf between Bangladesh and

Myanmar are yet to be determined by the CLCS and that, therefore, without the appropriate outer limits demarcated, the continental shelf beyond 200 nm cannot be effectively delimited. ITLOS too, acknowledging the situation, observed in its judgment as follows:

> *"in order to fulfil its responsibilities under Part XV, Section 2, of the Convention in the present case, it has an obligation to adjudicate the dispute and to delimit the continental shelf between the Parties beyond 200 nm. Such delimitation is without prejudice to the establishment of the outer-limits of the continental shelf in accordance with article 76, paragraph 8, of the Convention."*[26]

The decision of ITLOS in this case is noteworthy because it did not wait for the CLCS to determine the outer limits of the continental shelf of Bangladesh and Myanmar respectively, as would be the default situation. ITLOS proactively formulated a framework for delimitation of maritime boundary claims for continental shelf beyond 200 nm between the two States thus saving time and increasing the efficiency of the dispute settlement mechanism. Both parties have accepted the decision of ITLOS thus laying to rest a 36-year-old fight between Bangladesh and Myanmar in a span of just two years. The judgment of ITLOS in this case has formulated comprehensive principles to be applicable in issues concerning the delimitation of maritime boundary claims between competing States and has thus made remarkable contributions towards the development of the law of the sea. ITLOS's judgment in this case has also assisted the Convention to stay relevant in addressing contemporary maritime disputes.

- **Philippines vs. China Case**

In January 2013, the Philippines initiated an international arbitration against China before the Permanent Court of Arbitration (PCA) under the compulsory dispute settlement provisions of the Convention seeking to resolve long-pending maritime disputes between them. The Philippines requested the arbitral tribunal to decide on fifteen issues, which may be broadly classified into three important aspects, namely, China's claim to sovereign jurisdiction within the nine-dash line based on historic rights; whether the features in the South China Sea, that China claims, generate maritime zone entitlements under the Convention; and lastly, whether China violated its obligations under the Convention in terms of interfering with the Philippines' exercise of its sovereign rights. China failed to officially participate in the proceedings but nonetheless expressed its views in the case to the Tribunal through a 'position paper'. The Tribunal after considering the contentions of both the nations in detail delivered its final award in July 2016 in accordance with the principles established under the Convention.

With respect to China's claim to sovereign jurisdiction within the nine-dash line based on historic rights, the tribunal held,

> *"as between the Philippines and China, China's claim to historic rights, or other sovereign rights or jurisdiction, with respect to the maritime areas of the South China Sea encompassed by the relevant part of the 'Nine-dash line' are contrary to the convention and without lawful effect, to the extent that they exceed the geographic and substantive limits of China's maritime entitlements under the Convention"* [27] *(emphasis applied)*

The tribunal also observed that,

> *"the Convention superseded any historic rights, or other sovereign rights or jurisdiction, in excess of the limits imposed therein."*[28]

With respect to whether China's interference with the Philippines exercise of its sovereign rights violates the Convention, the Tribunal held as follows,

> *"Based on the considerations outlined above, the Tribunal finds that China has, through the operation of its marine surveillance vessels with respect to M/V Veritas Voyager on 1 to 2 March 2011, breached Article 77 of the Convention with respect to the Philippines' sovereign rights over the non-living resources of its continental shelf in the area of Reed Bank. The Tribunal further finds that China has, by promulgating its 2012 moratorium on fishing in the South China Sea, without exception for areas of the South China Sea falling within the exclusive economic zone of the Philippines and without limiting the moratorium to Chinese flagged vessels, breached Article 56 of the Convention with respect to the Philippines' sovereign rights over the living resources of its exclusive economic zone."*[29] *(emphasis applied)*

Although China has rejected the judgment of the arbitral tribunal and fails to comply with it, as per the Convention, the judgment of the arbitral tribunal is final and binding upon both the Philippines and China. Thus, the order of this Tribunal has laid to rest China's sovereign claim within the waters comprising the Nine-dash-line. The Tribunal has also clarified an important principle of the law of the sea that the Convention has superseded all sovereign claims to maritime territory by States based on historical rights.

This case is important for three reasons: Firstly, the issues involved in this dispute, namely, China's claims to sovereign jurisdiction in the South China Sea based on historic rights and its nine-dash-line, are similar or closely related to issues in most disputes, that are arising out of the South China Sea today and therefore, this decision, the first such case, would set a precedent. The judgment of the arbitral tribunal also clarified, though broadly, the important aspects of the Law of the Sea Convention pertaining to sovereign claims based on historic rights; Finally, the case also exposes a critical lacuna within the Convention, namely, the lack of enforcement provisions to the compulsory dispute resolution mechanism that was created by the Convention. Each of these aspects has been discussed in this paper.

- **Timor Liste vs. Australia Case**

In the case of Timor Liste vs. Australia, Timor Liste initiated conciliation proceedings under the United Nations Compulsory Conciliation (UNCC), Annex V of the Convention, against Australia seeking to settle their disputes pertaining to de-limitation of their maritime boundaries.[30] Both States successfully settled their maritime boundary dispute; however, this case presents a peculiar challenge where their mutually agreed maritime boundary is not in accordance with the delimitation procedure established under the Convention.

The Convention provides for de-limitation of the territorial sea between States with opposite or adjacent coasts.[31] Eventually, the international courts and tribunals established under the Convention have developed the law with respect to delimitation of the EEZ and continental shelf within and beyond 200 nm between States with opposite or adjacent coasts and have also laid down the framework for such disputes in the future. It is these principles of de-limitation that have proved ineffective to address the maritime de-limitation between Timor Liste and Australia. Thus, in spite of the resilience of the international courts and tribunals to develop the law of the sea, the case of Timor Liste and Australia clarifies the escalating gap between the Convention and the emerging maritime challenges.

Therefore, though the international courts and tribunals established under the Convention have significantly contributed to the development of the law of the sea by addressing challenges brought before them, as we have seen, many challenges still remain unaddressed by the Convention.

21st Century Maritime Challenges

The nearly four-decade-old Convention is regarded as the most successful multilateral treaty adopted by the international community following the Charter of the United Nations. However, what is practically different about the twenty-first century is that maritime disputes now are taking place within a broader context: there is a significant shift in the nature and scope of maritime order; power is now more diffuse; security and economic interests of States are increasingly overlapping and global challenges often intersect with national prerogatives, thereby adding multiple layers of complexity to the original fundamental task of the Convention, that is, safeguarding the oceans and seas.[32] International courts and tribunals established under the Convention, as we have seen above, are struggling to keep pace in addressing the emerging challenges arising from the 'global maritime commons'. While they have successfully resolved many disputes, many more maritime disputes still remain unresolved by the Convention. An analysis and understanding of the current maritime disputes should throw enough light on the legitimacy and relevance of the Convention to address 21st-century maritime challenges.

To examine the legitimacy of the Convention, this paper relies on the constitutional model of legitimacy of law coined by Mattias Kumm.[33] According to this model, examining four important principles would lead to assessing the legitimacy of law:

(i) *Formal Legitimacy/Principle of International Legality*—this principle requires that its addressees must obey it. It is based on the belief that in order for international law to achieve its purpose, those for whom it is addressed are morally required to generally comply, even when they disagree with its content.

(ii) *Jurisdictional Legitimacy/Principle of Subsidiarity*—the principle of subsidiarity, in essence, tests whether international law justifies a special need to replace application of established local laws. It is not enough to justify an international law as essential for the welfare of the public; the justification must clearly explain what exactly would be lost if States act upon their own domestic policy considerations.

(iii) *Procedural Legitimacy/Principle of Adequate Representation and Accountability*—Procedural legitimacy focuses on the procedural quality of the decision-making process and tests whether the decision-making institutions are in fact responsive to their addressees' concerns.

(iv) *Outcome Legitimacy/Principle of Achieving Reasonable Outcomes*—this principle is based on the premise that bad outcomes affect the legitimacy of a decision and tends to undermine the authority of the decision maker.

Thus, whether or not the Convention suffers from a legitimacy and relevance crisis is determined by examining a few important issues threatening the global maritime domain today.

Lack of Enforcement Provisions

The Philippines vs. China arbitration case, discussed above, exposes the absence of the 'compulsoriness' in the 'compulsory dispute settlement mechanism' contained in Part XV of the Convention. China, being bound by the order of the international arbitral tribunal in the above case, has refused to comply with it.

In another such instance,[34] Russia refused to participate in an international arbitration initiated against it by the Netherlands under Annexure VII of the Convention. The Netherlands claimed that Russia violated the provisions of the Convention by seizing the Dutch-flagged vessel M/V *Arctic Sunrise* and arresting 30 environmental activists for disrupting the activities of the Gazprom drilling platform in the Pechora Sea, which lies within 200 nm of Russia's EEZ. The vessel with its activists were allegedly holding protests as part of the 'Save the Arctic' campaign that fights for banning of offshore oil drilling and industrial fishing in Arctic waters. Russia did not participate in the arbitration at any stage. It also refused to follow the provisional order passed by ITLOS on 22 November 2013 directing it to immediately release the vessel and all the persons detained. The Arbitral Tribunal in its final order held that Russia had violated the Convention on multiple counts: by seizing the *Arctic Sunrise*, by arresting, detaining, and initiating judicial proceedings against the thirty persons on board that vessel ("*Arctic 30*"), by Russia's non-participation in the proceedings before the arbitral tribunal, by its failure to pay its share of the fees and expenses of the arbitration as requested by the Tribunal and also its failure to comply with the ITLOS order dated 22.11.2013. Further, the arbitral tribunal through its order dated 10.07.2017 directed Russia to pay € 5.4 million in damages to the Netherlands. Russia immediately disregarded the order of the Tribunal, but eventually settled the case with the Netherlands, two years later, on 17.05.2019 for a compensation of € 2.7 million.[35]

These two recent incidents of China and Russia, categorically refusing to follow the orders of the international arbitral tribunals exposes the lack of enforcement provisions in the Convention to execute the orders passed by courts and tribunals established under it. As noted above, the Convention in its Part XV has provided three forums; two tribunals (ITLOS and arbitration tribunals established under Annexure VII and Annexure VIII) and the ICJ, with the power and jurisdiction to adjudicate disputes under the Convention.

The framers of the Convention agreed to have a compulsory dispute settlement mechanism contained in Part XV of the Convention as an integral and important aspect of the Convention. The compulsory dispute settlement mechanism is considered to have established one of the most comprehensive and sophisticated dispute settlement systems to date.[36]

This tenor of 'compulsoriness' in the dispute settlement mechanism was also carried forward in the provisions of the Convention. As per Article 296(1) of the Convention,[37] a decision made by any of the three forums, i.e., ITLOS, ICJ and Arbitral Tribunals (Annexes VII & VIII) is final and must be complied with by the parties to the disputes. Additionally, Article 33(1) of Annexure VI and Article 11 of Annexure VII of the Convention also provide that an order of ITLOS or an award of an arbitral tribunal constituted under Annexure VII is final and that the parties to the dispute must comply with it.[38]

Further, Article 12 of Annexure VII titled 'interpretation or implementation of award' provides that any controversy between the parties to the dispute about the manner of implementation of the award can be submitted to the arbitral tribunal that rendered the award. While the Convention is silent about the implementation of an order of ITLOS or the ICJ, an order of the ICJ can be implemented by recourse to the UNSC which is empowered under Article 94 of the UN Charter to take necessary measures to give effect to the judgment.[39]

However, in today's emerging peculiar situations where the-veto wielding powers like China and Russia consciously disregard an order of an international arbitral tribunal as seen above, even the UNSC would be incapable of enforcing it if the order is against the interests of a veto power or its allies. Hence, for all practical purposes, enforcement of orders passed by international courts and tribunals under part XV of the Convention are left solely to the mercy of the good faith obligations of the parties to the dispute.[40]

Thus it is clear that though the Convention intended that all disputes that arise under it are compulsorily resolved between the parties by recourse to its provisions by incorporating a 'compulsory dispute settlement mechanism', the lack of enforcement provisions in the Convention, make the orders of the international courts and tribunals, except those that are expressly accepted by both the parties, ineffective. Such instances, however few today, threaten the very foundation of an international-rules-based-order, which is the 21st century objective of most maritime nations.

Additionally, the lack of enforcement provisions to the compulsory dispute mechanism enumerated under the Convention fail the decision-making process under the Convention and hence fails the Convention on its third test of jurisdictional legitimacy.

Non-compliance to the Provisions of the Convention

Non-compliance means and includes not adhering to the rules and laws framed under the Convention. International scholars argue that there are about 168 parties to the Convention and that at least one-third of them are in breach of at least one significant provision of the Convention.[41]

Though divergences in the application of international law in case of ambiguity in its interpretation may be acceptable, until its appropriate resolution according to law, casual disregard to the provisions of the Convention, based upon individual nationalistic interests of States would undermine the democratic use of ocean space and may lead to serious consequences. More so, such a huge degree of non-compliance clearly undermines the integrity and legitimacy of the Convention and fails the Convention on its first test of formal legitimacy.

Maritime Territorialisation

In 2006, an international Law Discussion Group found that today, "An acre of sea might be worth more than an acre of barren land, especially if there is oil and gas on the subsoil or on the seabed".[42] In recent times, maritime sovereignty disputes have clearly become highly visible consequences of broader contests. According to Edyta Roszko, the term "maritime territorialisation" refers to the ways in which States treat the sea as "land".[43] According to the Westphalian order, land territory was indivisible from statehood and States have traditionally claimed exclusive sovereignty over a defined land territory.[44] The maritime space however is different. Traditionally, waters beyond 3 nm have been regarded as global commons under the 'cannon-shot' principle developed by a Dutch legal scholar, Hugo Grotius, who argued that waters could not be occupied or seized and therefore could not be exclusively owned as property.[45]

In the 20th century however, the Convention provided the coastal states with exclusive sovereignty over the territorial sea and exclusive sovereign rights and jurisdiction over its EEZ and continental shelf. The layers of 'sovereign authority' of the Coastal State through the maritime zones enumerated in the Convention are designed to balance the needs of the coastal states with that of the international community.[46] This balance has given Coastal States some sovereign rights without the exclusivity that is typically associated with sovereign territory; for example, in the EEZ, where the coastal states enjoy exclusive sovereign rights over all natural resources in the water column and sea bed, other States enjoy freedom of navigation, over flight and also have the power to lay their submarine pipes and cables.[47]

These sovereign entitlements under the Convention together, with the growing strategic importance of the world's oceans, have altered the way the States increasingly perceive the seas as analogous to land territory. This process of maritime spaces being increasingly equated to state sovereignty is termed 'maritime territorialisation'.

The seas matter for materialist reasons as they provide critical trading thoroughfares and they are also rich in living and non-living resources. Traditionally, competition among States for these material factors has caused conflicts in the maritime domain. Recent maritime conflicts, however, have witnessed linkages of national identity, status and prestige of a nation to its maritime sovereignty claims. China's claim to the nine-dash-line as well as the current prolific contests over maritime territory between the littoral States of the South China Sea, East China Sea and other maritime spaces in the world are examples of the escalating disputes relating to maritime territorialisation.

States are increasingly applying varying interpretations of the Convention to suit and support their maritime sovereignty claims. The Convention which is a broad framework of principles concerning the law of the sea lacks specificity and clarity in its principles, thus leading to varying interpretations of its provisions by States to suit their sovereign interests. Overlapping maritime sovereignty claims between neighbouring nations are a cause for most maritime disputes today. As seen in the case of Philippines vs. China above, the dispute settlement mechanism, which is entrusted to resolve disputes arising in relation to the interpretation of the Convention, has proven ineffective, thus failing the Convention. Thus, maritime territorialisation, unaddressed by the Convention, is a new and daunting challenge threatening the global maritime domain today.

Sovereignty Claims over Features, Islands, Rocks and Artificial Islands

In the South China Sea, China officially claims indisputable sovereignty over all four major archipelagic groups in the South China Sea namely, the Spratlys (Nansha Qundao), Paracels (Xisha Qundao), Pratas (Dongsha Qundao), and the Macclesfield Bank and Scarborough Shoal (Zhongsha Qundao).[48] These archipelagic groups comprise groups of islands/islets, rocks and features, most of which China claims as its sovereign land territory. By claiming indisputable sovereignty over islands, rocks and features within the South China Sea, China claims sovereignty over the land territory comprising the island, features or rock as well as and in consequence, by operation of the Convention, sovereign rights and jurisdiction over the maritime zones that the feature, island or rock may be entitled to under the Convention.

The Convention in its Article 121 provides definition and maritime entitlements of islands, rocks, and other features. Article 121 states as follows:

> *"1. An island is a naturally formed area of land, surrounded by water, which is above water at high tide. 2. Except as provided for in paragraph 3, the territorial sea, the contiguous zone, the exclusive economic zone and the continental shelf of an island are determined in accordance with the provisions of this Convention applicable to other land territory. 3. Rocks which cannot sustain human habitation or economic life of their own shall have no exclusive economic zone or continental shelf."*

Additionally, the Convention leaves open the maritime zone entitlements of rocks which can sustain human inhabitation, the status of semi-submerged features, and procedure to determine the status of the features are some issues of practical difficulty. The Convention is also silent about how to determine disputing claims of sovereignty over islands, rocks, features or artificial islands, which in essence comprise sovereignty claims over land territory. Further, the Convention in its preamble provides that for matters that are not regulated by it, principles of general international law would apply. Thus, maritime disputes relating to sovereign claims over islands, reefs, rocks and features are beyond the scope of the Convention thus leaving open conflicting and unresolved sovereignty claims over maritime features, islands and rocks to be determined by principles of general international law. For this reason, too, the Convention has failed to meet the test of time.

Status of Artificial Islands

Another interesting maritime challenge arising out of the South China Sea is the rampant construction of artificial islands over semi-submerged or totally submerged atolls and reefs. Since early 2014, China has been carrying out land reclamation activities on a number of its occupied atolls and reefs on an industrial scale, thereby fundamentally changing both the political and ecological status quo of the area.[49]

An American report suggests that,

> *"the total extent of land reclaimed by China reached 12.8 square kilometres by January 2016. Fiery Cross Reef (Yongshu Jiao), occupied by the PRC since 1988, is now considered to be the largest new landmass in the Spratlys, with an additional expansion of 2.74 square kilometres. It has a port facility large enough to receive tankers and warships as well as a new 3,000-metre airstrip that is within strike fighter range of the Philippines, Vietnam and Malaysia."*[50] *(emphasis applied)*

According to BBC correspondents, the Spratly Islands in the South China Sea could potentially be a major geopolitical flashpoint as China has used land reclamation to expand disputed islands, and has built runways on them.[51] With the only exception of Fiery Cross Reef, the majority of Chinese-occupied features were totally submerged prior to the large-scale island construction campaign being undertaken by China.[52]

China is not the only nation conducting land reclamation activities and constructing military installations on tiny atolls and reefs in the Spratly sub-archipelago but, as per the report of the Centre for Strategic and International Studies (CSIS) in Washington, "Vietnam has been building up its military facilities on Sand Cay and Western London reef, the Philippines has upgraded its naval port facilities on Spratly Island, and Taiwan has extended its airstrip on Itu Aba to 1,195 metres."[53] The fundamental difference, however, lies in the scale and speed of China's build-up of occupied maritime features.

The Convention, thus, does not comprehensively define the meaning and scope of maritime entitlements of maritime features, rocks, islands and artificial islands found at sea. Although artificial islands do not acquire maritime entitlements under the Convention, the determination of whether an island is artificial or natural is an area on which the Convention remains silent. This silence of UNCLOS and its lack of clarity over such important aspects are leading to competing claims between States resulting in smart nations taking advantage.

Oil and Gas Exploration in Disputed Boundaries

The rising energy demand is also playing an important role in the escalation of maritime disputes between nations. China and Vietnam, both littorals of the South China Sea, have since the last two decades, exploited their oil exploration licences to defend their maritime claims.[54] Competition over the allocation of oil and gas exploration contracts between the two States is now on the rise with an increase in the number of stakeholders. For example, in 2012, a few months after Petro Vietnam signed joint exploration contracts with Exxon Mobil, Gazprom and India's Oil and Natural Gas Corporation (ONGC), China National Offshore Oil Corporation (CNOOC) issued new concessions to international bidders in overlapping Vietnamese blocks.[55] Though China began offshore oil exploration in the South China Sea way back in 1970, Chinese oil companies refrained from operating in disputed areas until recently.[56] This was probably due to the significant geological and technological constraints that require enhanced expenditures. This historical restraint by China to operate oil rigs in disputed waters changed by the action of CNOOC in 2014 to move the mobile oil rig, *'Haiyang Shiyou 981'*, into waters just 17 nautical miles away from the Paracel Islands and 120 miles from the coast of Vietnam for the purposes of exploration and drilling.[57] Additionally, the action of China to move the oil rig led to massive anti-Chinese riots in Vietnam which escalated to the evacuation of Chinese nationals and the destruction of hundreds of foreign-owned businesses in Vietnam.[58]

The Convention provides Coastal States sovereign rights to explore and exploit living and non-living resources within its EEZ. Further, the Convention and the international courts and tribunals established under the Convention have laid out the law applicable to delimitation of maritime boundaries between competing adjacent or opposite States. However, as seen in the dispute between China and Vietnam, unresolved overlapping maritime sovereignty claims between them are causing new challenges. In such situations, the Convention is silent about the remedies available to a coastal state to exclusively exploit resources in its disputed EEZ. Thus, this new challenge of oil and gas exploration in contested territory remains unaddressed by the Convention.

Fishing Rights in Disputed Waters

The Convention provides Coastal States rights and jurisdiction to exclusively exploit the living resources including fisheries within its EEZ. However, in situations of overlapping EEZs between two or more coastal States, the exclusivity of the Coastal States' exercise of its sovereign rights of fishing in its EEZ is severely threatened.

The competition over dwindling fish stocks is also on the rise. Fish stocks are shrinking in size owing to serious coastal pollution, unsustainable fishing practices, and the destruction of marine ecosystems, leading to the heavy exploitation of various species of fish like tuna, mackerel, shrimp and shellfish.[59] Additionally, as a consequence of technological advancements and over exploitation, fishing fleets are venturing into deeper waters more frequently, thus leading to escalating disputes between fishing fleets of neighbouring coastal states over exclusivity of their respective fishing rights in the disputed/ overlapping maritime territory. Recent incidents however, have exposed state support and assistance to fishing activities undertaken in disputed waters.

One such example is the Chinese Coast Guard supported fishing incursions into Indonesian waters off the Natuna Islands in the South China Sea.[60] Indonesia claims that the Chinese fishing vessel *'Kway Fey 10078'* which intruded into Indonesia's EEZ carried out illegal fishing in its waters. Indonesia's Minister of Maritime and Fisheries Affairs also claimed that the Chinese Coast Guard vessel escorting the fishing vessel *Kway Fey 10078* interfered with Indonesian authorities in their lawful exercise of Indonesia's sovereign fishing rights within its EEZ. The sequence of events as narrated by the Minister is as extracted below:

> *"The vessel continued to try to escape in a zigzag way so the surveillance vessel, the Him 11 vessel approached and could not avoid crash with the Chinese vessel, Susi said, adding that at least three personnel of Him 11 vessel jumped on the Chinese vessel and managed to arrest its crew.*
>
> *However, the Indonesian Navy vessels failed to bring the vessel as evidence because the Chinese coast guard vessel that has a bigger size and is equipped with weapons tried to hinder the Indonesian Navy. The Indonesian Navy, which lacks weaponry, finally released the illegal fishing boat, which was taken by the Chinese coast guard vessel outside the Indonesian waters. We lost evidence. I saw that the Chinese coast guard vessel did not want the vessel to be sunk and we regret that."*[61] *(emphasis applied)*

Indonesia announced a diplomatic protest with China over the alleged illegal fishing by Chinese boats escorted by the Chinese Coast Guard within its EEZ and sent its protest note to China.[62] Though China does not claim the Natuna Islands, which are considered to be a part of Indonesian territory, China's nine-dash-line claim includes the waters just north of the Natunas, which Indonesia insists falls within its EEZ. More importantly, these waters contain the world's largest offshore gas fields with an estimated 1.27 trillion cubic metres of recoverable gas.[63] Reports suggest that recently too, in 2019, Chinese fishing vessels escorted by Chinese coast guard vessels confronted the Indonesian authorities around the Natuna Islands, which led to diplomatic protests by Indonesia.[64]

Therefore, though Indonesia, under the Convention, has legitimate and exclusive rights to exploit fishing resources within its EEZ, it is unable to stop incursions by Chinese fishing vessels as China too claims exclusive sovereign rights over these waters.[65] The Convention on the other hand, does not provide remedial measures in such instances and hence fails to redress emerging maritime challenges.

Freedom of Navigation in EEZ

Today's competition amongst Coastal States to acquire maritime territory and its consequential sovereign entitlements over maritime space is threatening the historic principle of the law of the sea: freedom of navigation. The principle of freedom of navigation is derived from a

400-year international norm called *'res communis'* which means the 'common right' of all nations to use the seas, for the purposes of navigation and trade.[66]

The Convention, through Article 56(1), entitles Coastal States to exercise their sovereign rights for the exploration and exploitation of natural resources, both living and non-living, within the waters comprising its EEZ. The Convention, in Article 56(2), provides a Coastal State jurisdiction to establish and use artificial islands, installations and structures in its EEZ; carry out marine scientific research and protect and preserve the marine environment. Further, Article 58 of the Convention provides all States certain freedoms within the EEZ of a coastal state which includes freedom of navigation and over flight, freedom to lay submarine cables and pipelines, etc. Thus, the Convention has strived to balance the sovereign entitlements of the Coastal States with the freedom of navigation of the international community within the EEZ of a coastal State. Yet, discrepancies loom large.

Today, the South China Sea disputes are increasingly threatening the freedom of navigation through its waters. The South China Sea is critical for international shipping with over 40,000 ships passing through it every year, constituting about 40 per cent of the global sea trade.[67] One of the straits of the South China Sea, the Strait of Malacca, offers the shortest navigational route between Europe and Asia Pacific, and is also the transit passage for super-tankers transporting oil from Africa and the Middle East to the resource-dependent East Asian nations.[68]

A littoral of the South China Sea, China, today claims exclusive sovereign rights and jurisdiction over major parts of the South China Sea. While it has not yet used the nine-dash-line as an inviolable border to its sovereignty, it has officially not explained the meaning of the line, raising suspicion over its intentions.[69] This has led to a fear among the world's maritime nations, including the USA, that,

> *"Beijing's behaviour in the South China Sea raises serious concerns that it may be intending to control the South China Sea by force, possibly establishing military bases to advance power projection capabilities."*[70]

The South China Sea has consequently been witnessing increased naval activities and freedom of navigation exercises by many countries, including and not limited to the USA, Japan and Australia, since the turn of this century.[71] Freedom of Navigation Operations/Exercises (FONOPs) are a method of enforcing the Convention by reinforcing freedom of navigation through practice by using ships to sail through all areas of the sea permitted under the Convention, especially those areas that Coastal States have attempted to close off to free navigation.[72] China, however, has declared these freedom of navigation operations as provocative.[73]

It must be recollected that the drafting of the Convention was driven in part over concern by the States that strong national maritime interests of Coastal States could lead to excessive maritime claims over coastal seas, which would in turn threaten the freedom of navigation.[74] Thus, the Convention has failed to achieve its primary objective of ensuring freedom of navigation, a fundamental principle of the law of the sea.

Exclusion of the USA, an Important International Maritime Actor

The geo-strategic rivalry in the South China Sea between the two superpowers of the 21st century—the USA and China—one existing and another aspiring, is increasing. Further, recent clashes between the two states: *"The EP-3 incident in April 2001, involving a collision between a US Navy plane and a PLA F-8 jet fighter, the clash between the US naval ship Impeccable and Chinese vessels just 75 nautical miles south-east of Hainan Island in March 2009, and the confrontation between a US Navy P-8 Poseidon plane and a PLA Su-27 fighter in August 2014, all reveal a pattern of low-level conflict that throws light on the growing suspicions between the two states."*[75]

The Convention has received near universal acceptance with 168 of the world's 193 nations as its members. Fourteen UN member-States have signed the Convention but have failed to ratify it including the USA, Afghanistan, North Korea, UAE and a few others.[76] Though the USA participated in all the discussions that led to the Convention and significantly contributed to its shaping, it has not yet ratified it, allegedly due to its reservations with the provisions of Part XI of the Convention.[77]

The ratification of the Convention by the USA is important not just because it is a super power with the world's largest navy but, during this period of escalating geo-strategic rivalry between it and China, the USA, has certainly weakened its position by not being a member of the Convention. In this peculiar situation, where a member of the Convention violates a provision of the Convention, it is necessary to rely on principles of general international law and customary maritime law to question China's unlawful actions. Further, the USA will be unable to utilise the services of the law of the sea specialised institutions set up under the Convention. It would, therefore, have to resort to global international institutions like the ICJ, which lack the expertise. Thus, the USA would lack the support of both the substantive international laws and the expertise of the judicial institutions. Further, the exclusion of the USA, an important international maritime actor, from the membership of the Convention, by itself challenges the USA's commitment to an international maritime-rules-based order.

Some American scholars argue that most of the principles contained in the Convention form part of principles of customary international law. Thus, the USA had nothing to lose by not ratifying the Convention. This argument is maybe more valid now than it ever was in view of the Convention itself losing relevance in many situations as seen above.

Further, the Convention, no doubt a highly specialised legislation concerning the law of the sea, is only a general compilation of broad principles concerning many aspects of the law of the sea and hence does not comprehensively deal with all the aspects it enumerates. The Convention, as seen in many instances above, leaves a lot of scope for varying interpretations by State parties thus making its non-compliance more attractive to them. Further, the principles contained in the Convention also form part of customary international law. Hence, the Convention does not provide any special justification to compel the States to follow it. The Convention has thus failed the test of jurisdictional legitimacy, when the USA failed to ratify the Convention on the ground that it was not different from customary international law.

China's Maritime Ambitions and Actions

As seen above in various instances, China's aggressive maritime ambitions and actions have not just violated the Convention on multiple occasions, but pose a grave threat to the global maritime domain. The recent press statement[78] of Michael R. Pompeo, Secretary of the State of the USA on 13.07.2020, is of particular relevance to understand the threat posed to the global maritime domain by China's maritime ambitions and actions. While explaining the USA's position on the South China Sea, Pompeo, reaffirming America's commitment for a free and open Indo-Pacific and the South China Sea, categorically criticised Beijing as follows:

> *"[...] We are making clear: Beijing's claims to offshore resources across most of the South China Sea are completely unlawful, as is its campaign of bullying to control them."*

Referring to the commitment of the world's nations to an international rules-based order and their commitment to the shared interests in the South China Sea, namely, preserving peace and stability, upholding freedom of the seas in a manner consistent with international law and maintaining the unimpeded flow of commerce, the statement read:

> *"These shared interests have come under unprecedented threat from the People's Republic of China (PRC).*
>
> *Beijing uses intimidation to undermine the sovereign rights of Southeast Asian coastal States in the South China Sea, bully them out of offshore resources, assert unilateral dominion, and replace international law with "might makes right." Beijing's approach has been clear for years. In 2010, then-PRC Foreign Minister Yang Jiechi told his ASEAN counterparts "China is a big country and other countries are small countries and that is just a fact." The PRC's predatory worldview has no place in the 21st century. [...]*
>
> *The world will not allow Beijing to treat the South China Sea as its maritime empire. America stands with our Southeast Asian allies and partners in protecting their sovereign rights to offshore resources, consistent with their rights and obligations under international law. We stand with the international community in defence of freedom of the seas and respect for sovereignty and reject any push to impose "might makes right" in the South China Sea or the wider region".*[79] *(emphasis applied)*

Beijing thus threatens the authority of the Convention; the authority of international law/international-rules-based-order; the littoral States of the South China Sea their maritime territory and their lawful maritime rights and entitlements in the South China Sea; the global commons by impending the free flow of navigation and trade through the South China Sea. China's aggression in the South China Sea and international affairs leads to the understanding that it is unlikely to retard as its technological prowess grows.[80] To conclude, China's current positioning in the maritime domain reveals its growing resolve to enforce its maritime claims while maintaining an advantageous position in the resource competition. International scholars have held that though China is not alone in its nationalistic stance, what distinguishes China's position from those of other claimant States is the scale, speed and intensity of its rights enforcement campaign."[81]

It is important to be reminded that the central political impetus behind the drafting of the Convention was to safeguard the oceans and seas by ensuring equity between richer nations and the developing states. China is today seeking to replace established international law, i.e., the Convention with its 'might makes right' principle, which throws light on the magnitude and scale of the maritime challenges staring at us today.

Conclusion

The oceans and seas have historically been governed by customary state practices, which eventually came to be termed as customary international law. Lack of internationally standard norms, differing customary state practices and its resulting disturbances, necessitated the need for a common international legal order for the seas. After a failed attempt by the League of Nations, the UN's member-states successfully codified the law of the seas into a Convention that evolved over the years to its current version, UNCLOS III.

The Convention has, indisputably, been a successful legislation for standardising and codifying many customary state practices and also introducing new regimes to address the 20th century maritime challenges like the EEZ, 'The Area', and the compulsory dispute settlement mechanism, to name a few. The international courts and tribunals established under the Convention have been struggling to keep pace with the changing dynamics in the maritime domain in the 21st century.

ITLOS and the arbitral tribunals established under the Convention have made significant and noteworthy contributions to the clarification and development of the law of the sea. However, a closer examination of the current global maritime challenges reveals that the Convention is unable to effectively address many of them. The old and outdated Convention has left many maritime disputes unresolved due its silence over those aspects or because of the insufficiency of its provisions.

The Convention has failed the test of legitimacy in all the four principles of the Constitutional model of legitimacy of international law. The Convention has failed the test of formal legitimacy due to its large-scale non-compliance by States and it has failed the test of procedural legitimacy due to an ineffective dispute resolution mechanism caused by the lack of enforcement provisions. Further, the principles contained in the Convention also form the principles of customary international law and thus the Convention does not incentivize its ratification by States. Additionally, the failure of the United States of America to ratify the Convention is an example of the Convention failing the test of jurisdictional legitimacy. The Convention also fails the test of outcome legitimacy due to its broad principles that leave scope for differing State interpretations that consequently undermine its authority. Therefore, an analysis of the contemporary global maritime challenges reveals that the Convention suffers from a legitimacy crisis and its role, as the 'Constitution for the Oceans', has little relevance in modern times.

Furthermore, an examination of the global maritime challenges, more specifically, the China vs. Philippines arbitration case and the Netherlands vs. Russia case leads us to question the legitimacy and relevance of the United Nations and its allied institutions. In the case of the Philippines vs. China, the enforcement wing of the UN, the United Nations Security Council, loses both legitimacy and relevance as it would fail to uphold the international rule of law by enforcing the decision of the arbitral tribunal against a veto-wielding China. Therefore, on a larger perspective the global maritime challenges today threaten the legitimacy and relevance of the UNSC and consequently the UN itself. Therefore, to conclude, and at the core, the future of an effective international-maritime-rule-based order begins with recognising the changes in the global balance of power since 1982. The ascendancy of the Asia Pacific and the growing economic might of its littorals along with the economic fall of the traditional European powers has led to a change in the balance of power, requiring a formal structural change in the existing international legal framework.

NOTES

1. Alfred T. Mahan, "The Influence of Sea Power Upon History", available at https://www.digitalhistory.uh.edu/disp_textbook.cfm?smtID=3&psid=4044 (Accessed on 29 July 2020).
2. Shunji Yanai, "Can the UNCLOS Address Challenges of the 21st Century," 57 *German Y.B.Int'l L.* 43 (2014), p. 43.
3. Dean Cheng, "The Importance of Maritime Domain Awareness for the Indo–Pacific Quad Countries," The Heritage Foundation global politics report, available at https://www.heritage.org/global-politics/report/the-importance-maritime-domain-awareness-the-indo-pacific-quad-countries. (Accessed on 29 July 2020).
4. Ibid.
5. UNCTAD "Review of Maritime Transport 2019," UNCTAD/RMT/2019, available at https://unctad.org/en/PublicationsLibrary/rmt2019_en.pdf. (Accessed on 29 July 2020).
6. Lutz Feldt, "The Importance of the Global Maritime Domain for World Politics and Security," *ISPSW Strategy Series: Focus on Defence and International Security*, Issue No. 382 (2015), available at https://www.files.ethz.ch/isn/194184/382_Feldt.pdf. (Accessed on July 29, 2020).
7. Available at https://chinapower.csis.org/much-trade-transits-south-china-sea/ (Accessed on 29 July 2020).
8. Srijan Shukla, "What is nine-dash line? The basis of China's claim to sovereignty over South China Sea," *The Print*, 29 July 2020, available at https://theprint.in/theprint-essential/what-is-nine-dash-line-the-basis-of-chinas-claim-to-sovereignty-over-south-china-sea/469403/ (Accessed on 29 July 2020).
9. K. Morton, "China's ambition in the South China Sea: Is a legitimate maritime order possible?," *International Affairs*, Vol 92, No. 4, (2016), pp. 909-940.
10. Md. Monjur Hasan et al. "Protracted maritime boundary disputes and maritime laws," *Journal of International Maritime Safety, Environmental Affairs, and Shipping*, Vol. 2, No. 2 (2019), pp. 89-96, available at https://doi.org/10.1080/25725084.2018.1564184 (Accessed on 29 July 2020).
11. Ibid.
12. The First United Nations Conference on the Law of the Sea resulted in the signing of the following four conventions at Geneva on 29 April 1958: Convention on the Territorial Sea and the Contiguous Zone, UNTS 516,205; Convention on the Continental Shelf, UNTS 499,311; Convention on the High Seas, UNTS 450, 11; Convention on Fishing and Conservation of the Living Resources of the High Seas, UNTS 559, 285.
13. L. Brilmayer and N. Klein, "Land and Sea: Two Sovereignty Regimes in Search of a Common Denominator," *NYU Journal of International Law and Politics*, Vol. 22 (2001), pp. 703-707.
14. The United Nations Convention on the Law of the Sea (hereafter, 'the Convention'),

the Preamble, available at http://www.un.org/Depts/los/convention_agreements/texts/unclos/unclos_e.pdf. (Accessed on 29 July 2020).

15. Christopher C. Joyner and Elizabeth A. Martell, "Looking Back to See Ahead: UNCLOS III and Lessons for Global Commons Law," 27 *Ocean Dev. & Int'l L.* 73 (1996).
16. The Convention. op cit, Article 76(8).
17. The Convention. op cit, the Preamble.
18. Division for Ocean Affairs and the Law of the Sea, "Declarations and statements under articles 287, 298 and 310 of the Convention," available at https://www.un.org/Depts/los/ convention_agreements/convention_declarations.htm. (Accessed on 29 July 2020).
19. Hasan, Md. Monjur, op cit, p. 91.
20. The International Tribunal for the Law of the Sea (ITLOS), *List of Cases*, available at https://www.itlos.org/cases/list-of-cases/. (Accessed on 29 July 2020).
21. International Tribunal for the Law of the Sea (ITLOS), Seabed Disputes chamber renders unanimous advisory opinion on responsibilities and obligations of States sponsoring persons and entities with respect to activities in the 'Area', *ITLOS/Press 161*, 01 February 2011, available at https://www.itlos.org/fileadmin/itlos/documents/press_releases_english/PR_161_E.pdf. (Accessed on 29 July 2020).
22. "Responsibilities and obligations of States with respect to activities in the Area, Advisory Opinion", *ITLOS Reports 2011*, 01 February 2011, p. 10, available at https://www.itlos.org/fileadmin/itlos/documents/cases/case_no_17/17_adv_op_010211_en.pdf. (Accessed on 29 July 2020).
23. Ibid.
24. International Tribunal for the Law of the Sea (ITLOS). Proceedings instituted in the dispute concerning the maritime boundary between Bangladesh and Myanmar in the Bay of Bengal. *ITLOS/Press 140*, 16 December 2009, available at https://www.itlos.org/fileadmin/itlos/documents/press_releases_english/PR.140-E.pdf. (Accessed on 29 July 2020).
25. International Tribunal for the Law of the Sea (ITLOS), Dispute Concerning Delimitation of the Maritime Boundary Between Bangladesh and Myanmar in the Bay of Bengal (Bangladesh/Myanmar), Judgment of 14 March 2012, ITLOS Reports 4, 2012, available at https://www.itlos.org/fileadmin/itlos/documents/cases/case_no_16/published/C16-J-14_mar_12.pdf. (Accessed on 29 July 2020).
26. Ibid.
27. Award on PCA Case No. 2013-19 in the matter of the South China Sea arbitration - before - an Arbitral Tribunal constituted under Annex VII to the 1982 UNCLOS between the Republic of the Philippines and the People's Republic of China, 12 July 2016, available at https://pca-cpa.org/wp-content/uploads/sites/175/2016/07/PH-CN-20160712-Award.pdf. (Accessed on 29 July 2020).
28. Ibid.
29. Ibid.
30. Permanent Court of Arbitration (PCA). Timor Sea Conciliation (Timor-Leste vs. Australia), available at https://pca-cpa.org/en/cases/132/. (Accessed on 29 July 2020).
31. The Convention. op cit, Article 15.
32. K. Morton. op cit, p. 910.
33. M. Kumm, "The Legitimacy of International Law: A Constitutionalist Framework of Analysis", *European Journal of International Law* 15, No. 5 (2004), pp. 907-31.

34. Permanent Court of Arbitration (PCA). Arctic Sunrise Arbitration (Netherlands vs. Russia), 18 July 2017, available at https://pca-cpa.org/en/news/arctic-sunrise-arbitration-netherlands-v-russia-3/. (Accessed on 29 July 29, 2020).
35. "Russia to pay 2.7 mln in Greenpeace ship settlement". *France24*, 17 May 2019, available at https://www.france24.com/en/20190517-russia-pay-27-mln-greenpeace-ship-settlement. (Accessed on 29 July 2020).
36. John E. Noyes, "Compulsory Third-Party Adjudication and the 1982 United Nations Convention on the Law of the Sea," *4 Connecticut Journal of International Law* 675 (1989) p. 675; A.O. ADEDE, "Settlement of Disputes Arising Under the Law of the Sea Convention," *69 American Journal of International Law* 798 (1975), p. 816.
37. The Convention. op cit, Article 296 (1): *"Any decision rendered by a court or tribunal having jurisdiction under this section shall be final and shall be complied with by all the parties to the dispute."*
38. The Convention. op cit, Article 33 (1) of Annexure VI: *"The decision of the Tribunal is final and shall be complied with by all the parties to the dispute." r.w.* Article 11 of Annexure VII: *"Finality of award: The award shall be final and without appeal, unless the parties to the dispute have agreed in advance to an appellate procedure. It shall be complied with by the parties to the dispute."*
39. Charter of the United Nations and Statute of the International Court of Justice, San Francisco, 1945, Article 94, available at https://treaties.un.org/doc/publication/ctc/uncharter.pdf (Accessed on 29 July 2020).
40. Hamsa Devineni and Gurpreet S. Khurana, "China and the South China Sea Arbitration: Analyses in the Indo-Pacific Context," *National Maritime Foundation*, 28 December 2018, available at https://maritimeindia.org/china-and-the-south-china-sea-arbitration-analysis-in-the-indo-pacific-context/. (Accessed on 29 July 2020).
41. Robin Churchill, "The Persisting Problem of Non-compliance with the Law of the Sea Convention: Disorder in the Oceans", *The International Journal of Marine and Coastal Law* 27 (2012), pp. 813-820. 10.1163/15718085-12341254.
42. Chatham House, "Methods of resolving maritime boundary disputes," *Meeting summary of International Law Discussion Group*, 14 February 2016, available at http://studylib.net/doc/7497535/methods-of-resolving-maritime-boundary- disputes. (Accessed on 29 July 2020).
43. Strating Rebecca. "Maritime Territorialization, UNCLOS and the Timor Sea Dispute." *Contemporary Southeast Asia*, Vol. 40, No. 1 (2018), pp. 101-125.
44. Ibid.
45. Lea Brilmayer and Natalie Klein, "Land and Sea: Two Sovereignty Regimes in Search of a Common Denominator", *NYU Journal of International Law and Politics*, Vol. 22 (2001), pp. 703–707.
46. Chelsea Purvis, Comment on "Coastal State Jurisdiction Under UNCLOS: The Shen Neng 1 Grounding on the Great Barrier Reef" https://digitalcommons.law.yale.edu/cgi/viewcontent.cgi?article=1398&context=yjil. (Accessed on 29 July 2020).
47. Strating, Rebecca, "Maritime Disputes, Sovereignty and the Rules Based Order in East Asia," *Australian Journal of Politics & History*, Vol. 65, No. 3 (2019) pp. 449-465.
48. Zou Keyuan, *"Law of the sea in East Asia: issues and prospects,"* (London: Routledge, 2005).
49. Shannon Tiezzi, 'The environmental costs of China's South Sea construction', *The Diplomat*, 18 September 2015.
50. CSIS Asia Maritime Transparency Initiative, available at http://amti.csis.org.

(Accessed on 29 July 2020); Derek Watkins, 'What China has been building', *New York Times*, 27 October 2015; James Hardy and Sean O'Connor, "China completes runway on Fiery Cross Reef," *HIS Jane's Defence Weekly*, 15 September 2015.

51. "Australia conducting 'freedom of navigation' flights in South China Sea," *BBC News*, 15 December 2015, available at https://www.bbc.com/news/world-australia-35099445. (Accessed on 29 July 2020).
52. K. Morton, op cit, pp. 909-940.
53. "CSIS Asia Maritime Transparency Initiative," *Island Tracker*, available at http://amti.csis.org/island-tracker/. (Accessed on 29 July 2020).
54. K. Morton, op cit, p. 923.
55. Rakesh Sharma, "ONGC to continue exploration in the South China Sea," *Wall Street Journal*, 19 July 2012.
56. Charlie Zhu, "China optimistic of finding gas off Vietnam, could test ties further," Thomson Reuters, Eikon, 29 May 2014.
57. Ibid.
58. Agence France-Presse, Beijing, "Chinese flee Vietnam as Hanoi counts cost of riots," *Guardian*, 19 May 2014, available at www.theguardian.com/world/2014/may/19/chinese-flee-vietnam-hanoi-riots. (Accessed on 29 July 2020).
59. United Nations Food and Agriculture Organization, *"State of the world fisheries and aquaculture report 2014: opportunities and challenges"* (Rome, 2014).
60. Francis Chan and Wahyudi Soeriaatradja, "Indonesia to charge Chinese fishing crew with poaching," *Straits Times*, 23 March 2016.
61. "Indonesian Sends a Note of Protest against China in South China Sea Fishing Dispute," Cabinet Secretariat of the Republic of Indonesia, available at https://setkab.go.id/en/indonesian-sends-a-note-of-protest-against-china-in-south-china-sea-fishing-dispute/ (Accessed on 29 July 2020).
62. Ibid.
63. "Indonesia Air Force Exercises Conducted around Resource rich, and contested, Natuna Islands," *RWR Advisory Group Report*, 07 October 2016, available at https://www. rwradvisory.com/indonesia-air-force-exercises-conducted-around-resource-rich-and-contested-natuna-islands/. (Accessed on 29 July 2020).
64. Derek Grossman, "Why Is China Pressing Indonesia Again Over Its Maritime Claims?" *World Politics Review*, 16 January 2020, available at https://www.worldpolitics review.com/insights/28476/why-is-china-pressing-indonesia-again-over-the-natuna-islands. (Accessed on 29 July 2020).
65. K. Morton, op cit, p. 922.
66. https://en.wikipedia.org/wiki/Freedom_of_navigation. (Accessed on 29 July 2020).
67. United Nations Conference on Trade and Development (UNCTAD), Review of maritime transport, Geneva, 2015, available at http://unctad.org/en/pages/Publication Webflyer.aspx?publicationid=1374. (Accessed on 29 July 2020).
68. K. Morton, op cit, p. 915.
69. https://en.wikipedia.org/wiki/Nine-dash_line. (Accessed on 29 July 2020).
70. John Chen and Bonnie Glaser, "What China's militarization of the South China Sea would actually look like," *The Diplomat*, 05 November 2015.
71. https://en.wikipedia.org/wiki/Freedom_of_navigation. (Accessed on 29 July 2020).
72. Aceves William Joseph, "The Freedom of Navigation Program: A Study on the Relationship between Law and Strategy," (Masters Dissertation, *University of Southern California*, 1990), available at https://search.proquest.com/docview/1643255666.

(Accessed on 29 July 2020).

73. Keyuan Zou, "Navigation in the South China Sea: Why Still an Issue?," *The International Journal of Marine and Coastal Law,* Vol. 32, No. 2 (2017), pp. 243-267.
74. Kraska James, and Raul A. Pedrozo, "*International Maritime Security Law*" (Leiden: Martinus Nijhoff Publishers, 2013).
75. The EP-3 incident in April 2001 involved a collision, 70 nautical miles from Hainan Island, between a US navy EP-3 reconnaissance plane and a PLA naval F-8 jet fighter that crashed into the sea. Following an emergency landing on Hainan Island, the Chinese authorities detained the US crew for eleven days on the accusation that they had entered Chinese airspace without permission. See Shirley A. Kan, ed., "China–US aircraft collision incident of April 2001: assessments and policy implications," *CRS report for Congress,* 10 October 2001, available at www.fas.org/sgp/crs/row/RL30946.pdf. The USNS *Impeccable* incident in March 2009 also took place in waters close to Hainan Island. Five PRC vessels forced an unarmed US Navy vessel to take emergency action in order to avoid a collision. The ship returned the next day under the escort of a guided-missile destroyer. Captain Raul Pedrozo JAGC, "US Navy close encounters at sea: the USNS *Impeccable* incident," *Naval War College Review,* Vol. 62, No. 3 (Summer 2009), pp. 101–111.
76. https://en.wikipedia.org/wiki/List_of_parties_to_the_United_Nations_Convention_on_the_Law_of_the_Sea. (Accessed on 29 July 2020).
77. Baker Spring and Brett Schaefer, "Report on The United Nations Convention on the Law of the Sea: The Risks Outweigh the Benefits," *The Heritage Foundation,* 16 May 2007, available at https://www.heritage.org/report/the-united-nations-convention-the-law-the-sea-the-risksoutweigh-the-benefits. (Accessed on 29 July 2020).
78. Press Statement by Michael R. Pompeo, "U.S. Position on Maritime Claims in the South China Sea," US Department of State, available at https://www.state.gov/u-s-position-on-maritime-claims-in-the-south-china-sea/. (Accessed on 29 July 2020).
79. Ibid.
80. K. Morton, op cit, p. 924.
81. Ibid., p. 925.

Rule of Law and UNCLOS: Harmonious Settlement of Bay of Bengal Maritime Dispute

11

Role of UNCLOS in Facilitating Peaceful Settlements of Disputes—India–Bangladesh: A Case of Harmonious Maritime Dispute Resolution

Tariq Karim

The Bangladesh Perspective

Bangladesh had been seized with the existential importance of the Bay of Bengal to itself practically from the very early days of its emergence as an independent sovereign nation state, but particularly since 1973 onwards. While conventional wisdom in those days thought largely in terms of fisheries, tourism and connectivity potentials, the report by external geological experts consulted by Bangladesh also triggered expectations about vast mineral and hydrocarbon resources that could be extractable, and which would exponentially augment the nation's wealth.

The nine-month long war of liberation had turned Bangladesh into a wasteland, with its entire infrastructure in complete shambles, an empty treasury, and practically no resources left save its teeming millions. Therefore, the prospect of striking oil and gas was fantasized by many, particularly by leaders and policy makers desperately seeking resources to augment national income and rebuilding the country from scratch.

The existence of oil and gas fields in the neighbouring northeast of India convinced many that if Bangladesh's geological formation was a natural extension of the former, and there were indications of gas deposits either identified or under exploitation, then investing in more exploration must be undertaken. However, a consensus emerged that it was more likely to be found offshore than onshore.

The existence of areas of contestation in the Bay of Bengal between Bangladesh, India and Myanmar were known to pre-exist since Bangladesh's birth, and the country's founding father, Bangabandhu Sheikh Mujibur Rahman, was intensely aware of the importance of arriving speedily at agreed arrangements with Bangladesh's neighbours. When senior officials of the Foreign Ministry pointed out to him some of the arguments that could be used to present a possible legal case, he brushed them aside impatiently and asserted that given the *bonhomie* that existed between Bangladesh and India and between him personally and India's Prime Minister, Mrs. Indira Gandhi, arriving at a cordial mutually acceptable solution benefiting both would not be a problem.

The commissioning of the Farakka Barrage coinciding with Bangladesh's birth and the concerns in Bangladesh of the possible adverse impact on agricultural production because of a reduced flow of water in the Ganga had already triggered increasing anxiety in the minds of Bangladeshis. Even in those early days of *bonhomie*, inevitably an undercurrent of resentment against India had already started surfacing. India's claims on New Moore Island (South Talpatty to Bangladesh) after the emergence of that island, essentially a massive shoal mass in 1970, following the devastating Bhola cyclone, had also aroused and stoked fears in Bangladesh on this issue.

The conviction that great wealth lay on the Bay of Bengal's floor waiting to be tapped fanned hopes and anticipation of finding oil and gas. It was further fuelled by geological reports that served to accentuate the conviction that the solution to the new nation's acute economic and financial crisis lay in the finding of oil and gas in the Bay of Bengal. Consequently, Bangladesh also engaged with enthusiasm and great seriousness as an eager and proactive participant in all the meetings and protracted deliberations of the United Nations Convention on the Law of the Seas (UNCLOS). Its active participation was primarily geared towards building a strong case for access to maritime resources. Indian maritime claims must be understood in this context. Even though they remained muted in the early years, they served to gradually fuel the expanding resentment among Bangladeshis from a perceived sense of denial by a 'larger and more powerful neighbour'.

The early years of Bangladesh were therefore marked by great expectations as well as great accompanying angst centring on how to delimit the maritime boundary from the baggage of the Radcliffe Award that had partitioned Bengal. There were passionate internal debates on how to draw the base line from which to commence delineation, given the complex and unevenly broken configuration of the deltaic coastline.

Initial Bangladeshi Arguments: The SONG and the South Talpatty "island"

One element that was mentioned and considered seriously as a possible argument in favour of Bangladesh early on was 'Swatch of No Ground' (SONG). The SONG or the Ganga Trough, situated on the southern side of the Ganga-Brahmaputra Delta is a marine valley or canyon, which is shaped like a trough that crosses the Continental Shelf of the Bay diagonally. The mouth of the Indus River is also home to delta-front troughs known as the Indus Trough with similar formations off the west side of the Mississippi Delta called the Mississippi Trough. The SONG has a comparatively flat floor 5 to 7 km wide. Sediments are tunnelled through sandbars and ridges present near the mouth of the Ganga-Brahmaputra Delta, which point towards the SONG and feed the deeper part of the Bay of Bengal with sediments.

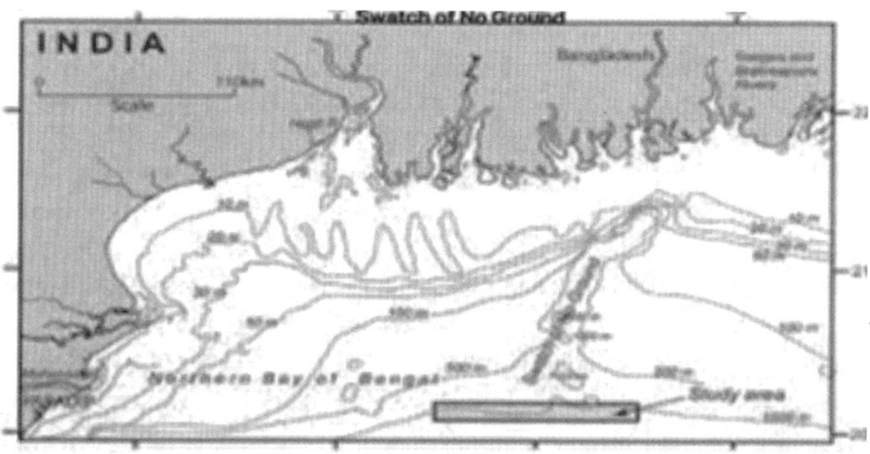

It is a treasure trove of marine life—globally famous for its cetaceans (whales, dolphins and porpoises) population.

The Bangladesh side considered whether they could use this geo-morphological argument on which to rest her case reasoning that progressive accumulation of sediment siltation would accrue in land extension of Bangladesh's coastal territory, giving the densely packed land more precious space for a rapidly growing population whose growth in those days was well over three per cent.

Then there was the matter of the South Talpatty/New Moore "island". This was essentially a large shoal formation or offshore sandbar landform in the Bay of Bengal, off the coast of the Ganges-Brahmaputra Delta region. It emerged in the Bay of Bengal in the aftermath of the Bhola cyclone in 1970.[1] India and Bangladesh immediately laid claim to this island, which became a critically important central focus for basing their respective claims.

This shoal formation was about 3.5 kilometres (2 miles) long and 3 kilometres (1.5 miles) wide. It had no human habitation. There were also no permanent pre-existing structure on it, but India sent some paramilitary soldiers and the navy in 1981 to hoist its National Flag on it. This became a big focus of a negative media campaign in Bangladesh and was capitalised by many to whip up anti-India sentiments. Ironically, in March 2010, the New Moore/South Talpatty 'island' disappeared as suddenly as it had surfaced, again as the consequence of natural causes, this time flowing from global warming and sea water expansion (inundating other smaller islands as well in the Sundarbans Region).[2]

The Politics

The deeply divided domestic politics within Bangladesh triggered mirroring reactions within India. The brutal assassination of Sheikh Mujibur Rahman and the senior most-leaders of his party in 1975 deepened the political divide within Bangladesh as well as across borders between Bangladesh and India. The Awami League's complete relegation to political exile for the subsequent 18 years and military/quasi military rule in Bangladesh, which was hostile to India, made progress towards any settlement on any issue excruciatingly difficult. When Sheikh Hasina succeeded in returning with an Awami League-led coalition in 1996, fresh hope was awakened on both sides of resolving long-festering disputes and making a fresh beginning. Consequently, the 30-year Ganga Treaty and the Chittagong Hill Tracts Accord ending all insurgency were signed. However, this was a very short window that closed quickly. The next such window of opportunity opened with the landslide victory of the Awami League led by Sheikh Hasina in December 2008, which gave a clear mandate. A dramatic turnaround took place, with the commencement of serious interlocution to reconfigure relations. Prime Minister Sheikh Hasina's state visit to India in January 2010 marked a game-changing turning point in the two neighbour's bilateral relations.

Reconfiguring Bangladesh-India Relations

Commencing seriously mandated negotiations on various long outstanding issues, the long pending Protocol to the 1974 Land Boundary Agreement (otherwise known as the Indira Mujib LBA) was completed and signed in September 2011. However, its ratification by India was delayed until May 2015, on account of internal political divisions within India. Subsequently, economic and trade concessions were extended by India unilaterally without insistence on reciprocity, as a gesture of goodwill. Bangladesh also permitted India to move over dimensional cargo (ODC) through Bangladesh waterways from Kolkata to Agartala for a vitally needed Indian power project. The first big line of credit of USD 1 billion was extended by India to Bangladesh almost at International Development Association (IDA) rates. All these steps put

Bangladesh-India relations back on track and on forward movement on the maritime boundary was therefore a critically important factor.

Never having lost sight of the importance of resolving its maritime boundary contestations in the Bay of Bengal, Bangladesh also decided in 2009 to take the maritime boundary issues with Myanmar and India for arbitration to the International Tribunal on Law of the Seas (ITLOS), a dispute-resolution body available to all parties under UNCLOS. There was a moment of surprise and some demurring on this decision on both sides—but the rationale became increasingly clear and was largely accepted by all.

UNCLOS—ITLOS vs. Bilateral Resolution

As bilateral relations were back on an even keel, and a vast *bonhomie* and spirit of cooperation existed between the two leaderships, there was a strong opinion that favoured bilateral negotiations. This was in keeping with this new state of mind towards resolving long festering disputes, as happened in the case of the Land Boundary Agreement (LBA). However, it was soon realised, and quite rightly so, that both the governments would be condemned, whatever they did or agreed to, as had happened in the case of the 1996 Ganga Treaty. Moreover, in the case of the LBA, the key principles had already been agreed to by the two Prime Ministers (Sheikh Mujib and Indira Gandhi) in 1974—but circumstances such as the Berubari case HC judgment, legal challenges and Mujib's assassination amongst others had intervened and put everything on hold.

As a result, Bangladesh initiated arbitration proceedings in respect of its case with India, in October 2009, under Article VII of the UNCLOS. It did the same with Myanmar in December 2009. Going in for ITLOS appeared a much safer option as, whatever be the outcome, it could easily be attributed to the International Tribunal under UNCLOS to which both countries were parties, thereby avoiding brickbats for the political leadership in both the countries.

ITLOS—the Process

The political bonhomie perhaps was the most important factor—both leaders at the highest level mutually agreed and their bureaucracies went along to take the contentious dispute for arbitration to ITLOS. For ITLOS to agree to take on the case, both sides had to commit themselves to certain basic principles that would enable ITLOS to proceed. These included a convergence on composition of members of the Tribunal, willingness to listen to each other and translate their political will down to operational levels, and finally a commitment to abide by the dynamics of the process.

Remarkably, there were no significant efforts to procedurally stall or filibuster. At the same time, perhaps Bangladesh felt it prudent to adopt the same route for resolution as had been adopted for Myanmar by the Tribunal in their case with India, so as not to prejudice either case. Interestingly, ITLOS was able to consider the case between Bangladesh and Myanmar, and decide upon it, earlier than the case between Bangladesh and India. The reason perhaps was the possible existence of a more complicated historical baggage to wade through in the latter's case. It made eminent sense, therefore, to deal with the much easier Bangladesh-Myanmar case and use the judgment to establish the Bangladesh-India case. Consequently, the two rulings turned out to be consistent with each other.

It was even more significant that there was a convergence on basic modalities. Importantly, both parties agreed that the Radcliffe Award of 1947, in conjunction with the Notification by the Governor of Bengal in 1925 were the acceptable starting points. In case of the latter, Bangladesh did some very laborious research, and went to the India Office Library in London to dig out old maps and documents of the British colonial period that were hitherto in the realm of hearsay—and India, much to its credit, accepted it, graciously.

Both the parties also accepted the jurisdiction of the Tribunal to adjudicate and agreed to abide by the final award. They agreed to let the Tribunal determine the location of the Land Boundary terminus resulting from the Radcliffe Award; and both requested the Tribunal to draw a single maritime boundary line delimiting the three maritime zones—this was decidedly very complex, but both sides decided to leave it to the Tribunal's better judgment than each arguing his own case ad infinitum. Most noteworthy of all, there was constantly a palpable demonstration of clear political will by both sides, representing a rare occasion for law and power arriving at equilibrium, and deliberately nesting itself on a high moral ground. The judges were unanimous on all except the last (delimitation) item, on which Justice Rao recorded dissent.

The Award: Final Resolution

The final delimitation line that Tribunal drew resulted in a "grey area" which lies beyond the 200 nautical mile-limit of Bangladesh, in which Bangladesh only has rights to the seabed and subsoil of the continental shelf, but not to superjacent waters of the exclusive economic zone which fall within 200 nautical miles of India and thus belong to the latter.[3] The ITLOS awarded Bangladesh an area of 19,467 sq km,[4] four-fifths of the total area of 25,602 sq km, which was at stake due to a disputed maritime boundary in the Bay of Bengal. Bangladesh's maritime boundary has been extended by 118,813 sq.km, comprising 12 nautical miles of territorial sea and an Exclusive Economic Zone extending up to 200 nm into the high seas.[5] Both countries accepted the award with commendable grace.

Tribunal's Delimitation, Final Delimitation and Grey Areas

There was a residual complication: this grey area also partially overlaps with similar a grey area created by ITLOS in the Bangladesh-Myanmar

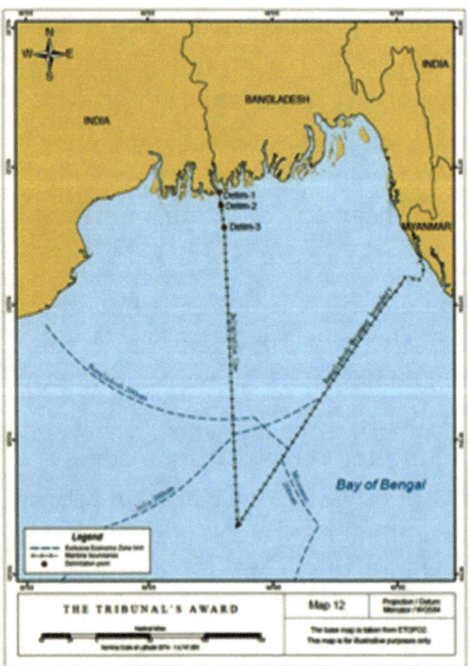

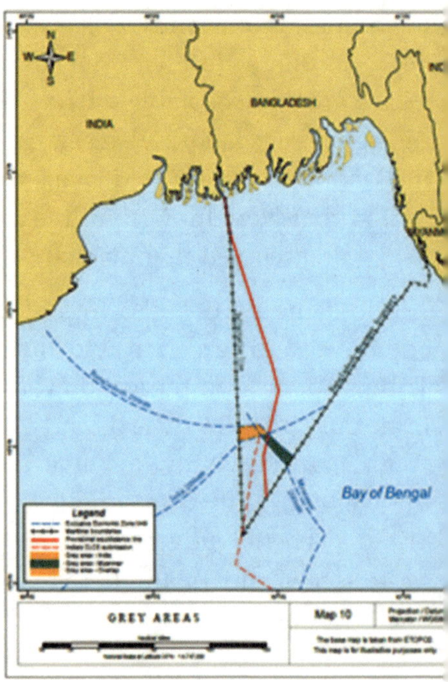

case. The Tribunal hoped that the neutralisation of ill will between the three parties by their accepting the respective awards would generate sufficient sustaining goodwill for them to be able to arrive at a final resolution of this small grey area.

Implications

This path-breaking development opened the door for exploration of oil and gas in the Bay of Bengal—the site of huge energy reserves with enormous economic significance for a small state like Bangladesh. According to some estimates after the arbitration award, the possible natural gas reserves of Bangladesh are estimated at around 200 trillion cubic feet, which make them the largest gas reserves in the Asia-Pacific.[6] Consequent to the dispute resolution with its two partners, Bangladesh has offered 26 offshore blocks for exploration, which include 11 shallow blocks and 15 deep-sea blocks.[7]

Bangladesh's maritime dispute with India deterred many international petroleum companies from investing in the sea-blocks previously offered. The verdict, additionally, also recognised India's sovereignty over New Moore Island, enabling India to receive nearly 6,000 sq. km. of the contested zone where the island had once existed. This also enabled both the countries to cooperate in jointly promoting the preservation of biodiversity that is critically important. The dispute resolution is also good news for millions of fishermen in both the countries, as they can fish in areas that were not available to them for fishing earlier on account of the dispute. Importantly, the parties agreed to exercise their sovereign rights and perform their duties under the Convention with due regard to the rights of the other.

The Tribunal also encouraged India and Bangladesh to determine the measures they considered appropriate, including through the conclusion of further agreements or the creation of a cooperative arrangement. More importantly, considering a notable departure from the past behavioural pattern displayed by the post-colonial neo-Westphalian order that emerged after 1945, it was an important signal to break free of the 'Partition Syndrome' that had not only divided just the land and communities, but also the hydrosphere and ecosphere. Despite a bitter colonial legacy, it enabled everyone to stop worrying about the trampling of their sovereign rights, and move towards collaborating and addressing issues related to the commons that are the seas, skies, space, and cyber-space

This creation of mental space for conceiving cooperation in the Bay of Bengal opened up exciting vistas for moving forward gradually to a larger cooperative order in the largest Bay in the world. For example, Bangladesh and India signed a bilateral coastal shipping agreement. India and Myanmar also have a similar agreement. This has awakened interest on the part of Sri Lanka to join in but this is yet to happen. This could perhaps be the beginning of a sub-regional coastal shipping cooperation between Sri Lanka, India, Bangladesh and Myanmar!

This could then conceivably be extended to include Thailand also, thus, making it a BIMSTEC configuration. The countries of the region could then expand their horizons to envisage a BIMSTEC Plus configuration that would also include Malaysia and Indonesia that comprise the south-eastern flank of the Bay of Bengal. This could enable all the littorals to enter into a larger configuration, may be to form a Bay of Bengal Coastal and Maritime Shipping. Most importantly, this could enable the region to move towards the cherished goal of setting up a Bay of Bengal Community.

Some legal quibbling on some points of awards may still continue, spurred by narrower domestic political dynamics, particularly when such politics breaks through domestic limitation infringes, and negatively affects, domestic dynamics and the politics of the others. Nevertheless, the Award creates a historically important precedent in moving the realm of International Law beyond being merely customary—inching towards an enforceable regime. A cooperative political atmosphere has to be conducive for arriving at a culture of consensus acceptable to all, for the greater good of the many—analogous to the domestic political process of law-making. While still a far cry from an international government, it constitutes an important step towards an international regime of governance, at least in some areas, that could apply as a precedent for others. The Award and its subsequent implementation could work as a role model for resolving all such contentious maritime disputes across the globe.

NOTES

1. Sugata Hazra, et al, "Disappearance of the New Moore Island from the Southernmost Coastal Fringe of the Sundarban Delta: A Case Study", *Journal of the Indian Society of Remote Sensing* (February 2016), p. 479.
2. Ibid., pp. 483-484.
3. "Award", *In the Matter of the Bay of Bengal Maritime Boundary Arbitration between The People's Republic of Bangladesh and the Republic of India*, The Hague: Permanent Court of Arbitration, 07 July 2014, pp. 155-156.
4. Ibid., p. A-7.
5. Ibid.
6. Jack Detsch, "Bangladesh: Asia's New Energy Superpower?", *The Diplomat*, 14 November 2014.
7. "Bangladesh moves to go for auction to explore offshore gas", *Dhaka Tribune*, 26 August 2018.

12

Bay of Bengal Maritime Delimitation Cases:
Upholding the Rule of Law in International Relations

Aniruddha Rajput

Disputes are an inevitable reality in an interconnected world. What is important is how States address them, especially with respect to the use of the oceans and the regulation of their use through the United Nations Convention on the Law of the Sea (UNCLOS) that could result in disputes. The UN Charter[1] and various subsequent resolutions of the General Assembly, such as Declaration on Principles of International Law Concerning Friendly Relations and Co-operation among States in accordance with the Charter of the United Nations[2] and Declaration on the Inadmissibility of Intervention and Interference in the Internal Affairs of States[3] have reaffirmed these. The principles contained therein have been declared as customary international law by the International Court of Justice.[4] Adjudication is one of the important methods of peaceful settlement of disputes.[5] It has been given a special position in the architecture of UNCLOS.

China's failure to participate and comply with the decision of the arbitral tribunal in the South China Sea dispute is regularly mentioned as an instance of non-compliance with international law and the framework of UNCLOS. Despite this example, there is another example from Asia, which shows that States with relatively more power are willing to adhere to third party binding dispute resolution process and comply with those decisions although they may have to give away their maritime claims. These instances deserve celebration since they are examples of upholding the rule of law in international relations. The discussion in this article is about the maritime delimitation disputes in the Bay of Bengal between Bangladesh and India on one hand and Bangladesh and Myanmar on the other.

The Bay of Bengal is situated in the North-eastern Indian Ocean. The northern part of the Bay of Bengal, which was a subject of conflicting maritime claims, is shared by Bangladesh, India and Myanmar. The three States resolved a complex and a long drawn dispute regarding overlapping maritime claims between them by resorting to and complying with the UNCLOS framework. There were two independent cases relating to different parts of the Bay Bengal, one between Bangladesh and India and the other between Bangladesh and Myanmar. These cases are collectively referred to as the Bay of Bengal Maritime Delimitation Cases.

The Legal Framework

The United Nations Convention on the Law of the Sea (UNCLOS) contains a mandatory dispute resolution clause under Article 287. The dispute resolution clause is an inseparable part of the scheme of the UNCLOS, meaning thereby that a State cannot opt out of the dispute resolution provisions. This mandatory framework for compulsory dispute resolution, which was unique at the time when the UNCLOS was negotiated, was described as a 'package deal' by the President of the Third United Nations Conference on the Laws of the Sea.[6] The consequence of the 'packaged-deal' approach is that all aspects of UNCLOS are integral and binding. States cannot rely on a few and withdraw from the others, particularly provisions relating to compulsory dispute resolution.[7] Article 287 allows the States to choose from one of three modes: proceedings before the International Tribunal for the Law of the Sea (ITLOS), International Court of Justice (ICJ) or *ad hoc* arbitration proceedings under Annex VII of UNCLOS. The parties should have chosen the same forum for dispute resolution, otherwise an arbitral tribunal constituted under Annex VII of UNCLOS serves as a default option. None of the three States had made a declaration choosing the ITLOS or the ICJ. Bangladesh and Myanmar agreed to refer the dispute to ITLOS[8]. India and Bangladesh neither made any declarations regarding jurisdiction nor accepted to choose ITLOS or ICJ. The dispute thus went automatically for *ad hoc* arbitration under Annex VII of UNCLOS. Although the proceedings between Bangladesh and India commenced before the proceedings between Bangladesh and Myanmar, the Bangladesh Myanmar proceedings got over sooner. The Annex VII tribunal deciding the Bangladesh-India case took 53 months whereas the ITLOS deciding the Bangladesh-Myanmar case took 27 months.

The Bay of Bengal cases involved overlapping claims over four areas: the territorial sea, Exclusive Economic Zone (EEZ), continental shelf up to 200 nm and continental shelf beyond 200 nm (also called the 'extended continental shelf'). Overlapping claims over the territorial sea are regulated by Article 15, whereas Article 74 and Article 83 regulate overlapping claims over the EEZ and continental shelf within and beyond 200 nm, respectively. The claims over the extended continental shelf are determined by the Commission on Limitation of Continental Shelf (CLCS) under Article 76. There is no provision that has a direct reference to overlapping claims over the extended continental shelf, Article 83 that is the basis for delimitation of the continental shelf was used. All the States had made claims before CLCS for extended continental shelf claims. Yet, in both the cases, the tribunal decided to proceed and delimit rights over the extended continental shelf.[9]

The rules on maritime delimitation in the EEZ and continental shelf are the same and they are different from those on the delimitation of the territorial sea. There are two common features about delimitation rules regarding all the zones. Firstly, the coasts have to be adjacent or opposite each other. In the Bay of Bengal cases, the coasts of all the three States are adjacent. Secondly, the legal provisions would not operate if there is an agreement to the contrary between the parties. In the case of the EEZ and the continental shelf, there is an additional requirement that the agreement has to be as per international law specified in Article 38(1) of the ICJ Statute. This provision cannot have serious implications since all agreements would have to be in accordance with the law and all the sources of international law are comprehensively noted in Article 38(1) of the ICJ Statute. In both the cases, the parties argued that there was an agreement delimiting the maritime zones and was rejected in both the cases—discussed in detail below.

The other aspects of rules on maritime delimitation of different zones differ. The difference is due to the nature of rights exercisable in these areas. The rights of coastal States over the territorial sea are 'territorial'; thus, they enjoy sovereignty over the seabed, superjacent waters, and the air column.[10] Rights on the EEZ and continental shelf are mostly in relation to exploitation of natural resources.[11] The focus of delimitation in the territorial sea is on an equidistance line, whereas in the case of other zones it is on an equitable solution. Therefore, no precise methodology is provided for delimitation in the EEZ and the continental shelf unlike the territorial sea.[12]

The maritime delimitation of the territorial sea is based upon an equidistance line, which is a median line, every point on which is at an equal distance from both the coasts. The rule of an equidistance line would not apply in the territorial sea in case of a 'historic tile' or 'other special circumstances'. In the Bay of Bengal cases, claims of historic title were not involved.[13] But the parties argued that there were special circumstances (discussed in detail below). In the EEZ and the continental shelf, different methods for finding an equitable solution for delimitation have been developed and parties to the dispute relied on them (discussed in detail below)

The following section focuses on the legal arguments of the parties and the conclusions of the tribunals. The discussion would show that the arguments were purely technical in nature. There were some sensitivities involved with the legal issues involved in the case, yet the analysis and conclusions were strictly legal. They represent the neutrality of the legal rules that flows from technicality and that they are insulated from the political underpinnings and consequences of those rules.

The Land Boundary Terminus

The particularly sensitive issue was the determination of the land boundary terminus in the Bangladesh-India case. The land boundary terminus is a point on the land from where the maritime delimitation line between the States is drawn. The parties agreed on the role and importance of the land boundary terminus in law but disagreed about its precise location,[14] thus, in effect, disagreeing with the precise location of the land boundary between them. As it is, the determination of land boundaries is a sensitive issue between States. What aggravated the sensitivity was that the determination of the land boundary terminus required interpretation and application of two critical awards: the Bengal Boundary Commission (known popularly as the 'Radcliffe Award') and the India-Pakistan Boundary Disputes Tribunal (known as the 'Bagge Tribunal'). The Radcliffe Award is particularly infamous in the subcontinent and is politically emotive since it formed the basis of the partition of India and Pakistan in 1947, which resulted in the loss of human life and property in large proportion.[15]

The Radcliffe Award declared the land boundary between India and East Pakistan (that became Bangladesh in 1971) to be the line that ran southwards along the districts between Khulna and 24 Parganas, where it met the Bay of Bengal. This line that ran southwards between the mentioned districts was specified in detail in the notification of 1925. India argued that the line contemplated under the 1925 notification was fluid. It relied on the 1925 notification specifying that the line and correspondence between two officials of India and East Pakistan (which later became Bangladesh) had so agreed. Bangladesh, on the other hand, argued that the line was fixed and was so recognised in the Radcliffe Award and reaffirmed in the Bagge Award. According to India, the line was to be decided on the date of demarcation and not as was decided by Radcliffe in 1947. The parties presented several arguments along with evidence in the form of maps and other government records to support their positions. The Tribunal determined the land boundary terminus had been finalised in the Radcliff Award and thus was the one as noted in 1947. The interpretation of the Radcliff and Bagge Awards left no doubt that Bangladesh's argument was correct. It was not fluid as India was arguing but fixed as defined in the Radcliff Award and confirmed in the Bagge Award.[16] Furthermore, the correspondence between two officials of India and East Pakistan relied upon by India cannot undo the boundary determined in the Radcliff Award and confirmed in the Bagge Award.[17]

Base Points and the Delimitation of the Territorial Sea

The first stage in maritime delimitation is the determination of base points, since it is on their position that maritime zones are measured. In situations where there are no conflicting claims, the base points of coastal states are not normally under challenge. But in situations of maritime delimitation, they could be a very controversial matter. In the Bangladesh-India case, this was technically a complex matter of political significance.

There were several challenges in the choice of base points, but the important one was regarding an island. Bangladesh objected to base points on South Talpatty or New Moore Island. According to Bangladesh, the island had disappeared in the late 1980s or early 1990s and satellite images after 1989 do not show the island.[18] India maintained that the island was visible during low tide and that it could not be spotted during the site visit because the weather was bad on the day of the visit.[19] The Tribunal did not accept the base points of South Talpatty or New Moore Island because they did not fall on the coastline and did not constitute a protuberant coastal point.[20] The effect of the award is that it negates the relevance of islands that are alongside the coast.

The conclusion of the tribunal for excluding the South Talpatty and New Moore Islands is unconvincing. If a low tide elevation is situated within the claimed area of the territorial sea, then it may be used as a baseline for measuring the territorial sea.[21] The islands in question were low tide elevations and since they fell within the territorial sea, there was no reason to exclude them as base points for drawing the baseline. If not base points, they certainly qualified as a special circumstance for India to adjust the equidistance line. The Tribunal could have rather considered the evidence of the latest satellite imagery to consider whether the islands did in fact exist or not and whether they were represented in the maps. Baselines are to be essentially identified based on maps so produced by the coastal State and so deposited with the Secretary General of the United Nations.[22]

Regarding the methodology for delimitation within the territorial sea, Bangladesh argued that 'special circumstances' play an important role and have been expansively interpreted in recent jurisprudence.[23] India argued that special circumstances were an exception and could not be treated as a rule.[24] The Tribunal did not accept Bangladesh's argument that there were special circumstances because the geographical peculiarity noted was the Raimangal estuary, which was common to both States. It could therefore not constitute a special circumstance.[25] Additionally, the concavity of the coastline of the Bay of Bengal did not produce and significant cut-off of the territorial sea. Therefore, no adjustment of the median line was necessary.[26]

The next question was of the relevant coast for delimitation. Since the land dominates the sea, the seaward projection of the coast that could generate entitlement for the territorial sea is the relevant coast. There was an agreement between the parties regarding the relevant coast for Bangladesh and it was based on the decision of ITLOS between Bangladesh and Myanmar.[27] Bangladesh disputed India's claims of the relevant coast. The Tribunal accepted India's claim that the relevant coast of India would be from the land boundary terminus to the north of Devi Point since it could generate projections that overlap with the claims of up to 200 nm by Bangladesh.[28]

In the Bangladesh-Myanmar case, there had been long negotiations between the parties, with the recent one in 2008, which continued unaffected by the pending judicial proceedings. This represents that the parties were trying to resolve their dispute although the matter was being considered by a judicial body. The issue was whether the parties had already delimited the territorial sea through agreement minutes of 1974 and 2008 or by a tacit agreement. The negotiations continued to be cordial.[29] According to Bangladesh, the dividing line between Bangladesh and Myanmar was agreed to in 2008.[30] Myanmar contended this position and argued that there was only a conditional agreement and that a final agreement had not been reached yet.[31] It was a record of minutes of the meeting rather than an agreement.[32]

The Tribunal was thus first to determine whether there was an agreement for maritime delimitation under Article 15 of UNCLOS. The Tribunal firstly observed that for Article 15, the agreement had to be a legally binding agreement.[33] The agreed minutes of 1974 were treated only as a conditional understanding during the course of negotiations rather than as a final agreement under Article 15.[34] The circumstances in which the minutes were agreed do not suggest that the territorial sea was intended to be comprehensively delimited. Myanmar always wanted a comprehensive agreement on all zones; territorial sea, continental shelf, and EEZ.[35] The Burmese official who engaged in the proceedings did not have the authority to bind the Burmese Government.[36] Thus, the 1974 agreed minutes did not amount to an agreement and were not binding and the same problems persisted with the conclusions of the meeting in 2008 hence the meeting too was not binding.[37]

In the absence of an express agreement, Bangladesh argued that there was a tacit agreement, because the parties had behaved in accordance with the agreed minutes for more than three decades. Bangladesh fishermen had been fishing in those waters and naval vessels had been patrolling those areas.[38] The Tribunal did not accept the argument of a tacit agreement because the standard of evidence for a tacit agreement has to be compelling and thus very high; this was not met in this case.[39] Since there was an absence of sufficient evidence to show that the parties had administered the sea in accordance with the Agreed Minutes of 1974, it could not be said that estoppels was proved and Myanmar could not challenge the recorded minutes of 1974.[40]

Since the presence of an actual or tacit agreement or estoppels was not proved, the Tribunal proceeded to delimit the territorial sea. In the territorial sea, the only controversial aspect was the importance to be given to St Martin's Island. Myanmar argued that St. Martin's Island, which was located immediately off its coast, but belonged to Bangladesh, was a special circumstance that required adjustment of the median line.[41] Bangladesh was arguing that since it is an island, it should be given the full effect.[42] If the island was treated as a special circumstance, Myanmar would have received a large section of the territorial sea. If it was given full effect as an island, it would have its own territorial sea of 12 nm, and would thus further reduce Myanmar's entitlement.

The Tribunal viewed that the effect to be given to an island would depend on whether the delimitation concerned the territorial sea or EEZ or the continental shelf.[43] St. Martin's Island was a significant geographical feature with a significant population, and economic and other activities. It could not be treated merely as a 'special circumstance'. It has to be given full effect as an island.[44] St. Martin's Island was edging the continental shelf and EEZ of Myanmar thus cutting off Myanmar's access to these areas. It was necessary that Myanmar had a free and unimpeded right to navigate through the territorial sea around St. Martin's Island. Bangladesh made a statement that it had accepted that Myanmar would have free and unhindered access to navigation around the territorial sea of St. Martin's Island.[45] This was indeed an expression of a spirit of goodwill and concession of States in dealing with each other.

Unlike the Bangladesh-India case, there was no dispute regarding the land boundary terminus for maritime delimitation in the case of Bangladesh-Myanmar.[46] Also, there was hardly any disagreement regarding the base points, thus making the process of delimitation simple.[47] Nevertheless, the outcome of delimitation of the territorial sea depended on the cooperation and goodwill of the parties.

Overlapping Claims over the Exclusive Economic Zone and the Continental Shelf within 200 nm

As discussed in the section relating to the legal framework, the principles of delimitation in the territorial sea are different from those of the EEZ and the continental shelf. While the equidistance line is the pivotal criteria for delimitation of the territorial sea, an equitable result is the objective in the delimitation of the EEZ and the continental shelf.

Bangladesh argued that since an equitable outcome was desired, the equidistance rule had no role to play.[48] It, therefore, argued that the Tribunal should apply the angle-bisector method since the coast was unstable.[49] According to the angle bisector method, a line bisecting the general direction of the coast or perpendicular to the straight line joining the coastline may be drawn.[50] This line does not correspond to the equidistance method since each point on this line need not be at an equal distance from the coasts of both the States. The consequence of the angle-bisector method in the present case would have been that a straight line would have to be drawn that would be perpendicular to the coastline. Such a line would have given more area in favour of Bangladesh, unlike what it would have obtained if an equidistance line had been drawn. India argued that although an equitable solution was the objective, the methodology adopted in the jurisprudence is three-staged: first, establishment of a provisional equidistance line; second, special or relevant circumstances to be taken into account and if there are such compelling reasons then the equidistance line could be abandoned; and third, if there are no reasons to abandon the equidistance method, then the provisional equidistance line could be adjusted depending on the special circumstances.[51]

In exceptional situations, the angle bisector method could be used, but it does not represent transparency and therefore the Tribunal declined to apply it.[52] Further, the Tribunal noted that the methodology for delimitation in the EEZ and continental shelf was different from the territorial sea because there is no obligation to follow the equidistance rule.[53] Yet, equidistance is the first stage in delimitation and has to be employed, unless there are supervening factors in the nature of special circumstances that desire adoption of another approach.[54] As a general principle, there is a single line of maritime delimitation, hence the relevant base points and coasts remain the same and it is only the delimitation line in the territorial sea that is to be further extended and altered based on the rules regulating the EEZ and continental shelf. The Tribunal accordingly drew a provisional equidistance line.[55]

The Tribunal did not accept Bangladesh's argument that instability of the coast was a relevant circumstance for adjusting the equidistance line.[56] However, regarding the concavity of the coast, the Tribunal found that the equidistance line would result in a cut-off of the seaward projections of the Bangladesh coast and adjusted the equidistance line to avoid the cut-off effect,[57] thereby reducing the area of the EEZ and the continental shelf that India was claiming.

Bangladesh also insisted that its population depended on fishing and that too should be considered as a relevant factor to adjust the equidistance line for an equitable result. The Tribunal noted that although fishing interests were taken into consideration for establishing delimitation in the *Jan Mayen* case, Bangladesh had not produced sufficient evidence and therefore the equidistance line should not be adjusted.[58]

As was argued against India, Bangladesh argued that the angle bisector method may be used due to the specific configuration of the coast and its concavity.[59] Like the Tribunal in the Bangladesh-India case, the Tribunal declined to apply the angle bisector method since it would not have resulted in an equitable solution. Also, the equidistance method is a settled method in the jurisprudence.[60] The Tribunal followed the three-stage method that was followed by international courts and tribunals in relation to the delimitation of the EEZ and continental shelf.[61]

The concavity of the coast, does not by itself amount to a special circumstance, but if it results in a cut-off effect then it is. In this case, it resulted in the cut-off for the maritime entitlements of Bangladesh; therefore, it is a special circumstance.[62] Although St. Martin's Island was not a special circumstance for delimitation in the territorial sea because it was an island, it continued not to be a special circumstance for adjustment of the equidistance line for the EEZ and continental shelf delimitation. The reason for not considering it was that it would result in blocking the seaward projections of Myanmar's coast and result in unwarranted distortions in the delimitation line—hence, it was best ignored.[63] The depositional system of Bangladesh due to the physical, geological and geo-morphological connection between Bangladesh's land mass and the Bay of Bengal sea floor was not a special circumstance to warrant readjustment of the equidistance line.[64] The provisional equidistance line was adjusted at relevant process (Points ?) to avoid the cut-off effect for Bangladesh due to the concavity of its coast.[65]

Delimitation of the extended continental shelf is complex. In the absence of any precise rules in that regard, the Tribunal relied on Article 83 since the entire continental shelf within or outside 200 nm is continuous.[66] The claims of all the three States for extended continental shelf claims were pending with the CLCS. The CLCS is a body constituting of experts in geology, geomorphology, bathymetry, etc. ("The Commission shall consist of 21 members who shall be experts in the field of geology, geophysics or hydrography, elected by States Parties to this Convention from among their nationals, having due regard to the need to ensure equitable geographical representation, who shall serve in their personal capacities") from the rules. (The rules refer to Article 2 Annex II of the UNCLOS) of CLCS find out exact qualifications and put it here). They are an expert body, better qualified in technical areas than lawyers that adjudicate delimitation disputes. The issue of determination of extended continental shelf was left by UNCLOS to CLCS. Since CLCS rules provide that the CLCS cannot proceed in cases of conflicting claims (find the exact provision and language and put in foot note), ITLOS has viewed that it needs to take over that function because the disputes would otherwise remain unresolved. (find exact para from Bangladesh Myanmar in footnote). It is indeed advisable that all disputes should be resolved, but CLCS is not stopped from proceedings if parties so agree.

If parties intend to resolve their conflicting claims over the extended continental shelf then they need to agree that they be decided by CLCS. In any event, CLCS does not decide conflicting claims; it only determines whether geographically, the claim of extended continental shelf claim is sustainable. It is possible that CLCS may conclude that the claim of the coastal State is unfounded or much lesser than claimed, thus reducing the overlapping claims. By usurping the functions of CLCS, the tribunals in both the cases—purportedly relying upon expert evidence—determined claims over the extended continental shelf. This keenness to decide has resulted in the new concept of 'grey area', where one State has continental shelf claims and the other has extended continental shelf claims. Both the tribunals held that it is possible for States to concurrently exercise rights over those areas.

In the Bangladesh-India case, this was an area that fell within 200 nm of India and beyond the 200 nm continental shelf of Bangladesh. According to the Tribunal, in the grey area, the right of Bangladesh over the seabed and the subsoil as a part of its extended continental shelf could co-exist along with the right of India over the EEZ rights over the superjacent waters.[67] There are several areas where States enjoy shared rights under UNCLOS according to the Tribunal hence the States can share this area.[68] In a dissenting opinion, Mr. Rao disagreed with the conclusions of the majority since there is no sufficient basis for declaring a grey area. The disputes were thus not conclusively decided.[69] Similarly, in the Bangladesh-Myanmar case, a grey area was declared over an area beyond 200 nm of Bangladesh and within 200 nm of Myanmar.[70] Since the nature of rights differs, the States could exercise their rights concurrently.[71]

Thus, in both the cases, despite proceedings pending before the CLCS, the Tribunal proceeded to delimit the extended continental shelf.[72] Concavity continued to be a relevant circumstance for claims beyond 200 nm.[73]

Conclusion

These cases show that the domain of law is distinct from the domain of politics. The cases of maritime delimitation are purely technical in nature. The example of change of methodology adopted by Bangladesh represents this. Such application of legal rules may result in a party winning a certain issue and losing on another. It is difficult to assert in these proceedings that one party has won and the other has lost. Indeed, the practical effect would be more for one party as compared to the other. International adjudication in a sense removes the outcome of the controversy from the paradigm of success or loss.

Most importantly, these cases also represent the willingness of States to undertake mandatory dispute resolution despite a failure to reach a peaceful settlement through negotiations. Both the cases were filed by Bangladesh. States prefer to leave complicated questions to be decided by an independent judicial body that commands respect. It is thus better to resolve disputes on purely legal grounds by seeking to find political solutions. This shows the willingness of States to leave certain complex and politically difficult questions to an international court or tribunal. Also, it is easier for States to comply with the decisions on the ground that the State wants to be seen as a responsible State willing to comply with its international law.

The cases involved States with asymmetrical power. India is geopolitically stronger and an influential player in the SAARC region. Bangladesh is less powerful in comparison to India. Although Bangladesh and Myanmar are comparable, Myanmar had recently come out of political turmoil and uncertainty. Economically as well as geopolitically, it is weaker in comparison to Bangladesh (Bangladesh has a GDP of $ 221.4 billion[74] compared to Myanmar whose GDP is $ 67.4 billion;[75] further the value of Bangladesh's exports is around $ 36 billion, and imports are worth around $ 48 billion[76] as compared to $11.7 billion and $ 16 billion for Myanmar, respectively[77]). The asymmetry of power did not stop these States from taking their disputes to international adjudication, participating in the judicial process and complying with the judicial process. It is an example of compliance with a rule-based order. The stronger party lost its claims as compared to the weaker party. In the India-Bangladesh case, India did not get the area it claimed since Bangladesh was awarded a total area of 19,467 square kilometres out of 25,602 square kilometres of the disputed area.[78] In the Bangladesh-Myanmar case, out of a total relevant area of 283,471 square kilometres,[79] Bangladesh was awarded 111,631 square kilometres and 171,832 square kilometres were awarded to Myanmar.[80] The size of the disputed area should not undermine the value and importance of the decision. If the issue between the States was trivial indeed and one State was willing to throw it away in favour of another, they would have simply negotiated and agreed to a settlement to that effect. Parties had attempted negotiations several times. India and Bangladesh had 11 rounds of negotiations and Bangladesh and Myanmar had 14 rounds between 1974 and 2010.[81] The parties could not agree to a solution and chose to refer the matter to arbitration and one of the parties invoked the binding dispute resolution provision under UNCLOS. It is not that States have not been at loggerheads on trivial issues and declined to participate or comply with international law in the past.

It certainly cannot be denied the governments of these three States were ready to comply with international legal obligations. Should this be seen as a matter of praise and pride that some States are willing to comply with obligations and be hailed as a success of international law? The role of important and influential powers is crucial in upholding the international rule of law. If they comply with their obligations, they would set a precedent for other States to follow.

These decisions are indeed important for long-term stable international relations. In the words of the Bangladesh-India tribunal: The Tribunal notes that maritime delimitations, like land boundaries, must be stable and definitive to ensure a peaceful relationship between the States concerned in the long term.[82]

International law is decried as ineffective. What is forgotten is that a law is effective only if its users want it to be. It is necessary that rising powers like India and China that intend to take a larger role in international relations and global institutions show their commitment towards international law and particularly the law of the sea. It is only if they lead the way that the rest can follow suit and make international law and particularly UNCLOS an effective instrument for stability in the future world order and value-based international relations.

The author would like to thank Mr. Kartik Ashta for the research assistance.

NOTES

1. Article 2(3) and Chapter VI, UN Charter.
2. Declaration on Principles of International Law concerning Friendly Relations and Co-operation among States in accordance with the Charter of the United Nations, UNGA Res 2625 (XXV), 24 October 1970, available at http://www.un-documents.net/a25r2625.htm
3. Declaration on the Inadmissibility of Intervention and Interference in the Internal Affairs of States, UNGA Res 2131 36/103, 09 December 1981, available at http://www.un.org/documents/ga/res/36/a36r103.htm
4. Case Concerning Military & Paramilitary Activities in and against Nicaragua (Nicaragua vs. United States of America, Judgment of 27 June 1986, para 187; *Armed Activities on the Territory of the Congo (Democratic Republic of the Congo vs. Uganda),* Judgment of 19 December 2005, para 162.
5. UN Charter, Article 33.
6. 'A Constitution for Oceans', Remarks by Tommy T.B. Koh, President of the Third United Nations Conference on the Laws of the Sea, 06 December 1982, available at http://www.un.org/depts/los/convention_agreements/texts/koh_english.pdf
7. H. Caminos and M.R. Molitor, 'Progressive Development of International Law and the Package Deal' (1985) 79 *AJIL* pp. 871–890; Yoshifumi Tanaka, *The International Law of the Sea* (Cambridge: Cambridge University Press, 2nd edn), pp. 28-32.
8 Dispute Concerning Delimitation of the Maritime Boundary Between Bangladesh and Myanmar in the Bay of Bengal (Bangladesh vs. Myanmar) Merits, Judgment of 14 March 2012, [2012] ITLOS Reports 4, paras 3,4 and 47.
9. Ibid. (paras 369-394); Bay of Bengal Arbitration (Bangladesh vs. India) Award of 7 July 2014, Case No. 2010-16 PCA, paras 76-83.
10. Maritime Delimitation and Territorial Questions between Qatar and Bahrain (Qatar vs. Bahrain), Merits, Judgment, I.C.J. Reports 2001, p. 93, paras 173-174, referring to Delimitation of the Maritime Boundary in the Gulf of Maine Area, I.C.J. Reports 1984, p. 327, para 194.
11. *Report of the International Law Commission to the General Assembly on the Work of its Eighth Session,* 11 U.N. GAOR, Supp. No. 9 at UN Doc (A/3159) *reprinted in* [1956] 2 Y.B. Int'l L. Comm'n. 295-296, U.N. Doc. A/CN.4/104; Yoshifumi Tanaka, *The International Law of the Sea* (Cambridge: Cambridge University Press, 2nd edn.), pp. 128-31, 142-4.
12. Bangladesh vs. Myanmar, para 225.
13. Bangladesh vs. India, para 227; Bangladesh vs. Myanmar, para 130.
14. Bangladesh vs. India, paras 58-9.
15. See Larry Collins & Dominique Lapierre, *Freedom at Midnight* (Simon & Schuster, 2017).
16. Bangladesh vs. India, para 137.
17. Ibid., para 165.
18. Ibid., para 197.
19. Ibid., para 205.
20. Ibid., paras 261-3.
21. United Nations Convention on the Laws of the Sea, Article 13.
22. Ibid., Article 16.
23. Bangladesh vs. India, paras 228-31.
24. Ibid., paras 232-3.

25. Bangladesh vs. India, para 248.
26. Ibid., para 272.
27. Bangladesh vs. India, paras 28-36.
28 Bangladesh vs. India, para 301.
Agreed Minutes between the Bangladesh Delegation and the Burmese Delegation regarding the Delimitation of the Maritime Boundary between the Two Countries, para 58.
29. Bangladesh vs. Myanmar, paras 60-4.
30. Ibid., para 66.
31. Ibid., paras 76-8.
32. Ibid., para 89.
33. Ibid., para 92.
34. Ibid., paras 92-3.
35. Ibid., para 96.
36. Ibid,, para 98.
37. Ibid., para 101-3.
38. Ibid., paras 117-8.
39. Ibid., para 125.
40. Ibid., para 131.
41. Ibid., paras 140-2.
42. Ibid., para 148.
43. Ibid., paras 151-2.
44. Ibid., paras 170-6.
45. Ibid., para 157.
46. Ibid., para 161-2.
47. Bangladesh vs. India, paras 314-9.
48. Ibid., paras 323-9.
49. Ibid., paras 427-8.
50. Ibid., paras 319-21.
51. Ibid., para 345.
52. Ibid., para 339.
53. Ibid., paras 341-5.
54. Ibid., paras 368-70.
55. Ibid., para 399.
56. Ibid., para 408.
57. Ibid., paras 422-4.
58. Bangladesh vs. Myanmar, para 213.
59. Ibid., paras 235-9.
60. Ibid., para 240.
61. Ibid., paras 290-7.
62. Ibid., paras 317-9.
63. Ibid., paras 321-2.
64. Ibid., paras 329-30.
65. Ibid., para 454-5.
66. Bangladesh vs. India, para 505.
67. Ibid., para 507.
68. Bay of Bengal Arbitration (Bangladesh vs. India) Award of 7 July 2014, Case No. 2010-16 PCA, Concurring and Dissenting Opinion of Dr. P.S. Rao, paras 10-3, 24-37.

69. Bangladesh vs. Myanmar, para 463.
70. Ibid., paras 474-476.
71. Bangladesh vs. India, paras 458, 509-1; Bangladesh vs. Myanmar, para 410.
72. Bangladesh vs. Myanmar, para 461.
73. World Bank Open Data, available at: https://data.worldbank.org/indicator/NY.GDP.MKTP.CD?locations=BD
74. Ibid., available at: https://data.worldbank.org/indicator/NY.GDP.MKTP.CD?locations=MM
75. UN DATA, available at: http://data.un.org/Data.aspx?q=bangladesh+Imports&d=ComTrade&f=_l1Code%3a1%3brtCode%3a50
76. Ibid., available at http://data.un.org/Data.aspx?q=myanmar+Imports&d=ComTrade&f=_l1 Code%3a1%3brtCode%3a104
77. Rupak Bhattacharjee, Delimitation of the India Bangladesh Maritime Boundary, 19 August 2014, available at https://idsa.in/idsacomments/DelimitationofIndo-Bangladesh_rbhattacharjee_190814
78. Bangladesh vs. Myanmar, para 496.
79. bid., para 499.
80. Bangladesh vs. Myanmar, para 36.
81. Bangladesh vs. India, para 215.

13

Myanmar and Bangladesh: A Case of Harmonious Maritime Dispute Resolution under UNCLOS

*Myo Htike Tan Thein**

With the adoption of the UNCLOS in 1982, ocean governance was codified successfully, and laws were put in place to regulate the activities of the stakeholders involved. The UNCLOS marked the first successful attempt at arriving at mutual consensus on the need for demarcation of oceanic boundaries and securing the rights of transit and passage. The convention thus became the landmark legal framework for marine and maritime activities.

The case had its genesis in the long, concave coastline of Bangladesh, which ensured that the usual application of equidistance principle[1] would inevitably lead to a maritime dispute. The dispute emanates from the fact that the equidistance line[2] demarcating exclusive economic zones (EEZs) between Bangladesh and Myanmar would cut the equidistance line between India and Bangladesh, less than 200 nautical miles from the coast of Bangladesh, thereby considerably reducing Bangladesh's EEZ and cutting off its access to the continental shelf. That would leave Bangladesh with a disproportionately small EEZ, with respect to the length of its coastline. Consequently, there were conflicting claims over

*With inputs from Alok Bansal and Deeksha Goel.

a section of the sea and sea bed that extended southwest from the seaward end of its land border.[3]

Myanmar and Bangladesh Historical Context

The maritime conflict between Myanmar and Bangladesh has its roots in the pre-colonial days of the 19th century. After three subsequent Anglo-Burmese Wars, Burma was annexed by the British and made an official colony from 1 January 1886. The annexed state of Burma then became a major province under British Rule in 1897.[4] The present borders had their beginning as a line dividing two districts of British India. It acquired greater salience in 1937, when British Burma was separated from British India.[5]

At the time of Burma's independence in 1948 and that of Pakistan in 1947, both countries inherited and accepted the de jure Burma-Bengal boundary line drawn by the British during the colonial period. This being the case, Myanmar lost its historically owned *Shinmaphyu* in Burmese (Shahpuri) *Island* and Ohnkyun in Burmese (St. Martin) *Island* to erstwhile East Pakistan, now known as Bangladesh. In 1971, Bangladesh emerged from what was until then East Pakistan and this historic line became the border between Bangladesh and Myanmar. The Naf River, an estuary, divides Arakan in Burma from Cox's Bazar district in Bangladesh. Although there is some difference about the length of the border as Bangladesh claims it to be 193 km, while Myanmar believes it to be 272 km.[6] The land and river boundaries between the two states have been properly demarcated in accordance with the international law of state succession. However, the most problematic aspect of the Myanmar-Bangladesh boundary remained the maritime boundaries, which cover the territorial sea, contiguous zone, Exclusive Economic Zone (EEZ), continental shelf and even internal waters as far as the riverine boundary between the two was concerned. For a casual reader these terms have been explained below:

(a) **Territorial Waters.** Territorial waters are defined as the area immediately adjacent to the shores of a country and which also fall under its territorial jurisdiction. The jurisdiction of this maritime zone is different from the high seas, which are open for all stakeholders or even the inland waters which lie within the national boundary of a country. However, when used informally, territorial waters include all maritime areas under a nation's jurisdiction including the internal waters, territorial sea, contiguous zone, exclusive economic zone and the continental shelf.

(b) **Internal Waters.** Internal waters are maritime spaces, including lakes and rivers, that are encompassed within the territory of a state or lie within the base line of a state and face internally towards the land of the state. The state has complete jurisdiction within these waters akin to its land territory and not even innocent passage is permitted. In case of an archipelagic state like Indonesia and the Philippines, all waters inside the archipelagic baseline are considered internal waters.[7]

(c) **Territorial Sea.** UNCLOS defines territorial sea as a belt of coastal waters that may extend up to 12 nautical miles from the coast of a country or its base line. The territorial sea is considered to be under the jurisdiction of the coastal state and its laws remain applicable in the territorial sea. However, innocent passage by ships both military and non-military, of any nationality is permitted through it. This sovereignty of space in the case of territorial seas is not restricted to the seas alone but also extends to the airspace above it and sea beds.[8]

(d) **Contiguous Zone**. Contiguous zone is the second layer of delimitation in the maritime boundary of a country. The contiguous zone extends up to 24 nautical miles from the baseline. A country may exercise control as necessary to prevent infringement of its Customs, fiscal, immigration or sanitary laws and regulations within its territory or territorial sea.[9]

(e) **Exclusive Economic Zone (EEZ)**. The EEZ extends from the baseline of the coastal state up to 200 nautical miles and thus includes both the territorial sea and the contiguous zone. A coastal state has sovereign rights in the EEZ for exploiting, conserving and managing both the living or non-living natural resources, on the waters superjacent to the seabed as well as on the sea bed and its subsoil. It also has complete rights to harness energy from its water, currents and winds.[10]

(f) **Continental Shelf**: The continental shelf of a coastal State consists of the sea bed and subsoil of the submarine areas that extend beyond its territorial sea throughout the natural prolongation of its land territory to the outer edge of the continental margin. There are various criteria for determining the continental shelf, but in no case can it extend beyond 350 nautical miles from the baseline of a coastal state.[11]

The first attempt at the delimitation of the international boundary between modern-day Bangladesh (erstwhile East Pakistan) and Myanmar (formerly Burma) was made on 9 May 1966 with the signing of the Naaf River Boundary Agreement.[12] However, this established a border along the Naaf River delta only, which ended at the river's mouth up to the Bay of Bengal and consequently dealt with internal waters only.

After the liberation of Bangladesh, it tried to take the boundary beyond the Naaf River Agreement. Consequently, eight rounds of bilateral negotiations were held between the two parties between 1974 and 1986 to delimit the territorial waters, EEZ and continental shelf. The two sides had then signed the agreed minutes of 1974 as an outcome of the talks held in Yangon (erstwhile Rangoon) in September 1974 and Dhaka (erstwhile Dacca) in November 1974.[13] As per the 1974 agreement, both the parties agreed to delimit their territorial waters between Point No. 1 on the Naaf River to the point of intersection of the arcs of 12 nautical miles from the southern tip of the St. Martin Islands and the nearest point on the coast of the Burmese mainland.[14] In designating such a boundary, the Burmese side was assured of safe and secure passage of its vessels around St Martin Island. However, no such decisions could be reached on the delimitation of the EEZ and Continental Shelves.

The second round of negotiations between the representatives of the two countries were then held in 2008 and have been documented as the agreed minutes of 2008. However, no mutually agreeable decisions were taken and thus the talks remained inconclusive.

The dispute re-emerged after over 30 years of these talks. For Myanmar, the 1974 minutes were a conditional agreement between the two countries for immediate redressal of the issue whereas Bangladesh claims the minutes to be valid, binding and effective. It was the reemergence of this dispute that resulted in the two countries approaching the International Tribunal on the Laws of the Sea (ITLOS) for a binding settlement of the maritime boundary dispute between them.

Bringing the Case before the International Tribunal for the Law of the Sea

It was on 8 October 2009, that the Government of Bangladesh initiated arbitral proceedings against the Republic of the Union of Myanmar "to secure the full and satisfactory delimitation of Bangladesh's maritime boundaries with [...] Myanmar in the territorial sea, the exclusive economic zone and the continental shelf in accordance with international law". Both Myanmar and Bangladesh accepted the jurisdiction of ITLOS in the case.[15]

In its written submission, Bangladesh requested ITLOS to declare the maritime boundary between the two countries based on the settlement of 1974, which was also re-affirmed in 2008, whose geographical coordinates are given below:

No.	*Latitude*	*Longitude*
1	20° 42′ 15.8″ N	92° 22′ 07.2″ E
2	20° 40′ 00.5″ N	92° 21′ 5.2″ E
3	20° 38′ 53.5″ N	92° 22′ 39.2″ E
4	20° 37′ 23.5″ N	92° 23′ 57.2″ E
5	20° 35′ 53.5″ N	92° 25′ 04.2″ E
6	20° 33′ 40.5″ N	92° 25′ 49.2″ E
7	20° 22′ 56.6″ N	92° 24′ 24.2″ E

Bangladesh further submitted that from Point 7 onwards, the boundary between the two countries should follow a geodetic azimuth of 215 degrees to a point located at 17° 25′ 50.7″ N – 90° 15′ 49.0″ E and thereafter follow the 200-m limit drawn from Myanmar's baseline to 15° 42′ 54.1″ N – 90° 13′ 50.1″ E.[16]

Myanmar, on the other hand, submitted that the single boundary between the two nations runs between points A to G whose coordinates are specified below:

S.No	*Latitude*	*Longitude*
A	20° 42′ 15.8″ N	92° 22′ 07.2″ E
B	20° 41′ 03.4″ N	92° 20′ 12.9″ E
B1	20° 39′ 53.6″ N	92° 21′ 07.1″ E
B2	20° 38′ 09.5″ N	92° 22′ 40.6″ E
B3	20° 36′ 43.0″ N	92° 23′ 58.0″ E
B4	20° 35′ 28.4″ N	92° 24′ 54.5″ E
B5	20° 33′ 07.7″ N	92° 25′ 44.8″ E
C	20° 30′ 42.8″ N	92° 25′ 23.9″ E
D	20° 28′ 20.0″ N	92° 19′ 31.6″ E
E	20° 26′ 42.4″ N	92° 09′ 53.6″ E
F	20° 13′ 06.3″ N	92° 00′07.6″ E
G	19° 45′ 36.7″ N	91° 32′38.1″ E

It further submitted that beyond Point G, the line of demarcation should turn southwest and follow the geodetic azimuth of 231° 37′ 50.9" until the rights of a third state come into play.[17] Myanmar also questioned the validity of agreements reached in 1974 and 2008 and considered them as non-binding, as they had not been registered with the Secretary General of the United Nations and were negotiated by individuals not having the authority to do so.[18] Myanmar, while accepting the jurisdiction of ITLOS in the dispute, contended that in this particular case the Tribunal does not have the jurisdiction to delimit the continental shelf beyond 200 nm.[19] The claims of both Bangladesh and Myanmar with respect to the territorial sea are shown in Figure 1.

After having had due deliberations and analyzed the agreed minutes from 1974 and 2008, ITLOS delivered its judgement in the delimitation case between the two countries on 14 March 2012. In its judgement, the judges of the ITLOS concurred with Myanmar's view of the 1974 and 2008 agreed minutes between the delegations of Burma and Bangladesh to be only consultative and not binding or obligatory on either of the parties. Nor did they agree with Bangladesh's contention that these negotiations resulted in delimitation of maritime boundaries. Citing the verdict delivered by the International Court of Justice (ICJ) in the Territorial and Maritime Dispute between Nicaragua and Honduras, the judgement by ITLOS read that the case of border settlement is a sensitive one and cannot be settled on a presumptuous basis.[20] The tribunal expressly rejected Bangladesh's contention that the Agreed Minutes of 1974 constituted an agreement in accordance with Article 15 of the UNCLOS.[21]

Another major contention of Myanmar was that St. Martin's Island, although fully inhabited, was an isolated geographical feature, located well south of their land border, and consequently it should be considered as a special case as it was located opposite the mainland of Myanmar and not Bangladesh. It therefore contended that the island should not be granted full effect for demarcating the territorial sea, otherwise this relatively small feature would create a huge distortion vis a vis the general configuration of the coastline.[22] On the other hand Bangladesh contended that St. Martin's Island, on account of its proximity to Bangladesh, as well as due to the presence of a large population on it and a significant economic role, should be considered an integral part of Bangladesh's coastline. It therefore asserted that the island was entitled to a full territorial sea of 12 nautical miles.[23]

The tribunal in a judgment of enormous significance did not agree with Myanmar's contention with regard to demarcation of the territorial sea and gave the island full effect by allowing a territorial sea of 12 nautical miles around it. However, it accepted Myanmar's contention as far as the EEZ and continental shelf were concerned. Consequently, St. Martin's Island was not taken into account while determining the equidistance line between the two countries to delineate the EEZ and continental shelf. This decision considerably reduced the impact the island would have had on the delineation of the maritime boundary.[24]

In its judgment, the tribunal ruled that since there was no dispute between the two parties on the starting point of the delimitation line, the coordinates were retained at 20° 42′ 15.8″ N and 92° 22′ 07.2″ E. Thereafter subsequent points were delineated providing a full territorial sea limit of 12 nautical miles around St. Martin's Island. The final points of delimitation carried in the judgement are as follows:

S.No.	*Latitude*	*Longitude*
1	20° 42′ 15.8″ N	92° 22′ 07.2″ E
2	20° 40′ 45.0″ N	92°20′ 29.0″ E
3	20° 39′ 51.0″ N	92° 21′ 11.5″ E
4	20° 37′ 13.5″ N	92° 23′ 42.3″ E
5	20° 35′ 26.7″ N	92° 24′ 58.5″ E
6	20° 33′ 17.8″ N	92° 25′ 46.0″ E
7	20° 26′ 11.3″ N	92° 24′ 52.4″ E
8	20° 22′ 46.1″ N	92° 24′ 09.1″ E

The delimitation line is shown in Figure 2. The tribunal sought an assurance from Bangladesh and obtained an assurance to allow vessels from Myanmar coming from or going to the Naaf River, free and unimpeded navigation in the territorial sea of Bangladesh around St. Martin's Island.[25]

Fig. 1: Joint Submission of Maritime Boundaries for Adjudication

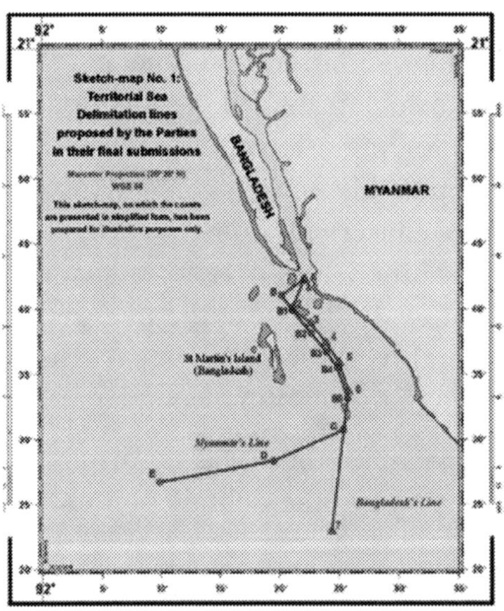

Source: Judgement 2012.

Fig. 2: International Tribunal Final Delimitation of Territorial Sea

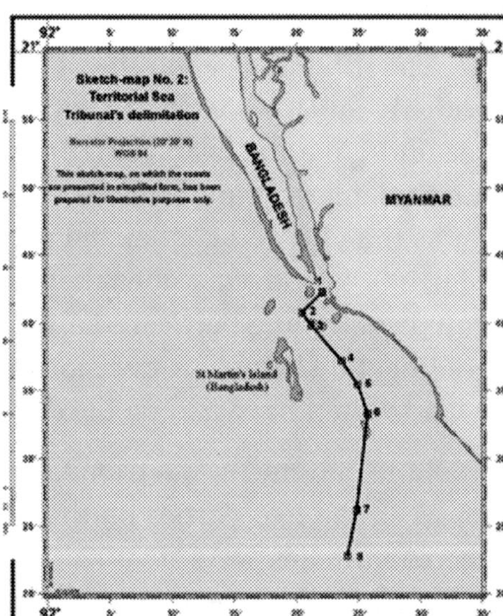

Source: Judgement 2012.

For demarcating the EEZ and Continental Shelf, while Myanmar stated the use of an equidistance line as stipulated in UNCLOS, Bangladesh contended that the equidistance model does not produce an equitable result and requested the application of the angle-bisector method for delimiting the EEZ and continental shelf between Bangladesh and Myanmar. It suggested the use of 215° azimuth line for delineating the boundary between them.[26]

The tribunal while delivering its judgement on the single-line delimitation line for EEZ and Continental Shelf between the two countries, cited Articles 74 and 82 of the UNLCOS, and stated that the principle of equidistance is the proper method to be applied to further the delimitation process. Thus, an equidistant line was first drawn between the two countries by establishing relevant base points. The tribunal rejected the proposal to use St. Martin's Island as the source of any base point, as it was located opposite the coast of Myanmar. After drawing the provisional equidistance line, the tribunal considered if there were special factors that required an adjustment in this line. While Myanmar contended that there were no relevant circumstances that required it, Bangladesh contested the non-existence of relevant circumstances advocated by Myanmar, by mentioning three peculiarities of its coast:

(a) Double concavity of Bangladesh's coast.
(b) Presence of St. Martin's Island which lies within the 5-nm boundary of Bangladesh's maritime border.
(c) Bengal Depositional System.

Based on these three peculiarities, Bangladesh maintained that equitable distribution would not be possible by using the provisional equidistance line.[27]

The tribunal, in its decision, accepted that the entire coast of Bangladesh, seen as a whole, is undoubtedly concave. It therefore felt that if the provisional equidistance line constructing it were not adjusted, it would invariably result in the cutting of Bangladesh's maritime projection. It would therefore result in a solution, which would not meet the requirements of equity, as required by Articles 74 and 83 of UNCLOS. While double concavity was factored in as relevant circumstances for adjustment, the cases of St. Martin's Island and Bengal Depositional System were turned down as being relevant circumstance in this case. Consequently, the tribunal adjusted the provisional equidistance line starting from Point X with coordinates 20° 03′ 32.0″ N, 91° 50′ 31.8″ E. The delimitation line from there follows a geodetic line along the azimuth of 215°. The final demarcation of the EEZ and Continental Shelf thus begins at 20° 26′ 39.2″ N, 92° 9′ 50.7″ E and follows a geodetic line until 20° 13′ 06.3″ N, 92° 00′ 07.6″ E (Point T1). From Point T1, the delimitation line follows a further geodetic angle up to Point 11 (X) denoted by 20° 03′ 32.0″ N, 91° 50′ 31.8″ E. From Point 11 (X) onwards a further geodetic angle of 215 degrees is formed until 200 nm from the baseline from where the breadth of the territorial sea of Bangladesh is measured.[28] The delimitation line is shown in Figure 3.

Lastly, the tribunal considered the case of the claims of the continental shelf beyond 200 nm. Myanmar contested the jurisdiction of the tribunal in ruling on the above subject but was overruled based on Articles 76 and 83 of UNCLOS which define continental shelf and have clauses for entitlement beyond 200 nautical miles. Despite both the countries contesting each other's claims of having entitlements beyond the EEZ, the tribunal continued the natural 215-degree angle prolongation of the demarcation line beyond 200 nautical miles to demarcate the continental shelf. It thereby created a grey area, which lay beyond the EEZ of

Fig. 3: Adjusted Equidistance Line

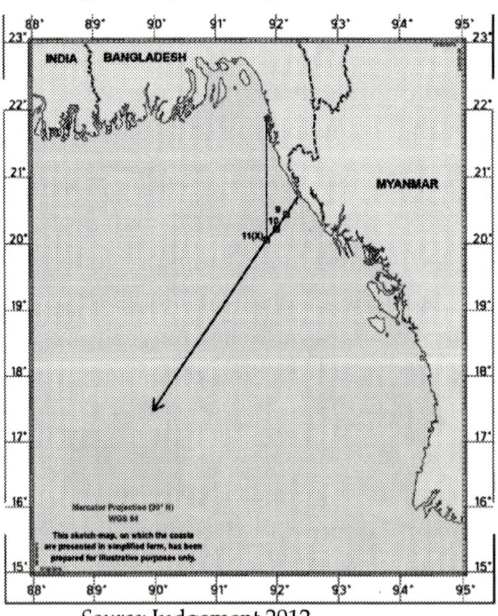

Source: Judgement 2012.

Fig. 4: Grey Area

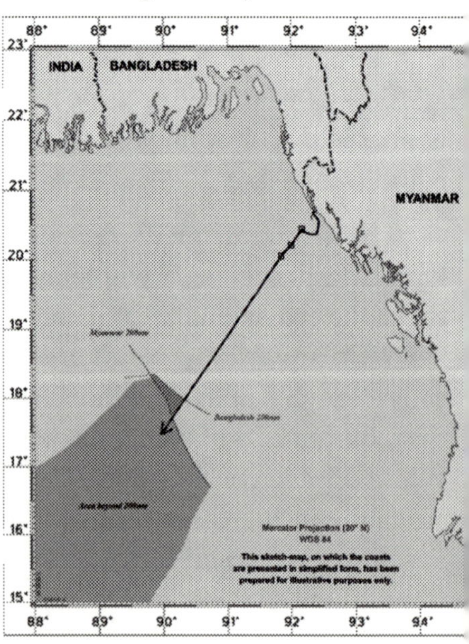

Bangladesh and within Myanmar's EEZ, but was on the Bangladesh side of the delimitation line. In this grey area, the tribunal accorded rights to Bangladesh with respect to the sea bed and subsoil of the continental shelf, without in any manner limiting Myanmar's rights with respect to the superjacent waters of its EEZ.[29] The demarcation is shown in Figure 4.

Conclusion

The judgment was a landmark judgment, as it was the first time ITLOS ruled on a maritime boundary dispute. The judgment was also significant in that it decided that it had the jurisdiction to decide not just the claims pertaining to territorial waters, but also the continental shelf. The verdict was also unique in that for the first time it created a 'grey area', where rights over the sea bed were given to Bangladesh, while Myanmar retained rights over superjacent waters. Some analysts apprehended this sort of dual jurisdiction could create problems of implementation. However, this verdict was used by the Permanent Court of Arbitration, which ruled on the India/Bangladesh boundary dispute in July 2014 and created another grey area.[30]

The judgement was widely acclaimed in Bangladesh, as it enabled it to access its full EEZ rights up to 200 nautical miles with undisputed rights of fishing and natural resources lying under its seabed. Besides, it also enabled it to claim the outer continental shelf, where it had rights over the sub-soil resources.[31] The tribunal gave full effect to St. Martin's Island in calculating the territorial sea for Bangladesh, to a full limit of 12 nautical miles around the island. Most significantly, the tribunal delimited the outer continental shelf, beyond 200 nm from the base line, again a first in the world, thereby giving Bangladesh a total area of almost 1.11 lakh square miles for sub-soil exploitation.[32]

Even in Myanmar, people were happy that their respective governments chose to resolve the dispute by peaceful means, and some praised their respective leaders for being pragmatic in making decisions and avoiding wars. The government in Myanmar not only accepted the verdict, but also stated that it would cooperate with Bangladesh on all maritime related matters in future. The fact that the demarcation was welcomed by both the countries has opened new vistas for regional cooperation.[33] In any case, ultimately, both countries had exercised the peaceful co-existence principle to find a solution.

The final judgement was accepted and adhered to by both the parties, Bangladesh and Myanmar. The 14 March 2012 ITLOS judgement is seen as a resolution that paved the way for both the littoral nations to explore and develop infrastructure necessary for the extraction of hydrocarbon gas reserves of the Bay of Bengal. The process for dispute resolution followed by the two countries exhibited an ideal example of how mature states resolve their bilateral disputes by going in for arbitration by international legal mechanisms. The sagacity shown by the two countries in resolving this vexed issue and subsequently by India and Bangladesh should be a role model as to how mature states resolve their disputes according to international law and norms. It is hoped that it becomes a template for the establishment of a 'Rule-based International Order' at sea and is replicated by other states, which have similar disputes at sea.

NOTES

1. The equidistance principle, also known as the principle of equidistance, advocates that when delimiting the maritime boundaries between two nations, the limits of an equidistance line should be adhered to.
2. The 1958 Geneva Convention defines the equidistance line as *"the line every point of which is equidistance from the nearest points of the baselines from which the breadth of the territorial sea of each of the Two States is measured."* An equidistance line is drawn to delineate the maritime boundaries between two maritime neighbours, whose maritime boundaries overlap. It is used to delimit territorial waters and secure every nation's rights in line with international treaties and regulations. The concept of equidistance line finds its mention in Article 15 of the UNCLOS with respect to the delimitation of maritime boundaries between two states.
3. Sarah Watson, "The Bangladesh/Myanmar Maritime Dispute: Lessons for Peaceful Resolution", *Asia Maritime Transparency Initiative,* 19 October 2015, available at https://amti.csis.org/the-bangladeshmyanmar-maritime-dispute-lessons-for-peaceful-resolution/ (Accessed on 21 September 2020).
4. *Imperial Gazetteer of India, Vol. IV (1908), The Indian Empire, Administrative,* Published under the authority of His Majesty's Secretary of State for India in Council, (Oxford: Clarendon Press), pp. xxx, 1 map, 552.
5. A.K.M. Ahsan Ullah, "Rohingya Refugees to Bangladesh: Historical Exclusions and Contemporary Marginalisation", *Journal of Immigrant & Refugee Studies,* Vol. 9, No. 2 (April 2011), p. 141.
6. Ibid.
7. "Territorial Sea and Contiguous Zone", available at https://www.un.org/Depts/los/convention_agreements/texts/unclos/part2.htm (Accessed on 21 September 2020).
8. Ibid.
9. Ibid.
10. "Part V Exclusive Economic Zone", available at https://www.un.org/Depts/los/convention_agreements/texts/unclos/part5.htm (Accessed on 21 September 2020).

11. "Part VI Continental Shelf", available at https://www.un.org/Depts/los/convention_agreements/texts/unclos/part6.htm (Accessed on 21 September 2020).
12. Treaties and International Agreements registered or filed and recorded with the Secretariat of the UN; Cumulative Index No. 17, available at https://treaties.un.org/doc/publication/cumulative%20index/unts%20volume%20no%201001-1050/cumindex.chrono.en.pdf
13. Reports of Judgements, Advisory Opinions and Orders, *"Dispute concerning delimitation of the maritime boundary between Bangladesh and Myanmar in the Bay of Bengal"*; Judgement of 14 March 2012; International Tribunal for the Law of the Sea, p. 21.
14. Agreed Minutes between the Bangladesh Delegation and the Burmese Delegation regarding the delimitation of the Maritime Boundary between the two countries as recorded in Reports of Judgements, Advisory Opinions and Orders, *"Dispute concerning delimitation of the maritime boundary between Bangladesh and Myanmar in the Bay of Bengal"*; Judgement of 14 March 2012; International Tribunal for the Law of the Sea, p, 24,
15. Reports of Judgements, Advisory Opinions and Orders, *"Dispute concerning delimitation of the maritime boundary between Bangladesh and Myanmar in the Bay of Bengal"*; Judgement of 14 March 2012; International Tribunal for the Law of the Sea, (ITLOS Case No. 16 - Bangladesh/Myanmar), pp. 9-10.
16. Ibid., pp. 16-17.
17. Ibid., p. 17.
18. Ibid., pp. 32-35.
19. Ibid., pp. 22-23.
20. Ibid., pp. 36-45.
21. Article 15 of UNCLOS states: *"Where the coasts of two States are opposite or adjacent to each other, neither of the two States is entitled, failing agreement between them to the contrary, to extend its territorial sea beyond the median line every point of which is equidistant from the nearest points on the baselines from which the breadth of the territorial seas of each of the two States is measured. The above provision does not apply, however, where it is necessary by reason of historic title or other special circumstances to delimit the territorial seas of the two States in a way which is at variance therewith"*.
22. ITLOS Case No. 16 - Bangladesh/Myanmar, op. cit., p. 46.
23. Ibid., p. 50.
24. Sarah Watson, op. cit.
25. ITLOS Case No. 16 - Bangladesh/Myanmar, op. cit., pp. 52-58.
26. Ibid., pp. 68-70.
27. Ibid., pp. 72-87.
28. Ibid., pp. 90-101.
29. Ibid., p. 136.
30. Sarah Watson, op. cit.
31. Moin Ghani, "A 'Great Win' for Bangladesh", *Daily Star*, 27 March 2012.
32. Rezaul Karim, "Bay is ours', *Daily Star*, 15 March 2012.

14

Maritime Dispute Resolution in the Bay of Bengal:

Leading to Greater Benefits

Sreeradha Datta

The Bay of Bengal is the largest bay off the coast of Bangladesh, India, Myanmar and Sri Lanka.[1] With the exception of Bangladesh, all the littoral states have reached agreements over their bilateral maritime boundaries. Although in the early 1980s, India faced some differences with Bangladesh over its maritime boundaries, the neighbours remained preoccupied with their land border issues. The maritime boundary became a source of worry in the mid-1980s with the Bay of Bengal becoming the theatre of aggressive posturing between Bangladesh and India as well as Bangladesh and Myanmar. Subsequently, India and Myanmar resolved their maritime boundaries based on the principle of an equidistance line through a bilateral agreement on 23 December 1986 (it came into force on 14 September 1987) but left their maritime boundaries with their common neighbour, namely, Bangladesh, unresolved. Each country has been keen to stake its claim on its territorial waters trying to maximise its sphere of control. The tensions over the maritime borders had largely risen due to the un-demarcated nature of the area causing overlapping claims of all the three states over the Bay of Bengal. The funnel-like shape of the Bay of Bengal, with concave edges, complicated a clear delineation of the maritime boundary.

In July 2014, the Permanent Court of Arbitration based in Hague had awarded an area of 19,467 sq. km. to Bangladesh, which is four-fifths of the total area of 25,602 sq. km. disputed maritime boundary with India in the Bay of Bengal. The maritime boundary between the two neighbours has been clearly delineated with the Exclusive Economic Zone (EEZ) and continental shelf within and beyond 200 nautical miles. The award ruled in favour of Bangladesh's maritime boundary being extended by 118,813 sq. km. comprising 12 nm of territorial sea and an extended EEZ up to 200 nm into the high seas.[2] The ruling also acknowledged sovereign rights of Bangladesh for undersea resources in the continental shelf, which extend as far as 345 nm in the high seas, taking the Chittagong coast as the base line. Bangladesh was naturally satisfied with the verdict, which was broadly accepted by India too resolving an old issue from festering further. Although the Tribunal's verdict was binding on all and there was no option for appeal, but any of the parties could ask for interpretation of the verdict, if it wished to do so.[3] But neither India nor Bangladesh felt the need to do so.

This chapter essentially argues that the maritime dispute resolution without any serious acts of aggression between India and Bangladesh was possible for a number of reasons. The verdict even if unexpected did not cause any further consternation and both states accepted the outcome graciously. Indeed, this was a festering issue and for long, the bilateral dialogue had not resulted in any positive direction. Thus, the Bangladesh decision to take the dispute for arbitration seemed inevitable. But the verdict that awarded greater EEZ to Bangladesh was seen as a marginal cost in the wake of the other bilateral and regional positive developments that were occurring around the same time. It needs to be remembered that the stakes involved were not large and all the three states—India, Bangladesh and Myanmar—were evenly poised and there existed no deep underlying hostility between the party states themselves. Much of this will be discussed in the second section. The first section of this chapter will briefly examine the history and causes of the hostility in the Bay of Bengal.

Brief History and Dispute

Bangladesh's disputes over territorial waters in the Bay of Bengal with both India and Myanmar were essentially over the baseline and the natural prolongation of the continental shelf. Each country was keen to stake claim on its territorial waters trying to maximise its sphere of control. The sudden escalation of activities in the Bay of Bengal by all the three states was a reflection of each claiming its stake on the rich natural resources that consists not only of fish and other marine resources but also of recently discovered hydro carbons. As per international maritime laws, a country can enjoy its right to marine resources as well as fishing and extraction of mineral resources in the exclusive economic zone, an area of up to 200 nautical miles from lawfully drawn baselines and extending seaward into an adjacent sea.

Quite clearly, the curvature coastal lines of India, Bangladesh and Myanmar lead to considerable overlapping of territory. Hence defining the maritime boundary cannot be resolved through any simple application of rules. This process would require technical expertise as well as international precedents to decipher the grey areas and arrive at mutually acceptable positions. Post UNCLOS III, the distance criterion has been established beyond past precedents. The three countries—India, Myanmar and Bangladesh—meet at a tri-junction point which gives Bangladesh 180 nm of EEZ, thus restricting its access to a Legal Continental Shelf. Given the energy deficit in the region and outside, the scramble for resources is neither unusual nor unexpected. With the discovery of energy resources in the Bay of Bengal since the late 1990s, the three littoral states sought to make the most of that opportunity. Thus, all the three states tried to stake their claim over the large and potentially rich continental shelf area.[4]

India and Bangladesh are energy deficit states, while energy export is Myanmar's largest source of foreign earnings. Thus, energy resource is a vital component for the economy of all the three states, compelling them to invest in oil exploration in the Bay of Bengal region. India's search for energy had led to the discovery of gas hydrates in the Bay of Bengal in the late 1990s.[5] During 2005-06, India discovered 100 trillion cubic feet (tcf) of gas reserves in the Bay of Bengal region.[6] Around the same time, Myanmar discovered seven tcf gas reserves, with significant gas discoveries in A1 and A3 gas fields in the Rakhaine coast in the Bay of Bengal, offshore of Myanmar's Sittwe region.[7] This area however was only 100 km from the Teknaf coast of Bangladesh. The initial discoveries had led to expectations of greater potential reserves waiting to be tapped. For its part, Bangladesh has been equally keen to explore and therefore initiate offshore oil exploration.[8] But this move was opposed by both India and Myanmar, insisting that Bangladesh's exploration moves were impinging upon their internal waters. The sudden spurt of activities by the three neighbours in their adjacent waters was to maximise their options by staking their legal claims to the resources they could exploit.[9] Thus, it became imperative to delineate bilateral maritime boundaries and settle the dispute without further exacerbation.

The disputes over the territorial waters in the Bay of Bengal amongst the three countries were mainly over the baseline and the natural prolongation of the continental shelf. With the application of the equidistance principle, Bangladesh's EEZ will be limited to less than 200 miles because these claims overlapped those of India and Myanmar. Therefore, without an amicable agreement and settlement of maritime boundaries Bangladesh would be left without a continental shelf zone.

For India, the resolution of the maritime boundary dispute between it and Bangladesh entails addressing two contentious issues—that of the baselines to demarcate maritime boundaries and delimitation of maritime boundaries including the outer limit of the overlapping extended continental shelf. The baseline needed determination that would establish the outer limits of maritime zones. This sets out the baseline of the state's internal waters. While India has applied this method to construct its baselines, Bangladesh has used the depth method, given the geographical peculiarities of the coastline in the region and the concave nature of its coast. Thus, according to Bangladesh's official position, neither the 'normal baseline' nor the 'straight baselines,' as contemplated in Articles 3 and 4 of the TS&CZ Convention fitted the 'local requirements.' Bangladesh, therefore, took the view that Article 4 needed to be amended to incorporate these basic attributes, and had proposed amendments at past sessions of UNCLOS III. The basic thrust of these amendments was to delineate the baseline by the depth-method, i.e., geographic coordinates at specific depths of the coastal waters are linked by straight lines to effectively demarcate the landward and seaward areas.[10]

Specifically, the problem surrounded the contrasting claims over what was known as New Moore in India and South Talpatty in Bangladesh. The dispute was over the ownership of this tiny island covering an area of two square miles lying in the estuary of the Haribhanga and Raimongal rivers in the Bay of Bengal. This island emerged after the Bhola cyclone of 1970 in the wake of acute volcanic activity in the area. The flow of the Haribhanga River has also been a major source of discord between India and Bangladesh, which has led to conflicting claims about the geographic proximity of the New Moore Islands to India and Bangladesh.

India's claim of it being towards the east was contested by Bangladesh. The island, which is a low tide elevation at the edge of the Sunderbans, was closer to the Indian coast at a distance of five km compared to seven km from the Bangladesh coast. According to Indian hydrographic surveys as well as satellite imagery, the navigable channels flow to the east of the island.[11] Over the years, due to land submergence, the island was visible only during low tide emerging in the estuary of the Haribhanga River, the bordering river flowing between South Pargana district in West Bengal and Satkhira district in Bangladesh, but according to a latest study, is unlikely to ever resurface.[12] Thus while at present their salience has diluted, there was a need to resolve this for future.

In May 1981, the lack of consensus led to threatening an Indian survey ship in the area by three Bangladeshi gunboats. The arrival of an Indian frigate, the INS *Andaman*, to the island prevented the conflict from further escalation. Since then India had maintained a minimal security presence on the island, although there are no permanent settlements. Arguably, the dispute over New Moore Island has more to do with the extent of the maritime zone to access the delta of the Ganga-Brahmaputra in the Bay of Bengal, which is potentially oil rich. If India was given sovereignty over the island, it could claim an additional 16,000 sq. metres of continental shelf but this would be much reduced if Bangladesh could prove its sovereignty over the island.[13]

Bangladesh and India discussed these issues for the first time in 1982 but without much success. For India, 'equidistance' is the guiding principle to determining the EEZ and not 'geography' or 'geomorphology' that Bangladesh insists on using as the criterion. Thus, based on the equidistance principle, Bangladesh stands to lose '5,000 square kilometres and a potential loss of related hydrocarbon and fish resources'.[14] India disagreed with the base point that Bangladesh had set for itself. Hence, the EEZ claims of India and Bangladesh overlap considerably; while India claims 22 oil blocks around the Islands, Bangladesh claims 14 oil blocks.[15] Bangladesh has claimed that the Indian oil blocks D-23 (8,706 square kilometres) and D-22 (7,790 square kilometres) have overlapped Bangladesh's oil block 21, declared in 1991.

In the past, India has rejected Bangladesh's suggestion for a joint survey to delimit the maritime boundary towards ensuring equitable distribution of the resources of the Bay of Bengal.[16] India believed its claims were backed by clear survey results and data generated, thus without any scope for any dispute. In the renewed round of talks, in September 2008, the two sides continued to have 'differences of opinion on the mid-flow of the Haribhanga. The technical experts used this platform to appraise each other of their positions. There has not been any definite shift in either of their positions from the 1980s. But with the impasse being broken and revival of talks, there was expectations on both sides that the next round of negotiations would help reach a consensus.

Bangladesh had feared that under the equidistant method, Myanmar could claim approximately 48,025 sq. km. of area and India 31,743 sq. kilometres from the area Bangladesh considers its own maritime zone of approximately 207,000 sq. km. Thus, Bangladesh's access to a Continental Shelf will be limited drastically.[17] Indeed, Myanmar's position was similar to that of India. It also insisted on the application of the equidistance method and maintained that the line must start on the basis of the equidistance method from the midpoint of St. Martins and Oyster Island. In the past, Bangladesh and Myanmar had drawn a 'friendship line', delimiting their bilateral maritime boundaries in 1974, which Bangladesh subsequently refused to recognise. Myanmar formally tabled a written proposal in November 1985, which was to draw a median line as the basis of the equidistant method. After 1986, Bangladesh and Myanmar resumed talks in 2008 to resolve the issue but Myanmar's insistence on the application of the equidistance line as the criterion led to an impasse. Bangladesh argued that with the application of the equidistance method, it would lose 48,025 square kilometres to Myanmar.

Bangladesh had also claimed that Myanmar had encroached 18,000 square kilometres into Bangladesh waters.

Ever since 2006, periodic hostility broke out between Bangladesh and Myanmar. However, when in 2009 Bangladesh signed a deal with international oil companies—ConocoPhillips (USA) and Tullow (Ireland)—to explore oil and gas in three offshore blocks in the Bay of Bengal, both India and Myanmar lodged strong protests. The three oil blocks that the two companies were working on overlapped with what India and Myanmar considered to be their territorial waters and hence, both decided to serve notices to the oil-exploring companies. While India protested, Myanmar took a more aggressive posture. The standoff between Myanmar and Bangladesh assumed greater intensity with the former bringing in heavy tanks, artillery guns and 12 warships along its border with Bangladesh.[18] In the meantime, on 28 December 2008, Myanmar submitted its claim to the UNCLOS for delimitation of the maritime boundary.

Specifically, according to Bangladesh, Myanmar and India have made overlapping claims on at least 18 out of Bangladesh's total 27 blocks.[19] For its part, India seemed complacent about the sound technical grounds it had juxtaposed in its arguments vis-à-vis Continental Shelf claims in accordance with UNCLOS. India believed its stand on the issue was very much in accordance with the UNCLOS regime and thus appeared to be in no hurry to discuss the problems bilaterally with Bangladesh. In September 2008, after a gap of 25 years, India and Bangladesh discussed the issue of maritime boundaries. The talks did not see any convergence. The underlying perception of a failed dialogue spurred Bangladesh to go for arbitration with India at the Adhoc Committee (Annexure VII).

Similarly, unable to come to any agreement with Myanmar on 8 October 2009, Bangladesh announced its decision to go to an arbitral tribunal of the International Tribunal for the Law of the Sea (ITLOS) to resolve its maritime boundary disputes with Myanmar.[20] Meanwhile, Bangladesh has appointed a Dutch firm at a cost of Tk 800 million ($11.77 million) to conduct a seismic survey in the Bay of Bengal to gather data before it submits its claims under Annexe VII of the UN Convention on the Law of the Sea (UNCLOS).

On 4 November 2009, however, Myanmar agreed to the jurisdiction of the International Tribunal for the Law of Sea in Hamburg, (ITLOS) towards resolving its maritime boundary dispute with Bangladesh.[21] The atmosphere was not very conducive as the talks were held against the backdrop of warship manoeuvres in the Bay of Bengal by both countries. The ITLOS ruling took the middle path. It modified the boundary that would have resulted from the equidistance approach (which sets the maritime boundary between two states by drawing a line equidistant from a series of "base points" on each state's coastline) in order to avoid cutting off Bangladesh from the outer reaches of its EEZ.[22] The resultant line was exactly in the centre of the boundaries as it was proposed by Myanmar and Bangladesh. Myanmar readily accepted the verdict and it did not allow this to come in the way of its bilateral issues with Bangladesh.

Bangladesh went to the Permanent Court of Arbitration at The Hague on 08 October 2009 seeking a judgment under the dispute clause of the UN Convention on the Law of the Sea and the submission of documents and oral hearings from both India and Bangladesh were concluded in December 2013.[23] As stated earlier, the Arbitral Tribunal which was constituted under Annex VII of the UNCLOS in the Bay of Bengal Maritime Boundary Arbitration (Bangladesh vs. India), rendered its Award on 07 July 2014 and confirmed Bangladesh's right to exploit the potentially rich waters in the Bay region. The UNCLOS gives a country 12 nautical miles of territorial control and ensures sovereign rights to explore, exploit and manage natural resources with 200 nm of EEZ.[24] While Bangladesh was happy with the extra-territorial waters it was awarded, India accepted the verdict hesitantly.

The Emergence of the Big Picture

One of the main factors that led to the verdict being accepted without any fuss was the low stakes involved and also because by the time the verdict was declared, the bilateral and regional atmospherics had changed over time. Firstly, the big picture that emerged between the neighbours weighed over the smaller issue of a maritime dispute. The dispute over the territorial waters at stake was not enormous and was unlikely to change the course of either the economic or the commercial expectations. Secondly, on the contrary, the political stakes were high, and India and Bangladesh were consolidating their bilateral ties that were also blossoming into regional engagement. More importantly, the neighbours were evenly poised. While India was a larger neighbour, the asymmetry between them was decreasing with the advances that Bangladesh had made not only in economic growth but also in several human development indices. Thirdly, for India, following the rule of order has been an article of faith and accepting an international verdict and adherence to it has never been an issue. On the contrary, going back on the letter and spirit of an agreement has not been India's preferred mode of practice in the international community and it will continue to pursue such a path. Fourthly, the cooperative regional landscape that was emerging was becoming more important to India and it hoped that the way forward would ensure greater regional collaborations. When Bangladesh decided to take the problem to the UNCLOS, the regional landscape had changed to a large extent and had led to an easier acceptance of the verdict that enabled both the powers to move ahead.

To recall briefly, the timing was critical. The Awami League coalition's win with over three-fourths majority in the 9th Jatiya Sangsad elections in December 2008 was extraordinary. After two years of an interregnum in Bangladesh, the domestic atmosphere changed dramatically. India too joined in with the celebrations and shared the dreams of close bilateral engagement. With an Awami League government in Dhaka, the future for Bangladesh held reasonable prospects and Sheikh Hasina's visit to India opened up the panorama of cooperation. The two friends had taken a leap of faith with this visit and the framework of cooperation was signed in 2010.

For India, not only was it a return of stability and a new phase of establishing a positive bilateral relation with Bangladesh, but New Delhi and Dhaka were also preparing to work on convergences and work out its divergences. Without a doubt, the big picture that had emerged for the two neighbours was important. It was a matured understanding of the ground reality that led India to put the verdict behind and work on the window of limitless opportunity that India and Bangladesh were hoping to create. The big picture of needing to signal a complete break from the past and take the two neighbours on a shared road of mutual gain and prosperity was imminent. The shared success will also follow in the path of the new policies that India and Bangladesh have initiated leading to regional growth. All elements within Bangladesh also saw that the need of cooperation and 'engagement was absolutely necessary to resolve issues between states; disengagement can only compound problems' has become the new buzz for the neighbours.[25] Hence, focusing on strengthening bilateral ties became more important.

Significantly alongside these bilateral developments, India and Bangladesh were working together to develop a regional hub inherent to the regional connectivity endeavour that India and Bangladesh agreed to undertake together. The Indo-Bangladeshi Joint Communiqué of 2010 had indicated a quantum leap from their past practices. It was a dramatic shift from the erstwhile policies of either of the governments. Not only did Bangladesh overcome its past reservations by allowing India transit passage, India also reciprocated in full measure by extending the highest line of credit for any neighbour. India's attitudinal change was also visible in it agreeing to allow Bangladesh transit from Nepal and Bhutan. For years, Bangladesh had been asking for unhindered transit to Nepal and Bhutan. To recall, the tri-nation gas pipeline from Myanmar fell through on this issue too. However, in the altered reality, in the words of the Bangladeshi Foreign Minister, Dipu Moni, 'India will be allowed to use Bangladeshi territory to reach seven landlocked north-eastern Indian states through establishment of road, water and railway connectivity, and Bangladesh will also be allowed to use Indian territory to reach Nepal and Bhutan, and will have direct access to the north-eastern Indian states.' Evidently, the changed Indian mindset 'displayed an awareness of its disproportionately greater responsibility as the regional pre-eminent power, according 'sovereign equality' to a less powerful neighbour, creating a new paradigm for intra-state relations in South Asia'.[26]

Thus, the renewed bilateral ties led to the scope for regional connectivity in South Asia. Improving regional ties became a distinct possibility and in recognition of the future possibilities, several multilateral institutions also agreed to lend their support to such endeavours. According to some estimates, the ADB had promised a support for $ 23 million for a sub-regional transport project preparatory facility in 2010, $ 120 million for regional transport connectivity in 2012,

$ 335 million for regional power generation and transmission in 2013 and $ 275 million for transport corridors in 2011 and 2013.[27] India and Bangladesh believed that the 'positive impact' of regional connectivity should be felt wider, beyond the borders of the two protagonists, India and Bangladesh. Nepal and Bhutan should also benefit from the result, gaining access to two Bangladeshi ports, and from better facilitation of intramural sub-regional trade among India, Bangladesh, Nepal and Bhutan.[28] Similarly, the electricity grid could also be extended to a regional grid, another issue that India had been reluctant to examine for years. The bilateral power grid through which India and Bangladesh began to trade energy is poised to grow into a regional grid and South Asian neighbours will now be able to share each other's energy potentials as never witnessed before. Bangladesh will thus transform itself into a transportation hub and realise its full potential as a regional hub very soon. With New Delhi responding to Dhaka's gestures, a new chapter in relations between two nations that share so much culture, language and history has begun.[29] India and Bangladesh would have shown their South Asian neighbours how to change the rules of business. It was hoped that the triumph of economics over political rhetoric not only between India and Bangladesh but also in the entire regional neighbourhood would take place. India was not going to derail any of these outcomes by squabbling over the maritime demarcation that may not have been as per Indian expectations.

Also, India was keen on reviving the Bay of Bengal initiative for Multi-Sectoral Technical and Economic Cooperation (BIMSTEC) that played an equally important role for India to focus on the positives and unhesitatingly adhere to the UNCLOS verdict. The BIMSTEC comprising seven member-states has seen a new spurt in activities in recent years. The Bay of Bengal directly touches the three littoral South Asian states of India, Bangladesh and Sri Lanka, while land-locked Nepal and Bhutan access the Bay through these South Asian states. Two South East Asian states, Myanmar and Thailand, together form a natural cluster at the Bay and have the semblance of a regional organisation. For India, making regionalism work in its own backyard was increasingly becoming a necessary imperative. Arguably, bilateral ties form the most important cornerstone for any nation state's diplomacy and India is no different. However, in contemporary international relations processes, multilateralism and regionalism have also been pursued for greater development, growth and integration amongst the comity of nations.

India's bilateral journey in the South Asian region had seen limited success and its sphere of influence remained heavily restricted, with serious and outstanding issues with some of its neighbours remaining unresolved. While it is increasingly being courted by extra-regional powers, it was hoping that with the new resurgence of regional ties, India would be able to engage more closely with its immediate neighbours. To address this, PM Narendra Modi unveiled a strong developmental plan consisting of building a network of roads and highways, organising investment fairs, encouraging tourism, establishing institutions of higher education and harnessing energy potential, but most importantly, establishing a connectivity to not only mainland India but also with its immediate neighbours in the East. A functional BIMSTEC organisation will not only be the precursor to establishing trade and connectivity and creating cross-border value chains with member-states but will also generate an economic momentum that will vitalise the land and sea route connections to mainland India. Bangladesh and Myanmar, two of India's eastern neighbours, are critical in making BIMSTEC operational. The bilateral cross-border connectivity and transport corridors India is developing with them will be woven into a regional transportation and connectivity network complementing many of the other BIMSTEC agendas.

Conclusion

Thus, while the world grapples with issues of boundary demarcation, both land and maritime, the surrounding context of the problem needs to be factored in. The dispute is often a reflection of the larger reality (read problem) that exists between states. The issue of boundary demarcation should be seen through the larger security prism the states view each other and not as an isolated instance of dispute. It needs to be understood within the broader context of bilateral and regional positions. Often muscle flexing over boundary issues is more a reflection of the nationalist narrative the state wishes to propound and less about the piece of land and a few stretches of water that it will give away or take over. Once the symbolism of strength and power play is taken away from the table, negotiations and adjustments are often easier to arrive at and provide a far greater enabling environment than anything a few swatches of land or water actually offer. For India, resolving its land borders and maritime delimitations with Bangladesh was critical to its bilateral partnership and the perceived negative outcome seemed to fade away in the face of a larger plan that the neighbours had for each other. Undoubtedly, the stakes in the maritime boundary demarcation were low and would not greatly affect any of the states involved but also more importantly the positive atmospherics made it possible to go beyond the verdict. The transformation of the bilateral political understanding has offered a level playing field that India and Bangladesh wished to capitalise on. The big picture of neighbourliness and peaceful cooperation emerged as a stronger development to rally around, and hopefully in South Asia, a cooperative framework will emerge as a stronger commitment over smaller individual gains. But for that political maturity, commitment to the rule of order and fair play is an underlying precondition.

NOTES

1. Bay of Bengal possesses a maximum depth of 4,700 metres, which is adequate for offshore oil gas exploration that are generally carried out up to a depth of about 2,000 metres.
2. Permanent Court of Arbitration, "Bay of Bengal Maritime Boundary Arbitration between Bangladesh and India (Bangladesh vs. India)", 08 July 2014, available at https://pca-cpa.org/en/news/bay-of-bengal-maritime-boundary-arbitration-between-bangladesh-and-india-bangladesh-v-india/
3. Haroon Habib, "Bangladesh Wins Maritime Dispute with India," *The Hindu*, 09 July 2014, available at https://www.thehindu.com/news/national/bangladesh-wins-maritime-dispute-with-india/article6191797.ece
4. Sreeradha Datta, "Bangladesh's Extended Continental Shelf: Navigating the Course with India and Myanmar", *Strategic Analysis*, Vol. 34, No. 5 (September 2010), pp. 728–743.
5. Successful seismic operations on India's east coast had led to oil and gas companies rushing to acquire exploration and drilling rights. Internationally renowned hydrate expert Yuri Makogon to review the seismic data collected by the Dehra Dun-based K.D. Malaviya Institute of Petroleum Exploration. Apparently, in a secret report, Makogon confirmed the presence of unparalleled gas hydrate deposits in the Andamans. Interestingly, not only is the area under contention between regional states but also intra has been a cause of vying to get a chunk of the resources. The West Bengal government has been reportedly sending feelers to the Government of India, suggesting the state should be given a 20 to 25 per cent share of the profits from exploration off the Bengal coast. Shantanu Guha Ray, 'Bay of Good Hope, Fresh findings off the east coast has world oil, majors excited', *Outlook*, 23 August 1999,

available at www.outlookindia.com/article.aspx?207956 (Accessed on 10 September, 1999).

6. India, Country Analysis, 'US Energy Information Administration March 2009' at March 2009, available at http://www.eia.doe.gov/emeu/cabs/India/NaturalGas.html (Accessed on 10 September, 2009).
7. "The new find in Block A-1 off Myanmar's Rakhine state contains a world-class commercial-scale gas deposit," *People Daily*, 13 December, 2006, available at http://english.peopledaily.com.cn/200612/13/eng20061213_332020.html (Accessed on 10 April 2009).
8. Bangladesh had allotted a few of its offshore blocks to multinationals ConocoPhillips and Tullow for oil exploration
9. India and Myanmar raised objections claiming that some of the Bangladesh areas in a number of blocks, including the three blocks that were awarded to ConocoPhillips and Tullow, had overlapped their territories, Early in November 2008, South Korea's Daewoo International Corp. for Myanmar started offshore oil and gas exploration activities in the disputed waters of the Bay of Bengal.
10. Rahul Roy-Chaudhury, "Trends in the Delimitation of India's Maritime Boundaries", *Strategic Analysis*, Vol. 22, No. 10 (January 1999), available at http://www.ciaonet.org/olj/sa/sa_ 99ror01.html (Accessed on 10 April 2009).
11. K.R. Srinivasan, "India's Maritime Boundaries," *USI Journal*, Vol. CXXXVII, (569) (July-September, 2007), pp. 329-339, available at www.usiofindia.org/article_Jul_Sep07_3.htm (Accessed on 10 April 2009).
12. According to the latest studies by Jadavpur University geologists the global warning has caused this island to submerge and it is unlikely to resurface ever again. For details, read Mark Magnier, 'Sunk by global warming? Wave goodbye to this disputed island,' *Los Angeles Times*, 25 March 2010, available at latimes.com/news/nationworld/world/la-fg-disappearing-island25-2010mar25,0,3895432.story
13. Note 7, ibid.
14. B.G. Verghese, "New Opening in Dhaka", *New Indian Express*, 22 January 2009, available at http://www.expressbuzz.com/edition/story.aspx?title=New+ opening+ in+ Dhaka&artid=4QxBHNuCzHc= (Accessed on 18 February 2009).
15. India's EEZ of 2.02 million sq. km.
16. Haroon Habib, "India-Bangladesh maritime boundary talks inconclusive", *The Hindu*, 19 September 2008, available at http://www.hindu.com/2008/09/19/stories/2008091956481400.htm, (Accessed on 20 January 2009).
17. Abu Syed Muhammad Belal, "Maritime Boundary of Bangladesh: Is Our Sea Lost?", *BIPPSS Focus*, available at http://bipss.org.bd/download/mb_bd.pdf (Accessed on 13 January 2010).
18. M. Abul Kalam Azad and Ahmede Hussain, "Myanmar brings in everything Troops, tanks, warships, frigate to spread tension further; Dhaka terms it routine exercise", *The Daily Star*, 12 October 2009, available at www.thedailystar.net/story.php?nid =109365 (Accessed on 10 April 2009).
19. This is possible if UNCLOS is applied with supporting national legislation on baselines.
20. "Bangladesh and Myanmar give ITLOS its first maritime boundary case", *Boundary News, Durham University*, 21 December 2009, available at http://www.dur.ac.uk/ibru/news/boundary_news/?itemno=9202&rehref=%2Fibru%2F&resubj= Boundary+ news%
21. ITLOS, "Proceedings instituted in the dispute concerning the maritime boundary

between Bangladesh and Myanmar in the Bay of Bengal," *Press Release* 140, 16 December 2009.

22. Sarah Watson, "The Bangladesh/Myanmar maritime dispute: Lessons for Peaceful Resolutions", *Asia maritime transparency Initiative,* 19 October 2015, available at https://amti.csis.org/the-bangladeshmyanmar-maritime-dispute-lessons-for-peaceful-resolution/
23. Harun ur Rashid, "India-Bangladesh: UNCLOS and the Sea Boundary Dispute", *IPCS 4557,* 14 July 2014, available at http://www.ipcs.org/comm_select.php?articleNo=4557
24. Noami Burke, Annex VII Arbitral Tribunal Delimits Maritime Boundary Between Bangladesh and India in the Bay of Bengal, Vol. 18, No. 20, 22 September 2014, available at https://www.asil.org/insights/volume/18/issue/20/annex-vii-arbitral-tribunal-delimits-maritime-boundary-between
25. Mashihur Rahman, "Agreement with India: Context and consideration", *Financial Express,* 26 February 2010.
26. Iftekhar Ahmed Chowdhury, "Hasina's Visit to India and Emerging Indo-Bangla Relations: Implications for the Region", *ISAS Brief No. 149,* 18 January 2010.
27. Syed Rezaul Karim, "Connectivity the key", *The Daily Star,* 29 May 2010.
28. Iftekhar Ahmed Chowdhury, "Hasina's Visit to India and Emerging Indo-Bangla Relations: Implications for the Region," *ISAS Brief No. 149,* 18 January 2010.
29. Philip Bowring, "India's opening with Bangladesh," *New York Times,* 12 January 2010.

Imbroglio in South China Sea: Problems of Non-compliance with UNCLOS

15

Maritime Confidence-Building Measures and the Code of Conduct at Sea

Yurika Ishii

Introduction

Maritime confidence-building measures (MCBMs) have emerged as an important means to overcoming stalemates relating to maritime disputes. A key issue in the negotiation and establishment of MCBMs is the balance between the freedom of the use of the sea and maritime safety. This article assesses state practices regarding MCBMs, with a particular focus on the code of conduct at sea.

The adoption of a legally binding code of conduct for the South China Sea has been long sought since the adoption of the Declaration on the Conduct in 2002[1] with little result. A code of conduct does not seem to be an effective solution for the South China Sea situation because of the two reasons. First, there are a number of overlapping areas, which include not only un-delimited maritime areas but also areas surrounding disputed features, and the rights and obligations of states in a disputed maritime area are a contentious theme to date. Therefore, states are not able to agree on what to shelve when they decide to refrain from certain conduct. Second, unexpected encounters between government vessels in this region often involve a private third party such as one or more fishery vessels. Precedents such as the code of conduct built during the

Cold War era differ in this respect as they dealt with government-to-government situations. Furthermore, there is an argument that such non-binding instruments are unlikely to enhance navigational safety or security and, in some respects, may even undermine them.[2]

This chapter examines whether such claims are fair and appropriate by analysing the relationship between international law and confidence-building measures concerning the safety of navigation.

The first part of this paper clarifies the concepts and content of a code of conduct, focusing upon its relationship with international law. The second part analyses relevant state practices. The analysis will be limited to a situation where military or government ships or aircraft confront each other beyond territorial sea and air. The scope of the study does not include a situation within a territory or a situation involving armed conflict.

I. THE CODE OF CONDUCT AND INTERNATIONAL LAW

Maritime Confidence Building Measures

The paper begins with an examination of MCBMs, which are a sub-category of confidence-building measures (CBMs). CBMs are defined as measures which address, prevent, or resolve uncertainties among states in order to prevent escalation of hostilities and to build mutual trust.[3] In general, a CBM consists of declaratory measures (demonstrating that a state does not have hostile intent), transparency measures (increasing the transparency and accountability of conduct), and constraint measures (limiting activities in order not to provoke an unintended consequence.[4] It encompasses various measures, including prohibition of dangerous or provocative activities, prior notification of missile experiments or military exercises, exchange of information, and strengthening of education or mutual understanding of domestic laws. It could be formal or informal, unilateral, bilateral, or multilateral and state-to-state or non-governmental.[5]

The origin of CBMs goes back to the 1970s in Europe, where the West tried to reconcile with the Union of Soviet Socialist Republics (USSR).[6] In that process, both sides have agreed on several CBMs to set aside conflict behind the scenes and to manage crises. In the long run, it is expected that states resolve conflicts themselves through the CBM process.

An MCBM is part of a crisis management mechanism when navies confront each other at sea. An MCBM, in a narrow sense, is a measure to prevent misunderstanding, miscalculation, or misperception between militaries or law enforcement agencies at sea. It includes measures to restrain the conduct of various parties, for example regulation of dangerous manoeuvres or prohibition of harassment or provocative actions at sea; to increase communication among states; and to maintain regular consultation and exchange of information between navies. In a broader sense, it includes search and rescue operations or cooperation in maritime management for marine protection.

Codes of Conduct at Sea

A code of conduct, which is part of an MCBM, is a set of rules which regulate the behaviour of naval vessels, government ships, and military and government aircraft at sea. The main content of a code of conduct include (1) an obligation to refrain from undertaking certain actions, such as a manoeuvre in certain areas or law enforcement action; (2) an obligation of due diligence when the state undertakes certain actions, such as an obligation to maintain a safe speed or distance; and (3) an obligation to communicate, such as the contact between vessels or the exchange of information between pertinent authorities. An analysis of state practices reveals that there is a tendency for states to choose to limit the scope of a code of conduct to an obligation of due diligence, particularly when the agreement covers a disputed maritime area.

Most existing codes of conduct are non-binding. The instrument is adopted to visualise possible options and enhance the foreseeability of the opponent party in the case of an unplanned encounter. In other words, while a non-binding code of conduct is not recognised as a source of law, it is recognised as an operational norm and is expected to function as a crisis management mechanism.

Legal Obligations to Maintain Maritime Safety

It should be noted that the obligation to maintain maritime safety is a legal one. The United Nations Convention on the Law of the Sea

(UNCLOS) obliges states to take such measures for ships flying their flag to ensure safety at sea in general terms.[7] In addition, the International Regulations for Preventing Collisions at Sea (COLREG) are the "rules of the road" at sea; they set out navigation rules in order to prevent collisions between vessels.[8] This instrument applies to "all vessels," including naval vessels, and in "all waters" connected with the high seas and navigable by seagoing vessels. These waters include territorial sea and internal waters. A general reading of the Convention may lead to an interpretation that it does not directly apply to military activities such as manoeuvres, simulated attacks, and military exercises as well as law enforcement activities within jurisdictional waters.

The South China Sea Arbitration Award of 2016 held that law enforcement activities conducted in a dangerous manner violate both UNCLOS and COLREG. In the Award, the Tribunal considered the lawfulness of the conduct of Chinese law enforcement vessels at Scarborough Shoal, when Chinese vessels had sought to physically obstruct Philippine vessels from approaching or gaining entrance to the Shoal. China argued in general terms that such action was based on its authority, stating that the waters surrounding the Shoal were within its sovereignty. The Tribunal decided that the Shoal had a legal status of "rock" which may possess territorial sea up to 12 miles but does not generate an exclusive economic zone (EEZ).

The Philippines claimed that Chinese law enforcement vessels had repeatedly approached Philippine vessels at high speed and sought to cross ahead of them at close distances, creating serious risk of collision and danger to the Philippine ships and personnel.[9] It submitted that COLREG are "generally accepted international regulations," which a flag state is obliged to ensure the implementation of under Articles 94(3) and (5) of UNCLOS,[10] citing the statement of the International Maritime Organization (IMO) that COLREG fulfilled the requirement of general acceptance.[11] The experts' report stated that the Chinese vessels "internationally endangered another vessel through high speed 'blocking' or harassment manoeuvres" and that the vessels showed "a flagrant disregard of the tenets of good seamanship."[12]

The Tribunal concluded that China had breached its obligations under both COLREG and UNCLOS. First, it determined that Article 94 of UNCLOS incorporates COLREG into the duties of a flag state by reference so that the latter binds a state even when it is not a party to the instrument.[13] Then, having determined that the conduct of China's law enforcement vessels was in "total disregard of good seamanship and neglect of any precaution,"[14] it held that these actions breached Rule 2(a). It stated that where the operational requirements of law enforcement ships stand in tension with COLREG, the latter must prevail.[15] In addition, the Tribunal held that the safe distance requirement (COLREG Rule 6) and the safe speed requirement (ibid., Rule 8) applies in the context of law enforcement, while recognising the fulfilment of these conditions should be done on a context-dependent basis.[16] It also concluded that rules relating to right-of-way (ibid., Rules 15 and 16) applied in the area of law enforcement.[17]

This decision did not prohibit states from conducting abordage or self-ramming. It required "precaution" to avoid causing any damage which is beyond reasonableness and necessity. However, it is fair to say that the Tribunal prescribed a high standard for state parties to comply with. It required compliance with due diligence obligations such as safe speed and distance and with rules relating to right-of-way, even in the context of law enforcement, as a matter of international law.

The South China Sea Arbitration Award is significant as it held that such activities are regulated under the general clause of UNCLOS as well as the technical clauses of COLREG. However, previously, a code of conduct was regarded as necessary in order to "supplement" general international law. It was difficult to proclaim that UNCLOS or customary international law prohibited conduct such a manoeuvre made in proximity to another party's military, harassment, or provocative actions, whether done on the high seas, in an exclusive economic zone (EEZ), or in a disputed area or whether in the air beyond a state's territorial area. One has to take into account a balance between the safety of navigation and the legitimate exercise of the rights of a state. When one takes such an interpretation, the main purpose of the code of conduct is to "shelve" these differences in order to secure the safety of navigation. However, unlike CBMs in general, a code of conduct is a direct regulation of the use of the oceans, so that it is difficult to reach an agreement if there is significant difference in the interpretation of international law.[18] In such a case, a code of conduct serves as an important tool for crisis management as it *affirms*, rather than *supplements*, the minimum content which both parties can agree with.

Bearing this in mind, the following will conduct case studies on actual agreements on (1) incidents at sea agreements (INCSEAs) and (2) maritime law enforcement cooperation.

II. CASE STUDIES

INCSEAs

The first precedent of MCBM in the form of a code of conduct was the INCSEA concluded in 1972 between the United States (US) and the USSR.[19] The USSR signed the same type of agreement with other states from Europe,[20] Japan[21] and South Korea,[22] from the end of the 1980s to the early 1990s. The USSR also concluded agreements on the prevention of dangerous military activities (DMAAs) with the US[23] and Canada,[24] among others, which focused on military activities beyond territorial sea. In the same period, West Germany and Poland concluded the same type of agreement with each other.[25]

One of the characteristics of these INCSEAs is that they concretely stipulate an obligation to refrain from certain actions. The agreements provide that ships shall avoid manoeuvring in a manner which would hinder the evolution of the formations of the other party.[26] It also prohibits formations from manoeuvring through areas of heavy traffic where internationally recognised traffic separation schemes are in effect.[27] Ships engaged in surveillance of other ships shall stay at a distance which avoids the risk of collision and avoid executing manoeuvres embarrassing or endangering the ships under surveillance.[28] It also provides for the prohibition of provocation. Ships shall not simulate attacks by aiming guns, missile launchers, torpedo tubes, or other weapons in the direction of a passing ship of the other party, nor launch any object in the direction of passing ships of the other party, nor use searchlights or other powerful illumination devices to illuminate the navigation bridges of passing ships of the other party.[29]

Secondly, it provides for a detailed obligation of due regard. The 1972 INCSEA was concluded because they needed certain rules of the road, while COLREG was not adopted as a convention at that time. The agreement thus provides that, when conducting exercises with submerged submarines, exercising ships shall show the appropriate signals prescribed by the International Code of Signals (ICS) to warn ships of the presence of submarines in the area.[30] Ships of one party, when approaching ships of another party conducting operations—particularly ships engaged in launching or landing aircraft as well as ships engaged in replenishment underway—shall take appropriate measures not to hinder the manoeuvres of such ships and shall remain well clear.[31]

In the course of negotiations of INCSEA, DMAA, as well as UNCLOS, the US did not agree with the following proposals made by the USSR. First, it fiercely opposed the so-called "fixed distance formula," that vessels or aircraft have to keep a certain distance from each other.[32] Second, it did not agree with the obligation to fix the area when it conducts a military exercise beyond territorial sea. Third, it did not accept the regulation of submarines. Lastly, it did not agree with regulation of manoeuvres made in proximity of territorial sea. This negotiation process shows the tension between the freedom of navigation and the necessity to secure the safety of navigation.

The number of incidents of encounters at sea did not decrease after the conclusion of these agreements. However, the mechanism of cooperation allowed states to minimise harm when an incident occurred.[33] There are a number of studies on why the INCSEA succeeded. Winkler describes the main factors as the mutual interest of the states, simplicity, practicability, and professionalism.[34] In addition, in a larger picture, the MCBM was designed to enable the state parties to prepare for incidents, exercise discretion, and allow them to engage in verification and accountability. Cooperation between the two states was based on hospitality of both sides.[35]

INCSEA-Type Agreements

After the "success" of the US–USSR INCSEA, the following states concluded similar agreements, with some modifications. The most significant difference between the US–USSR INCSEA and these agreements was that, in the latter cases, there existed disputed areas among the state parties.

(a) Greece–Turkey INCSEA Agreement of 1988

The first was the Greece–Turkey INCSEA agreement in 1988. After a series of crises between the two states regarding use of the Aegean Sea beginning in the late 1970s, over which Greece went to the International Court of Justice (ICJ),[36] and a serious crisis which came close to the outbreak of military conflict in 1987, the parties agreed to adopt guidelines and a memorandum of understanding (MOU).

The guidelines comprehensively regulated the activities of naval units and aircraft. They provided that the naval units of the parties would refrain from acts of harassment while operating on the high seas, in accordance with international law and custom;[37] that they would act in full conformity with international law, rules, regulations, and procedures as well as *military custom and courtesy* (emphasis added);[38] and that naval units engaged in the surveillance of ships of the other party would maintain a position which would not hamper their smooth conduct.[39] By referring to military custom and courtesy, the agreement prohibited activities which were against good seamanship, which is a broader notion than the one provided in international law. Similarly, it provided that air force units conducting military activities in international airspace would do so in full conformity with international law and international custom;[40] pilots were to display utmost caution when in proximity to aircraft of the other party and not manoeuvre or react in a manner which would be hazardous to the safety of the flight or affect the conduct of the mission of the aircraft.[41] The MOU, on the other hand, provided more concrete rules which the state parties accepted. It stated that the planning and conduct of national military exercises on the high seas or in international airspace which required the promulgation of a notice to airmen (NOTAM) or any other notification or warning should be carried out in such a way as to avoid, to the maximum extent possible, the following: the isolation of certain areas; the blocking of exercise areas for long periods; and their conduct during the tourist peak period and main national and religious holidays.[42] They agreed on the same sort of understanding as to the use of airspace in September 1988.[43] However, the process came to wither by the end of 1989 and did not prevent the crisis in 1995–1996 between the two parties.[44]

(b) India–Pakistan Agreement of 1991

The second case is an agreement between India and Pakistan in 1991.[45] It was not an INCSEA agreement *per se* but contained a provision which regulated the activities of the state parties against a background in which collisions between the two states had increased, in the 1980s. The two states tried to conclude an INCSEA in 1991, but the attempt was in vain.[46] However, as illustrated below, this agreement regulated the conduct of the state parties in order to avoid collisions.

It provided that land, naval, and air forces had to avoid holding major military manoeuvres and exercises in close proximity to each other.[47] However, if such exercises were held at distances as prescribed in the agreement, the strategic direction of the main force being exercised was not to be towards the other side, nor were any logistics to be built up and carried out close to it.

For naval forces, any exercise involving six or more ships of destroyer or frigate size or above exercising in company and crossing into the other's EEZ was provided to be regulated. It also provides that a schedule of major exercises with troops will be transmitted in writing to the other side through diplomatic channels in advance.[48] The agreement also provided that aircraft of either country would refrain from buzzing surface units and platforms of the other country in international waters so as to prohibit harassment in such waters.[49] Interestingly, it provided that combat aircraft, including fighters, bombers, reconnaissance, jet military trainers, and armed helicopters would not fly within 10 kilometres of each other's airspace, including air defence identification zones, with certain exceptions.[50]

In 1998, the relations of the two countries worsened, after they conducted nuclear weapons testing. In 1999, the ministers of foreign affairs adopted the Lahore Declaration for peacekeeping. On that occasion, they also signed an MOU which promised conclusion of an agreement on the prevention of incidents at sea in order to ensure safety of navigation by naval vessels and aircraft.[51] The agreement was never implemented, although they continued a track-two effort to promote CBMs in the region.[52]

(c) Indonesia–Malaysia MALINDO Guideline of 2001

The third case is the so-called MALINDO Guideline concluded between the defence authorities of Indonesia and Malaysia in 2001. It was a guideline which naval forces were to follow in case of unplanned encounters at sea.

This guideline basically followed the line of the INCSEAs. However, there were some differences in wording. One of the characteristics of this agreement was that it applied to "all maritime regimes relevant to UNCLOS of 1982 including disputed maritime territories." It is the only example which specifically mentions the inclusion of disputed areas.

It provided that ships of one party engaged in surveillance of ships of the other party should avoid executing embarrassing manoeuvres or endanger ships under surveillance.[53] Except when required to maintain course and speed under COLREG 1972, surveillance was to take early positive action so that, in the exercise of good seamanship, it would not embarrass or endanger ships under surveillance.[54] As for aircraft, it provided that captains of aircraft of the parties should exercise the greatest caution and prudence when approaching aircraft and ships of the other party, in particular ships engaged in launching or recovering aircraft.[55] In addition, it provided that simulated attacks, the performance of aerobatics over ships of the other party, the launching of any objects in the direction of ships of the other party, and deliberate jamming of any electronic equipment of ships or aircraft of the other party were not permitted.[56]

The inclusion of the disputed maritime area and the specification of the prohibited activities were signs of a successful MCBM. However, in practice, this guideline did not prevent disputes over maritime areas, nor was it referred to by the navies or law enforcement officers.

The two states resolved the territorial dispute over Ligitan and Sipadan, in which the ICJ held the territorial title for Malaysia in 2002.[57] Indonesia conceded the territorial title, redrawing its baseline. However, conflicts in other areas remained. In particular, the Ambalat boundary dispute in the western Sulawesi Sea had been causing disturbance in the relations of the two states.[58] Indonesia had already given licence to Ente Nazionale Idrocarburi (ENI) in 1999 and to UNOCAL Corporation in 2004 to exploit the overlapping area. In 2005, there was a serious confrontation between the two navies in the same area, when Malaysia granted oil exploration rights to Shell Oil Company and to its national oil company, Petronas.[59] The MALINDO Guideline was of no use in preventing these disputes.

(d) Arms Control and Regional Security in the Middle East Working Group Guideline of 1995

The last case is the guideline adopted by the Arms Control and Regional Security in the Middle East (ACRS) Working Group,[60] which is not available in the public domain. Nonetheless, the writings of David Griffiths and Peter Jones, who were involved in drafting the code, describe the content of the instrument in detail.[61] The background is that the ACRS Working Group was established in October 1991 as part of the peace process. An MCBM was chosen as one of the agendas. Since the 1970s, there had been several maritime incidents in the Red Sea and the Persian Gulf – partly because there existed a disputed area between Israel and Egypt while the former occupied the Sinai Peninsula, and partly because the navies were not experienced in naval operations. Beginning in May 1992, with the lead of the US, Russia, and later Canada, negotiations were undertaken in order to adopt a search and rescue agreement (SAR) and INCSEA. The important point is that they relied on the US–USSR INCSEA as a basic framework, although it was a multilateral agreement, and a disputed area among the states existed. While they discussed whether they should maintain the fixed distance formula or the application of the rule to submarines, they followed the INCSEA model, recognising the importance of the freedom of navigation. Due to complications in the peace process, the agreed measures have not been implemented, and ACRS has not held a formal plenary meeting since September 1995.[62]

CUES/MMCA

The 2000s saw an increase in the number of agreements, which mainly provide obligations of due diligence. The Codes for Unplanned Encounters at Sea (CUES),[63] adopted at the Western Pacific Naval Symposium in 2014, is considered a landmark instrument as it enjoys a wide range of participation, including that of China.[64] However, the content of CUES largely overlaps existing legal instruments, most importantly COLREG. The state parties tried to incorporate the obligation to avoid manoeuvres on certain occasions. However, such a proposal was rejected, and instead they inserted the safe speed and safe distance requirements. It is legally non-binding, and it frequently uses "should" or "may," which are themselves weak wordings.

The other example is the MOU concluded between China and the US regarding the Rules of Behaviour for Safety of Air and Maritime Encounters.[65] As described above, a Military Maritime Consultative Agreement (MMCA) was adopted in 1998, in which the two states agreed to hold annual meetings although it did not provide any obligation at sea. Furthermore, MOUs of 2014 and 2015 were derived, though in a different context, from the MMCA.[66] The characteristic of this US–China MOU is that it heavily cites existing legal instruments, in particular COLREG and CUES. There is nothing new besides confirmation of the political will of the two states to engage in cooperation.

Maritime Law Enforcement Cooperation

(a) Indonesia–Malaysia Agreement of 2012

An interesting trend in MCBMs is that states come to conclude a maritime law enforcement cooperation agreement. The first case was between Indonesia and Malaysia. There were frequent occasions of fishermen being captured or chased away by patrols when fishing near border areas.[67] The captures usually took place in a border area claimed by both countries, usually referred to as overlapping area.[68] No agreed maritime boundaries are in place, and border crossing is usually unilaterally justified.[69] After negotiations through a Joint Commission for Bilateral Cooperation (JCBC) between Indonesia and Malaysia, the two states reached an agreement in 2012 with regard to law enforcement cooperation.[70]

The agreement applies to all unresolved maritime boundary areas of the parties.[71] It is specifically mentioned that any action or omission undertaken pursuant to the provision of this MOU are without prejudice to the issues concerning maritime delimitation.[72] It is also provided that every action and manoeuvre undertaken by maritime law enforcement agencies should avoid any violence and be carried out without the use of force.[73] The parties agreed on the following points. First, an inspection request to leave the area shall be conducted promptly for all fishing boats except for those using illegal fishing gear such as explosives or electrical or chemical fishing gear.[74] Second, notification of the inspection and request to leave the area shall be reported promptly to Focal Points, which were designated in both sides under the MOU.[75] Third, they agreed to conduct open and direct communication among the maritime law enforcement agencies of the parties promptly and expeditiously.[76] In addition, the parties agreed that any difference or dispute between the parties concerning the interpretation, implementation, or application of a provision in the MOU shall be settled amicably through mutual consultation or negotiations between the parties through diplomatic channels, without reference to any third party or international tribunal.[77] By preserving the national interests of each side, the two states succeeded in reaching a practical framework for maritime security.

(b) Taiwan–Philippines Agreement of 2015

Taiwan and the Philippines followed this practice after their clashes in 2013 and 2015. In 2013, the Philippines Coast Guard (PCG) shot at a Taiwanese fishery vessel, *Guang Da Xing No. 28*, causing the death of one Taiwanese fisherman.[78] The Philippines claimed that the area was within its EEZ,[79] and Taiwan claimed that it was within the un-delimited EEZ between the two states.[80] Taiwan protested that the law enforcement measurement was an excessive use of force which violated the principle of avoiding the use of force and basic procedures for the use of force, the principle of proportionality, the principle of humanity, and the duty to provide assistance in international maritime law.[81] The Philippines could not prove its case because it did not record evidence, and its president later expressed his apologies.

In 2015, PCG arrested a Taiwanese fishing vessel, *Ming Jin Cai No. 6*, which led to a standoff with the Taiwanese Coast Guard (TCG). The vessel was released after four hours of negotiations.[82] While news media in the Philippines reported that the incident occurred within Philippine territorial waters, the Taipei Economic and Cultural Office (TECO) in the Philippines claimed that the location of the incident was within the un-delimited area between the two states and protested that the PCG's action was not in conformity with international law.[83] TECO's statement highlighted the necessity of an early conclusion of an agreement concerning cooperation and law enforcement in fishery matters "that would formalise how to resolve fishing disputes, including procedures on the detention and release of any fishing vessel or fisherman, so as to prevent the occurrence of similar incidents in the future."[84]

The two parties concluded the Agreement Concerning the Facilitation of Cooperation on Law Enforcement in Fisheries Matters in 2015.[85] The agreement contains three points of consensus, namely avoiding the use of violence or unnecessary force, establishment of an emergency notification system, and establishment of a prompt release mechanism.[86] Following the signing of the agreement, the two parties convened a working group meeting, which reached a consensus on two mechanisms: a one-hour advance notification to the other party and prompt release of detained vessels and crew (within three days). It was announced that the two parties would avoid the use of violence and unnecessary force when enforcing the law. Before taking law enforcement action against a fishing vessel from the other party, which is believed to be operating illegally in the overlapping EEZ, a one-hour advance notification will be given to the fisheries and coast guard agencies as well as the representative office of the other party. If the fishing vessel is found to have violated the law and subsequently detained, it will be released within three days after posting reasonable bond, other security, or payment consistent with the law of the arresting party.

These are important mechanisms which allow cooperation between authorities of the state parties in un-delimited maritime areas.

Conclusion

The findings of this study show that states do not establish any obligation through MCBMs even if they are non-binding. Instead, they tend to *confirm* existing rules through such agreements. When the interpretation of a rule is contentious, they typically do not reach to an instrument. Therefore, it is this author's opinion that a code of conduct would not harm the significance of the existing law of the sea. In the meanwhile, international law with regard to safety at sea is evolving, and the obligation of safe conduct at sea is now a positive rule. This development has important implications for maritime safety and security at sea.

NOTES

1. 2002 Declaration on the Conduct of Parties in the South China Sea, adopted by the Foreign Ministers of ASEAN and the People's Republic of China at the eighth ASEAN Summit in Phnom Penh, Cambodia, 04 November 2002.
2. Raul Pedrozo, 'US-China Incidents at Sea Agreement: A Recipe for Disaster' (2012) 6 *Journal of National Security Law and Policy* 207; James Kraska, 'Maritime Confidence-Building Measures for Navigation in the South China Sea' (2017) 32 *The International Journal of Marine and Coastal Law* 1.
3. United Nations Office for Disarmament Affairs, "Military Confidence-building", available at https://www.un.org/disarmament/cbms/
4. Susan Pederson and Stanley Weeks, 'A Survey on Confidence Building Measures: Asia Pacific Confidence and Security Measures' in Cossa Ralph (ed), *Asia-Pacific and Security Confidence Building Measures* (1995) 1.
5. Bonny Glaser, "Confidence Building Measures," Centre for Strategic and International Studies Website, available at https://www.csis.org/programs/international-security-program/international-security-program-archived-projects/asia-4.
6. Stanley Weeks, 'Measures to Prevent Incidents at Sea' (Jozef Goldblat ed, United Nations Institute for Disarmament Research 1992) 1.
7. United Nations Convention on Law of the Sea, adopted on 10 December 1982, entered into force on 16 November 1994, 1833 U.N.T.S. 3, Article 94(3).
8. Convention on the International Regulations for Preventing Collisions at Sea, adopted on 20 October 1972, entered into force on 15 July 1977, 1050 U.N.T.S. 16.
9. PCA Case No. 2013-19, In the Matter of the South China Sea Arbitration before an Arbitral Tribunal Constituted under Annex VII to the 1982 United Nations Convention on the Law of the Sea, the Republic of the Philippines vs. the People's Republic of China, Award, 12 July 2016 [hereinafter "South China Sea Arbitration Award"], paras. 1059-1075.
10. Ibid., para. 1063.
11. Ibid. See also International Maritime Organization, Implications of the United Nations Convention on the Law of the Sea for the International Maritime Organization, Doc. LEG/MISC/3/Rev.1 (January 6, 2003), pp. 10-11.
12. South China Sea Arbitration Award, para. 1069.
13. Ibid., para. 1083.
14. Ibid., para. 1094.
15. Ibid., para. 1095.
16. Ibid., paras. 1097-1101.
17. Ibid., paras. 1102-1104.
18. One should note that unifying the interpretation of the law of the sea is one form of MCBM. A prominent example is the US-USSR Joint Statement on the Uniform Interpretation of Rules of International Law Governing Innocent Passage. US-USSR Joint Statement on the Uniform Interpretation of Rules of International Law Governing Innocent Passage, 23 September 1989, *reprinted in* 28 I.L.M. 1444.
19. 25 May 1972, 23 U.S.T. 1168.
20. United Kingdom, 15 July 1986, 1505 U.N.T.S. 89; West Germany, 25 November 1988, 1546 U.N.T.S. 203; France, 04 July 1989, 1548 U.N.T.S. 223; Canada, 20 November 1989, 1568 U.N.T.S. 11; Italy Dec. 31, 1989, 1590 U.N.T.S. 22; Spain, 10 October 1991, 1656 U.N.T.S. 429; the Netherlands, 01 October 1991, 1604 U.N.T.S. 3.

21. 12 November 1993.
22. 02 July 1994, 1832 U.N.T.S. I-31353.
23. 01 January 1990, TIAS 11454; 28 I.L.M. 877.
24. 10 May 1991, *Canada Treaty Series* 1991/26.
25. 27 December 27, 1990, 1910 U.N.T.S. 39.
26. Article III(2).
27. Article III(3).
28. Article III(4).
29. Article III(6).
30. Article III(7).
31. Article III(8).
32. Timothy J Nagle, "Dangerous Military Activities Agreement: Minimum Order and Superpower Relations on the World's Oceans" (1990) 31 *Virginia Journal of International Law* 125.
33. Tetsuo Kotani, "Crisis Management in the East China Sea", (SIPRI 2015) 3.
34. David Winkler, *Preventing Incidents at Sea: The History of the Incsea Concept* (Centre for Foreign Policy Studies, Dalhousie University, 2008), p. 1; David Frank Winkler, *Cold War at Sea: High-Seas Confrontation between the United States and the Soviet Union* (Naval Inst Press, 2000), p. 1.
35. Winkler, *Preventing Incidents at Sea: The History of the Incsea Concept*, p. 1.
36. Aegean Sea Continental Shelf (Greece vs. Turkey), Interim Protection, Order of 11 September 1976, I.C.J. Reports 1976, p. 3.
37. Guideline, para. 2.
38. Ibid.
39. Ibid.
40. Guideline, para. 3.
41. Ibid.
42. MOU, para. 3.
43. International Crisis Group, "Turkey and Greece: Time to Settle the Aegean Dispute (Europe Briefing N°64, Istanbul/Athens/Brussels, 19 July 2011)," in *Policy Briefing* (2011), p. 3.
44. Ibid.
45. Agreement on Advance Notice of Military Exercises, Manoeuvres and Troop Movements, 06 April 1991, 1843 UNTS 71.
46. K.R. Menon, "Maritime Confidence Building Measures in South Asia," in *Maritime Confidence Building in Regions of Tension*, (ed.) Jill R. Junnola (1996); David Griffiths, "Maritime Aspects of Arms Control and Security Improvement in the Middle East," in *Policy Paper* (ed.) Institute on Global Conflict and Cooperation (2000); Ayesha Siddiqa-Agha, "Maritime Cooperation between India and Pakistan: Building Confidence at Sea," in *CMC Occasional Papers* (ed.) Cooperative Monitoring Centre (2000).
47. Agreement, Article 1.
48. Article 5.
49. Article 12.
50. Article 11.
51. Memorandum of Understanding signed by Indian Foreign Secretary K. Raghunath and Pakistan Foreign Secretary Shamshad Ahmad, Lahore, 21 February 1999, http://www.acronym.org.uk/official-and-govt-documents/lahore-declaration-and-

associated-memorandum-understanding, para. 3.
52. http://www.dal.ca/dept/cfps/Pillars/mspp/CCSAW.html.
53. Article 9.
54. Article 9.
55. Article 10.
56. Article 10.
57. Sovereignty over Pulau Ligitan and Pulau Sipadan, Indonesia vs. Malaysia, Judgment, 2002 I.C.J. Rep. 625.
58. Mark J. Valencia, "Regime-Building in East Asia : Recent Progress and Problems," in *The Future of Ocean Regime-Building* (ed.) Aldo Chircop, Ted L. McDorman, and Susan J. Rolston (2009); Areej Torla, Salma Yusof, and Mohd Hisham Mohd Kamal, "The Dispute between Malaysia and Indonesia over the Nd6 and Nd7 Sea Blocks," *Journal of East Asia and International Law* 8, No. 1 (2015); IBR Supancana, "Maritime Boundary Disputes between Indonesia and Malaysia in the Area of Ambalat Block: Some Optional Scenarios for Peaceful Settlement," *Journal of East Asia and International Law* 8 (2015).
59. Mark J Valencia, "Regime-Building in East Asia/: Recent Progress and Problems" in Aldo Chircop, Ted L McDorman and Susan J Rolston (eds), *The Future of Ocean Regime-Building* (2009); Areej Torla, Salma Yusof and Mohd Hisham Mohd Kamal, "The Dispute between Malaysia and Indonesia over the ND6 and ND7 Sea Blocks" (2015) 8 *Journal of East Asia and International Law* 171; IBR Supancana, "Maritime Boundary Disputes between Indonesia and Malaysia in the Area of Ambalat Block: Some Optional Scenarios for Peaceful Settlement" (2015) 8 *Journal of East Asia and International Law* 1.
60. Arms Control and Regional Security Working Group in the Middle East (ACRS Working Group), "Guidelines for Operating Procedures for Maritime Cooperation and Conduct in the Prevention of Incidents on and over the Sea."
61. David Griffiths, "US-China Maritime Confidence Building. Paradigms, Precedents, and Prospects," in *China Maritime Studies* (2010); Peter Jones, "Maritime Confidence Building Measures in Middle East," in *Maritime Confidence Building in Regions of Tension,* (ed.) Jill R. Junnola (1996).
62. "Maritime Confidence Building Measures in Middle East." See also United States Department of State, Fact Sheet, 01 July 2001, "Middle East Peace Process Arms Control and Regional Security (ACRS) Working Group", available at http://2001-2009.state.gov/t/pm/rls/fs/4271.htm.
63. http://news.usni.org/2014/06/17/document-conduct-unplanned-encounters-sea, 22 April 2014..
64. The twenty member states are Australia, Brunei, Cambodia, Canada, Chile, France, Indonesia, Japan, South Korea, Malaysia, New Zealand, Papua New Guinea, Peru, the Philippines, Russia, Tonga, Thailand, Singapore, the USA and Vietnam. There are three observer states, Bangladesh, India and Mexico.
65. U.S.-China Memorandum of Understanding (MOU) On the Rules of Behaviour for the Safety of Air and Maritime Encounters, 12 November 2014, Annex I, Terms of Reference of the Rules of Behaviour for Safety of Air and Maritime Encounters, available at http://www.defense.gov/pubs/141112_MemorandumOfUnderstanding RegardingRules.pdf.

    It is one of the two MOUs adopted in 2014. The other is Memorandum of Understanding on Notification of Major Military Activities Confidence-Building Measures Mechanism, 12 November 2014, Annex I, Notification of Major Security Policy and Strategy Developments; Annex II, Observation of Military Exercises and

Activities, available at http://www.defense.gov/pubs/141112_MemorandumOf Understanding OnNotification.pdf.

66. Pedrozo, "US-China Incidents at Sea Agreement: A Recipe for Disaster."
67. I Made Andi Arsana, "Indonesia-Malaysia Deal Is Good News for Fishermen," *Jakarta Post*, 30 April 2012.
68. Ibid.
69. Ibid.
70. Memorandum of Understanding in respect of the Common Guidelines concerning Treatment of Fishermen by Maritime Law Enforcement Agencies of Malaysia and Indonesia, 12 January 2012.
71. Article 5.
72. Article 2(c).
73. Article 2(b).
74. Article 3.
75. Article 3.
76. Article 3.
77. Article 10.
78. *See* The British Institute of International and Comparative Law, "Report on the Obligation of States under Articles 74(3) and 83(3) of Unclos in Respect of Undelimited Maritime Areas," (2016), para. 359.
79. Balintang Channel Incident Report, 07 August 2013, available at http://www.gov.ph/2013/08/07/balintang-channel-incident-report/
80. Ministry of Foreign Affairs, Republic of China (Taiwan), "Background Information: Philippines violated International Law in Guang Da Xing No. 28 Incident," 27 May 2013, No. 049, available at http://www.mofa.gov.tw/en/News_Content.aspx?n=2C62458194137213&s=97B8486A61EC2693.
81. Ibid.
82. The British Institute of International and Comparative Law, "Report on the Obligation of States under Articles 74(3) and 83(3) of Unclos in Respect of Undelimited Maritime Areas," para. 360.
83. Portal of Republic of China (Taiwan) Diplomatic Missions, "Press Releases: TECO's Official Statement on the May 25th incident," 05 July 2015, available at http://www.roc-taiwan.org/ct.asp?xItem=621191&ctNode=2237&mp=1, para. 5.
84. Ibid., para. 4.
85. Agreement Concerning the Facilitation of Cooperation on Law Enforcement in Fisheries Matters on 05 November 2015.
86. See Public Diplomacy Coordination Council, Taiwan, Press Release, "Taiwan and the Philippines sign agreement on law enforcement cooperation in fisheries matters," 09 November 2015, No. 269, available at http://www.mofa.gov.tw/en/News_Content.aspx?n=1EADDCFD4C6EC567&s=200FD620B9CCE60B.

16

Growing Problems of Non-compliance with UNCLOS

Vijay Sakhuja

The 1982 United Nations Convention on the Law of the Sea (UNCLOS) is a comprehensive framework for the regulation and management of the oceans and seas. Its 320 articles and 9 annexes span a broad spectrum of issues relating to the regulation and practice of navigation, marine protection, scientific research and seabed mining. The salient aspects of the Convention are:

(a) Drawing of base lines.
(b) Establishment of a 12 nautical miles territorial sea.
(c) Allowing unimpeded transit passage through international straits.
(d) Establishment of Exclusive Economic Zone (EEZ) extending up to 200 nautical miles.
(e) Acceptance of continental shelf regime and rights to manage living and non-living resources of the continental shelf to a minimum of 200 nautical miles.
(f) Concept of archipelagic waters and regulatory power over the ocean for archipelagic states.

The Convention establishes a comprehensive code of legal principles for resolving disputes relating to boundaries, passage rights, marine environment, and exploitation of marine resources, including safety and security of maritime transport. Under the 1982 UNCLOS, countries claim 12 nautical miles of territorial sea and a 200 nautical mile-EEZ that can extend out to 350 nautical miles if it is on the continental shelf'.[1] It also offers directions and regulations for the management of sea-based resources.

The 1982 UNCLOS has generated tensions among states, particularly in cases where states have declared national jurisdiction over disputed sea spaces, and have started exercising sovereignty over such areas and have even started exploiting resources from there. The situation is further complicated when states start responding through nationalist discourse, enacting laws including them in their provinces, start flag waving and construction of observation posts, meteorological stations, military garrisons, as well as naval anchorages.[2]

This paper attempts to understand the problems of non-compliance with 1982 UNCLOS. It lists a few case studies of compliance and non-compliance and analyses the Chinese refusal to participate in the contentious South China Sea island dispute. It also analyses China's decision to remain absent from the Permanent Court of Arbitration in The Hague, a mechanism convened under the compulsory dispute settlement provisions of the 1982 UNCLOS.

Issues of Contention

It is generally agreed that non-compliance of 1982 UNCLOS is primarily an issue of interpretation of law and in most cases driven by national interests. This approach not only 'undermines the integrity and legitimacy of the Convention' but is often the "cause of disputes and harm the marine environment".[3] Robin Churchill offers a select list to include:[4]

(a) Some State parties, including Bangladesh, Egypt, Myanmar and Vietnam, have drawn straight baselines in ways that do not meet the requirements of Article 7, even by the most generous interpretation of the admittedly imprecise provisions of that Article.

(b) Four State parties, namely, Benin, Philippines, Somalia and Togo, still claim a territorial sea with an extent that is in excess of the 12 nautical mile-limit permitted by Article 3 of UNCLOS.

(c) 12 State parties, including China, Haiti, India, Pakistan and Saudi Arabia, have included security as one of the matters in respect of which they claim to exercise jurisdiction in their contiguous zones, which is contrary to Article 33 of UNCLOS.

(d) A few State parties, including Japan, have sought to delimit an EEZ and continental shelf from uninhabitable rocks, which is totally contrary to Article 121(3).

(e) In addition, a significant number of flag State parties are in breach of their obligation under Article 94 of the UNCLOS to exercise effective jurisdiction and control in respect of the seaworthiness of ships having their nationality, as revealed by the record of inspections and detentions of unseaworthy ships carried out by port states under various regional Memoranda of Understanding (MoU) on port state control. In particular, such states include some of those on the black list of flag States, and possibly even those on the grey list, published every year by the Paris and Tokyo MoUs.

(f) A number of State parties are in breach of their obligations under Article 194(5) by failing to take the necessary measures to protect and preserve rare or fragile ecosystems, for example, by permitting fishing using explosives in the vicinity of tropical coral reefs or by permitting bottom trawling on seamounts and areas of cold-water coral reefs in their EEZs.

Military and Scientific Research Activities

During the debates concerning the UNCLOS negotiations, a majority of the participating States supported the view that 'military operations, exercises, and activities have always been regarded as internationally lawful uses of the sea and that the right to conduct such activities would continue for all States within the EEZs of other States'.[5] However, China and India preferred to counter this proposition and had argued against the prevalent view during the negotiations. Consequently, China reiterated its restriction on military activities by issuing a statement, immediately after ratification of UNCLOS, which stated that

> *The People's Republic of China reaffirms that the provisions of the United Nations Convention on the Law of the Sea concerning innocent passage through the territorial sea shall not prejudice the right of a coastal State to request, in accordance with its laws and regulations, a foreign State to obtain advance approval from or give prior notification to the coastal State for the passage of its warships through the territorial sea of the coastal State.*[6]

Similarly, the Government of India, in accordance with long-standing reservations on the presence of foreign warships near its coast, issued a declaration, while ratifying the UNCLOS, which stated that

> *The Government of the Republic of India understands that the provisions of the Convention do not authorize other States to carry out in the exclusive economic zone and on the continental shelf, military exercises or manoeuvres, in particular those involving the use of weapons or explosives without the consent of the coastal State.*[7]

Environment-Ecological Activism

International non-governmental organisations such as Greenpeace and Sea Shepherd have proactively engaged in international efforts to preserve the environment and ecology. For instance, in the Polar regions, the Greenpeace ship MV *Arctic Sunrise*, which had been protesting against drilling in the Arctic, was intercepted by Russia and charged with 'piracy'.[8] Similarly, MV *Bob Barker*, a ship operated by the Sea Shepherd Conservation Society, which was engaged in the preservation of marine life at sea near Antarctica was rammed many times by the Japanese whaling fleet's factory ship, MV *Nisshin Maru* in an area north of Australia's Casey Research Station in Antarctica.[9]

In 2013, Greenpeace had sought permission from the Russian Northern Sea Route (NSR) Administration to sail its icebreaker '*Arctic Sunrise*' registered in The Netherlands through the polar waters. Despite repeated applications and no decisions coming from the Russian authorities, Greenpeace activists sailed into the Russian Exclusive Economic Zone (EEZ) and attempted to board the oil rig, *Prirazlomnaya*, being operated by Russian energy company Gasport. The vessel was intercepted by the Russian Coast Guard and apprehended and escorted to the Russian port of Murmansk.[10] A Russian Court charged the 30

Greenpeace activists with 'piracy' and later, due to the international outcry, revised it to 'hooliganism'.[11]

The Netherlands approached the International Tribunal of the Law of the Sea (ITLOS), which on 22 November 2013 ordered Russia to release the ship and the crew 'upon The Netherlands's posting of a financial security in the amount of Euro 3,600,000 with the competent authority of the Russian Federation'. After serving nearly three months in detention, the Greenpeace activists were released as part of an amnesty to celebrate the 20th anniversary of Russia's post-Soviet constitution. However, the ship was released only in June 2014. Similarly, Sea Shepherd's ship *'Bob Barker'* had a skirmish with the Japanese ship, *Yushin Maru* engaged in whaling for scientific purposes. In 2012, a US court had passed an injunction against Sea Shepherd and ordered it to refrain from physically attacking and endangering vessels in the Southern Ocean and keep a distance of at least 500 yards from the Japanese whalers.[12]

Compliance and Non-compliance of 1982 UNCLOS

Some of the orders and commentaries on incidents where 1982 UNCLOS was complied with, and where it was not, are as follows:

2012: Dispute Concerning Delimitation of the Maritime Boundary between Bangladesh and Myanmar in the Bay of Bengal (Bangladesh/Myanmar)

Extract of the Case

The case had its origins in Bangladesh's long, concave coastline, which creates substantive grounds for a dispute on maritime boundaries. Under the usual application of the law for delineating maritime boundaries, the intersecting arcs of the EEZ of India and Myanmar would cut off Bangladesh's access to the continental shelf beyond 200 nautical miles and bestow it with a disproportionately small EEZ with respect to its long coastline. Consequently, both Bangladesh and Myanmar made conflicting claims to a part of the Bay of Bengal and its seabed extending southwest in a broadening sliver from the seaward terminus of their border on land.[13]

On 8 October 2009, Bangladesh initiated proceedings under Article 287 and annex VII of the 1982 UNCLOS against Myanmar regarding delimitation of the maritime boundary between the two countries in the Bay of Bengal. On 4 November 2009, Myanmar accepted the jurisdiction of the International Tribunal for the Law of the Sea (ITLOS).[14] The case has its genesis in as early as 1974 when both sides agreed on the delimitation of their respective territorial seas. They respected the arrangement in good faith for more than 30 years. However, "they could not reach agreement on the delimitation of the maritime areas beyond 12 nautical miles, i.e., exclusive economic zones and continental shelves, including in the areas beyond 200 nautical miles. The failure to reach an agreement has already had significant adverse consequences for the development of Bangladesh, in particular by limiting its ability to explore, exploit, and develop the natural resources to be found in the EEZ and continental shelf areas."[15]

Extract of the Judgment

The judgment by ITLOS ruled that St. Martin's Island has the full effect, as far as determination of territorial sea by equidistance principle between the two countries, up to 12 nm. However, for delimitation of EEZ and continental shelf, the island will have no effect. The judgment also used the delineation of EEZ based on an equidistance line adjusted to achieve equity. It also delineated the continental shelf by extending the line demarcating EEZ beyond 200 nm until it reached the point where the rights of a third State may be affected. This created a 'grey area' which lies on the Bangladesh side of the delimitation line, beyond 200 nm from its coast but within 200 nm from the coast of Myanmar. The judgment granted Bangladesh rights over the seabed and subsoil of the continental shelf in the grey area, without in any way limiting "Myanmar's rights with respect to the exclusive economic zone, notably those with respect to the superjacent waters."[16]

2015: The "Enrica Lexie" Incident (Italy vs. India)[17]

Extract of the Case

On 15 February 2012, two Italian marines belonging to the Italian Navy, who had been positioned on official duty on board the Italian tanker MV *Enrica Lexie* fired at an Indian fishing vessel *St Antony* and killed two fishermen. The incident occurred at a distance of approximately 20 nm from the coast of Kerala State in India, which is well within the Indian

Exclusive Economic Zone. India subsequently arrested and detained the vessel *MV Enrica Lexie* and the Italian marines. Italy sought an arbitration tribunal to be constituted under Annex VII of UNCLOS claiming that India had acted in breach of International Law and that the Italian marines, as State officials performing their duty, enjoyed immunity and Italy had, as the Flag State, the sole jurisdiction over the vessel and the marines with respect to the incident. It maintained that the dispute with India concerned the interpretation and application of UNCLOS, including, in particular, Articles 2.3, 27, 33, 56, 58, 87, 89, 92, 94, 97, 100 and 300. On the other hand, India contended that the incident and the subsequent assertion of jurisdiction over the vessel and the marines by India were not covered by the provisions of UNCLOS.[18]

Extract of the Order

The ITLOS, in its order dated 24 August 2015, ruled by a majority vote of 15 to 6 that "it is appropriate for the Tribunal to prescribe that both Italy and India suspend all court proceedings and refrain from initiating new ones which might aggravate or extend the dispute submitted to the Annex VII arbitral tribunal or might jeopardise or prejudice the carrying out of any decision which the arbitral tribunal may render". It also ruled that "since it will be for the Annex VII arbitral tribunal to adjudicate the merits of the case, the Tribunal does not consider it appropriate to prescribe provisional measures in respect of the situation of the two marines because that touches upon issues related to the merits of the case."[19]

In its Order, the Tribunal reaffirmed its view that "considerations of humanity must apply in the law of the sea as they do in other areas of international law". It also noted "the grief and suffering of the families of the two Indian fishermen who were killed" as well as "the consequences that the lengthy restrictions on liberty entail for the two marines and their families."[20]

1986: Nicaragua vs. United States of America

Extract of the Case

Nicaragua filed a suit against the USA for undertaking illegal military and paramilitary activities in and against Nicaragua. It contented that the USA was responsible for all such activities. The USA challenged the jurisdiction of the International Court of Justice (ICJ) and the admissibility of Nicaragua's application to it. Although the USA had accepted the mandatory justification of the court by a declaration in 1946, in 1984 it asserted that the declaration "shall not apply to disputes with any Central American State...."[21]

Extract of the Order

The USA did not appear before the ICJ at the merit stages, after refusing to accept the ICJ's jurisdiction to decide the case. The USA at the jurisdictional phase of the hearing, however, filed a Counter-Memorial stating that it acted according to its inherent right of collective self-defence guaranteed under Article 51 of the UN Charter and in pursuance of its obligations under the Inter-American Treaty of Reciprocal Assistance. It claimed to have responded to the requests by Costa Rica, El Salvador and Honduras for assistance to defend them against aggression by Nicaragua when it provided "upon request proportionate and appropriate assistance..." to Costa Rica, Honduras, and El Salvador in response to Nicaragua's acts of aggression against those countries.[22]

The USA also claimed that Nicaragua had "promoted and supported guerrilla violence in neighbouring countries," especially in El Salvador. It also submitted an affidavit by Secretary of State George P. Shultz, wherein he stated, "the Government of Nicaragua has actively supported armed groups engaged in military and paramilitary activities in and against El Salvador." He further added that besides supporting armed groups operating against the government of El Salvador, Nicaragua had also provided similar support, although on a much smaller level, "for armed groups engaged or which have sought to engage, in military or paramilitary activities in and against the Republic of Costa Rica, the Republic of Honduras, and the Republic of Guatemala."[23]

However, the Court ruled that the plea of collective self-defence taken up by the USA against an alleged armed attack on El Salvador, Honduras or Costa Rica, in order to defend itself, could not be upheld. It therefore ruled that the USA was in volition of "the principle prohibiting recourse to the threat or use of force" by way of its "assistance to the contras to the extent that this assistance involve[s] a threat or use of force".[24] It also stated that these acts could not be justified on grounds of collective self-defence, as the circumstances did not warrant it, nor was the USA justified in resorting to force in case of any intervention by Nicaragua in El Salvador.[25] It even decided by a majority vote of 12 votes to three that the United States of America had "an obligation to make reparation to the Republic of Nicaragua for all injury caused to Nicaragua by the breaches of obligations under customary international law."[26]

2015: Chagos Marine Protected Area Arbitration

Extract of the Case

On 20 December 2010, Mauritius initiated arbitration proceedings against the United Kingdom in accordance with Article 287 of UNCLOS as well as Article 1 of Annex VII to the Convention.[27] The dispute refers to the decision of the United Kingdom taken on 01 April 2010, whereby, it established a Marine Protected Area (MPA) around the Chagos Archipelago, which is under the administrative control of British Indian Ocean Territories (BIOT). The MPA covers an area of around half a million square kilometres and extends 200 nautical miles from the base line of Chagos Archipelago. According to Mauritius, the declaration of MPA violates UNCLOS, as the UK had no right to declare an MPA or other maritime zones as it is not the "coastal State" in accordance with Articles 2, 55, 56 and 76 of UNCLOS. Mauritius also contended that the declaration violates the rights conferred on it by the UK, while detaching Chagos Archipelago. It further violates the rights and obligations provided to Mauritius, including the fishing rights in Chagos Archipelago and its surrounding waters. The UK, on the other hand, challenged the Tribunal's jurisdiction over all aspects of the dispute and claimed that the proceedings were an artificial and baseless attempt by Mauritius to bring a dispute regarding sovereignty within the jurisdiction of the tribunal. [28]

Extract of the Judgment

The Tribunal in its ruling stated that the UK had not been able to provide any rational reasoning for its undue haste in proclamation of MPA and did not take into account the traditional fishing rights of Mauritius. The Tribunal accordingly concluded that the UK had breached Articles 2(3) and 56(2) and that the proclamation of the MPA was therefore incompatible with the Convention.[29]

The UK tried to justify the establishment of MPA on its obligation under Article 194 of UNCLOS. However, according to the Tribunal, in establishing the MPA, the United Kingdom was under an obligation to "endeavour to harmonize" its policies with Mauritius. More significantly, Article 194(1) is prospective and requires only the best efforts; it does not lay down any deadlines and does not lay down any requirement that such attempts should precede any action with respect to the marine environment. The Tribunal accordingly does not feel that in the limited life of the MPA to date that any obligation pursuant to Article 194(1) has been violated by the UK.[30]

The Tribunal considers Article 194(4) imposes a different type of obligation and requires that the UK "refrain from unjustifiable interference" to be similar to its obligation to give "due regard," under Article 56(2), or its obligation of good faith that emanates from Article 2(3). Similarly, Article 194(4) requires a balance between competing rights, based on the level of interference, the alternatives available, and the significance of the rights and policies in question. "Article 194(4) differs, however, in that it facially applies only to the 'activities carried out by other States' pursuant to their rights, rather than to the rights themselves. Mauritius' rights to the eventual return of the Archipelago and to the benefit of oil and minerals are prospective in nature: there are no activities presently carried out pursuant to these undertakings. Accordingly, the Tribunal considers that Article 194(4) is applicable only to Mauritian fishing rights, which in turn the Tribunal is considering only in respect of the territorial sea."[31]

The Tribunal did agree that for the purposes of Article 194(4), the possibility of environmental considerations could possibly justify the infringement of Mauritian fishing rights in the territorial sea. It however, considered that such a justification would require significant engagement with Mauritius, both to explain the necessity of the measure as well as to explore less restrictive alternatives. The Tribunal noted that such an engagement was not evident from the records submitted. "Accordingly, and for the reasons already largely set out in the application of Articles 2(3) and 56(2), the Tribunal concludes that the declaration of the MPA was not compatible with Article 194(4) and Mauritian fishing activities in the territorial sea."[32]

The Tribunal noted that there was an agreement in 1965 between

Mauritius and the UK on detachment of Chagos Archipelago, but the two countries disagreed on whether the consent was freely given or whether the agreement was legally binding. This is a significant point to decide the submissions by Mauritius about the sovereignty and identity of the coastal state.[33] The Tribunal by a majority vote of three to two concluded that it lacked jurisdiction to decide these two issues. It however unanimously ruled:

(1) that the United Kingdom's undertaking to ensure that fishing rights in the Chagos Archipelago would remain available to Mauritius as far as practicable is legally binding insofar as it relates to the territorial sea;

(2) that the United Kingdom's undertaking to return the Chagos Archipelago to Mauritius when no longer needed for defence purposes is legally binding; and

(3) that the United Kingdom's undertaking to preserve the benefit of any minerals or oil discovered in or near the Chagos Archipelago for Mauritius is legally binding.

It accordingly ruled that by establishment of the MPA around Chagos Archipelago, the UK had breached its obligations under Articles 2(3), 56(2), and 194(4) of the Convention.[34]

The Case of South China Sea

Extract of the Case

The Republic of Philippines by its notification and statement of claim dated 22 January 2013 initiated arbitration proceedings against the People's Republic of China in accordance with Articles 286 and 287 of UNCLOS 1982 and Article 1 of Annex VII. The Philippines sought an Award that:

(1) declares that the Parties' respective rights and obligations in regard to the waters, seabed and maritime features of the South China Sea are governed by UNCLOS, and that China's claims based on its "nine dash line" are inconsistent with the Convention and therefore invalid;

(2) determines whether, under Article 121 of UNCLOS, certain of

the maritime features claimed by both China and the Philippines are islands, low tide elevations or submerged banks, and whether they are capable of generating entitlement to maritime zones greater than 12 nm; and

(3) enables the Philippines to exercise and enjoy the rights within and beyond its exclusive economic zone and continental shelf that are established in the Convention.[35]

It clearly stated that it was neither trying to determine sovereignty over the islands, which are claimed by both, nor was it seeking delimitation of any maritime boundaries. China, on the other hand, presented a Note Verbale to the Philippines on 19 February 2013, rejecting the arbitration as well as returning the Notification and Statement of Claim. China claimed that its position on the matter "has been consistent and clear" and that "the core of the disputes between China and the Philippines in the South China Sea are the territorial disputes over some islands and reefs of the Nansha Islands." It further added that "two countries also have overlapping jurisdictional claims over parts of the maritime area in the South China Sea" and both had agreed to settle the dispute through friendly consultations and bilateral.[36]

Extract of the Order

On 22 January 2013, the Republic of the Philippines initiated arbitral proceedings against the People's Republic of China under Annex VII of UNCLOS to ascertain the role of historic rights and the source of maritime entitlements in the South China Sea. It also sought to ascertain the lawfulness of certain actions by China in the South China Sea that the Philippines alleged, were in violation of the Convention. China did not appoint an agent and adopted a position of non-acceptance and complete non-participation in the proceedings. The Permanent Court of Arbitration (PCA) served as Registry in this arbitration. In a Note Verbale by China to the PCA on 1 August 2013, and throughout the arbitration proceedings, China reiterated "its position that it does not accept the arbitration initiated by the Philippines." On 05 December 2014, Vietnam submitted a statement to the Tribunal and requested that the Tribunal should give due cognisance to Vietnam's position with respect to:

(a) advocating full observance and implementation of all rules and procedures of the Convention, including Vietnam's position that it has "no doubt that the Tribunal has jurisdiction in these proceedings";

(b) preserving Vietnam's "rights and interests of a legal nature";

(c) noting that the Philippines does not request this Tribunal to consider issues not subject to its jurisdiction under Article 288 of the Convention (namely questions of sovereignty and maritime delimitation);

(d) "resolutely protest[ing] and reject[ing]" any claim by China based on the "nine-dash line"; and

(e) supporting the Tribunal's competence to interpret and apply Articles 60, 80, 194(5), 206, 293(1), and 300 of the Convention and other relevant instruments.

Vietnam further added that none of the maritime features mentioned by the Philippines in the arbitral proceedings can "generate maritime entitlements in excess of 12 nautical miles since they are low-tide elevations or 'rocks which cannot sustain human habitation or economic life of their own' under Article 121(3) of the Convention." Viet Nam also sought to reserve "the right to seek to intervene if it seems appropriate and in accordance with the principles and rules of international law, including the relevant provisions of UNCLOS" and requested to receive copies of all relevant documents in the arbitration.[37]

The Tribunal on 29 October 2015 ruled that it was properly constituted and finds:

> *China's non-appearance in these proceedings does not deprive the Tribunal of jurisdiction;*
>
> *The Philippines' act of initiating this arbitration did not constitute an abuse of process;*
>
> *There is no indispensable third party whose absence deprives the Tribunal of jurisdiction;*
>
> *The 2002 China–ASEAN Declaration on Conduct of the Parties in the South China Sea, the joint statements of the Parties referred to in paragraphs 231 to 232 of this Award, the Treaty of Amity and Cooperation in Southeast Asia, and the Convention on Biological*

> *Diversity, do not preclude, under Articles 281 or 282 of the Convention, recourse to the compulsory dispute settlement procedures available under Section 2 of Part XV of the Convention;*
>
> *The Parties have exchanged views as required by Article 283 of the Convention. It FINDS that the Tribunal has jurisdiction to consider the Philippines' Submissions No. 3, 4, 6, 7, 10, 11, and 13, subject to the conditions noted in paragraphs 400, 401, 403, 404, 407, 408, and 410 of this Award;*
>
> *A determination of whether the Tribunal has jurisdiction to consider the Philippines' Submissions No. 1, 2, 5, 8, 9, 12, and 14 would involve consideration of issues that do not possess an exclusively preliminary character, and accordingly RESERVES consideration of its jurisdiction to rule on Submissions No. 1, 2, 5, 8, 9, 12, and 14 to the merits phase;*
>
> *Finally*
>
> *"DIRECTS the Philippines to clarify the content and narrow the scope of its Submission 15";*
>
> *"RESERVES consideration of its jurisdiction over Submission No. 15 to the merits phase";*
>
> *"RESERVES for further consideration and directions all issues not decided in this Award".*[38]

During the proceeding, the Chinese Ambassador to the Netherlands wrote repeated letters to individual members of the Tribunal, claiming the proceedings of the Tribunal to be null and void. On 23 June 2016, Malaysia, that had been an observer since 10 June 2015 of the proceedings, requested the Tribunal to show due regard to the rights of Malaysia. The tribunal acknowledged the communication and informed Malaysia that it had taken note of its Communication.[39]

The Tribunal in its final ruling on 12 July 2016, ruled that "China's claims in the South China Sea do not include a claim to 'historic title', within the meaning of Article 298(1)(a)(i) of the Convention, over the waters of the South China Sea." It also agreed with the contention of the Philippines that "no maritime feature claimed by China within 200 nautical miles of Mischief Reef or Second Thomas Shoal constitutes a fully entitled island for the purposes of Article 121 of the Convention." It added that "Mischief Reef and Second Thomas Shoal are low-tide elevations and, as such, generate no entitlement to maritime zones of their own"; consequently, "there are no overlapping entitlements to an exclusive economic zone or continental shelf in the areas of Mischief Reef or Second Thomas Shoal." It however, stated that "China's land reclamation and/or construction of artificial islands, installations, and structures at Cuarteron Reef, Fiery Cross Reef, Gaven Reef (North), Johnson Reef, Hughes Reef, Subi Reef, and Mischief Reef do not constitute "military activities", within the meaning of Article 298(1)(b) of the Convention". It also declared that UNCLOS defines the scope of maritime entitlement between China and the Philippines in the South China Sea. More significantly, it ruled that "China's claims to historic rights, or other sovereign rights or jurisdiction, with respect to the maritime areas of the South China Sea encompassed by the relevant part of the 'nine-dash line' are contrary to the Convention." It also found that "none of the high-tide features in the Spratly Islands, in their natural condition, are capable of sustaining human habitation or economic life of their own within the meaning of Article 121(3) of the Convention" and consequently entitled to an exclusive economic zone or continental shelf. It also declared that China failed to prevent its vessels from fishing in the Philippines EEZ and found it guilty of preventing fishermen from the Philippines from fishing in Scarborough Shoal, which has been a traditional fishing ground for fishermen of many nationalities. It also observed "that China's land reclamation and construction of artificial islands, installations, and structures at Cuarteron Reef, Fiery Cross Reef, Gaven Reef (North), Johnson Reef, Hughes Reef, Subi Reef, and Mischief Reef has caused severe, irreparable harm to the coral reef ecosystem."[40]

The Tribunal also found China guilty of not cooperating or coordinating with other States bordering the South China Sea with respect to the protection and preservation of the marine environment. It also found that the Chinese law enforcement vessels were guilty of creating serious risk of collision and danger to the ships and personnel of the Philippines in the vicinity of Sacramento Shoal, thereby, "violated Rules 2, 6, 7, 8, 15, and 16 of the Convention on the International Regulations for Preventing Collisions at Sea, 1972". It also found that China had built a large artificial island on Mischief Reef; while a dispute resolution mechanism was going on, thereby aggravating the dispute regarding their respective rights and entitlements in Mischief Reef. It finally declared that "China has breached its obligations pursuant to Articles

279, 296, and 300 of the Convention, as well as pursuant to general international law," as it was required to abstain from any measure that could have a prejudicial effect or "might aggravate or extend the dispute during such time as dispute resolution proceedings were ongoing."[41]

Issues for Debate

It is seen that there are many cases where many states, especially those which wield power have refused to comply with international law. This raises another question as to who would enforce international law and finally, is noncompliance primarily a problem of enforcement?

These questions have baffled practitioners and thinkers alike. Going as far back as Machiavelli who noted "A prudent Prince, neither can nor ought to keep his word when to keep it is hurtful to him and the causes which led him to pledge it are removed" has been at the heart of 'whether/why leaders should comply with their international commitments".[42] In 1625, Groitus also stated that 'pacts that leaders sign with one another are to be respected and fulfilled in good faith. This tenet forms the fundamental modern-day international legal principle of pacta sunt servanda ('agreements are to be observed'). He notes that "It is a rule of the law of nature to abide by pacts" Further, Grotius does attach certain exceptions to the good faith principle, for instance, when the contract is concluded under illegitimate circumstances or when the other party engages in large-scale noncompliance'.[43]

Finally, the above narrative showcases the general trends in the 'compliance' and 'non-compliance' of adjudication under the 1982 UNCLOS at the PCA and the ITLOS.

NOTES

1. Vijay Sakhuja, "Asian Maritime Power in the 21st Century: Strategic Transactions China, India and Southeast Asia", Singapore: Institute of South East Asian Studies, (2015), p. 41.
2. Ibid. p. 42.
3. Robin Churchill, "The Persisting Problem of Non-compliance with the Law of the Sea Convention: Disorder in the Oceans", *The International Journal of Marine and Coastal Law*, Vol. 27, No. 4 (01 January 2012), pp. 813–820.
4. Ibid.
5. Third UN Conference on the Law of the Sea, Plenary Meetings, Official Records, U.N Doc.A/CONF.62/WS/37 and ADD. 1-2, 244 (1973-1982) cited in "Military Activities

in an Exclusive Economic Zone (EEZ)", available at https://sites.tufts.edu/lawofthesea/chapter-4/ (Accessed on 30 October 2019).
6. Iskander Rehman, *India, China, and Differing Conceptions of the Maritime Order* (Washington DC: The Brookings Institute, June 2017), p. 8.
7. Ibid., p. 4.
8. Aditi Chatterjee, "Greenpeace Activism in the Arctic: Solution or Threat?" in Vijay Sakhuja and Gurpreet S. Khurana (eds), *Arctic Perspectives: 2015* (New Delhi: National Maritime Foundation, 2015), pp. 66-67.
9. Kim Choe, "Sea Shepherd claims victory in Southern Ocean after collisions", available at https://web.archive.org/web/20130926081649/http://www.3news.co.nz/Sea-Shepherd-claims-victory-in-Southern-Ocean-after-collisions/tabid/417/articleID/287594/Default.aspx (Accessed on 01 March 2020).
10. Shaun Walker, "Russia to charge Greenpeace activists with piracy over oil rig protest," *The Guardian*, 24 September 2013, available at https://www.theguardian.com/environment/2013/sep/24/russia-greenpeace-piracy-oil-rig-protest (Accessed on 01 March 2020).
11. "Russia must compensate Dutch over Greenpeace ship: international Court", available at https://www.straitstimes.com/world/europe/russia-must-compensate-dutch-over-greenpeace-ship-international-court (Accessed on 30 October 2019).
12. "Japan whalers given Sea Shepherd injunction by US court", available at https://www.bbc.com/news/world-asia-20778616 (Accessed on 30 October 2019).
13. Sarah Watson, "The Bangladesh/Myanmar Maritime Dispute: Lessons for Peaceful Resolution" *Asia Maritime Transparency Initiative*, 19 October 2015, available at https://amti.csis.org/the-bangladeshmyanmar-maritime-dispute-lessons-for-peaceful-resolution/ (Accessed on 01 January 2020).
14. Delimitation of the maritime boundary in the Bay of Bengal (Bangladesh/Myanmar), Judgment, ITLOS Reports 2012, pp. 10-11.
15. "Dispute Concerning Delimitation of the Maritime Boundary between Bangladesh and Myanmar in the Bay of Bengal," Memorial of Bangladesh submitted to ITLOS, Vol. 1, 01 July 2010, p. 2.
16. Delimitation of the maritime boundary in the Bay of Bengal (Bangladesh/Myanmar), Judgment, ITLOS Reports 2012, pp. 51-121.
17 "The "Enrica Lexie" Incident (Italy vs. India", available at https://www.itlos.org/fileadmin/ itlos/documents/press_releases_english/PR_237_EN.pdf (Accessed on 30 October 2019).
18. "The 'Enrica Lexie' Incident (Italy v India)", available at https://law.nus.edu.sg/cmlcmidata base/enrica-lexie-incident-italy-v-india (Accessed on 30 October 2019).
19. "The "Enrica Lexie" Incident" (Italy vs. India) List of cases: No. 24, Provisional Measures, Order of 24 August 2015, International Tribunal for the Law of the Sea Reports of Judgments, Advisory Opinions and Orders 2015, p. 204.
20. Ibid.
21. "Nicaragua vs. United States", available at https://www.casebriefs.com/blog/law/inter national-law/international-law-keyed-to-damrosche/chapter-2/military-and-paramilitary-activities-in-and-against-nicaragua-nicaragua-v-united-states/ (Accessed on 30 October 2019).
22. "Case Concerning Military and Paramilitary Activities in and against Nicaragua (Nicaragua vs. United States of America)", Merits Judgment of 24 June 1986 from

International Court of Justice, Reports of Judgments, Advisory Opinions and Orders 1986, p. 70.
23. Ibid., p. 71.
24. Ibid., p. 123.
25. Ibid., p. 128.
26. Ibid., p. 150.
27. "In the Matter of the Chagos Marine Protected Area Arbitration", Award of an Arbitral Tribunal Constituted under Annex VII of the United Nations Convention on the Law of the Sea between the Republic of Mauritius and the United Kingdom of Great Britain and Northern Ireland, Permanent Court of Arbitration, 18 March 2015, p. 5.
28. Ibid., pp. 1-3.
29. Ibid., pp. 209-210.
30. Ibid., p. 211.
31. Ibid.
32. Ibid., pp. 211-212.
33. Ibid., p. 163.
34. Ibid., p. 215.
35. "Award" of PCA Case № 2013-19 in the matter of the South China Sea Arbitration before an Arbitral Tribunal Constituted under Annex VII to the 1982 United Nations Convention of the Law of the Sea between the Republic of Philippines and the People's Republic of China, Permanent Court of Arbitration, 12 July 2016, p. 11.
36. Ibid., pp. 11-12.
37. Ibid., pp. 13-14.
38. Ibid., pp. 19-20.
39. Ibid., p. 37.
40. Ibid., pp. 471-475.
41. Ibid., p. 471-477.
42. Cited in Jana von Stein, "Compliance with International Law", available at http://www.janavonstein.org/uploads/4/6/1/9/46194525/isa-compendium-update.pdf (Accessed on 30 October 2019).
43. Ibid. H. Grotius, *On the Law of War and Peace* (Whitefish: Kessinger 1625).

17

Challenges in Implementation of UNCLOS in South China Sea

Ton Sinh Thanh

The Importance of the South China Sea

The South China Sea (SCS) is a vital waterway that links Northeast Asia and the Western Pacific to the Indian Ocean and the Middle East. It is an extremely significant trade route for almost all the countries of the region. It will therefore be a catastrophe for international trade if the South China Sea is blocked.[1] With an area of around 3.5 million square kilometres, the South China Sea is a large fishing ground for millions of people. The economy of almost all the littoral states depends heavily on fishing and other related industries in the South China Sea.[2] Moreover, many littoral states also depend economically on non-living resources such as oil and gas in the South China Sea.[3]

Decoding the Imbroglio in the South China Sea

However, the situation now in the South China Sea is extremely complicated and dangerous. If not properly managed, it can lead to a serious international conflict. There are two sets of disputes in the South China Sea: firstly, the territorial disputes over the sovereignty of various islands and, secondly, the disputes over maritime boundaries. These two sets of disputes are closely interrelated to each other.

The first set of disputes is mainly related to two major groups of islands in the South China Sea: the Paracel Islands and the Spratly Islands. Vietnam possesses full evidence and the legal foundation to claim its sovereignty over both these groups of islands.[4] However, given the fact that there are other claimants to these islands, Vietnam has expressed its willingness to resolve these territorial disputes by peaceful negotiations with other claimants in accordance with the international laws.[5] As a long-term solution to the disputes is pending from 1992 onwards, the countries of the Association of South East Asian Nations (ASEAN) have signed an agreement, which commits all of them not to change the status quo in the South China Sea. In 2002, ASEAN and China signed a Declaration of Conducts of Parties in South China Sea (DOC) with the same commitments, i.e., to respect the status-quo in the South China Sea and refrain from any act, which further complicates the problems.

However, China has not respected what it had committed and went ahead by occupying the Scarborough Shoal, which is claimed by the Philippines, in 2012. The Chinese have followed it up with a massive land reclamation programme in the islands since 2013. As part of this programme, the Chinese have constructed artificial islands on seven reefs in the Spratly Islands.[6] China has further complicated the situation by installing many sophisticated weapons and sensors on the Paracel Islands and the newly constructed artificial islands in the Spratly Islands. At the same time, China has refused to participate in any multilateral talks with all the claimants and have insisted on only bilateral talks with each of the claimants in the South China Sea. China has also refused the involvement of any third party, or any arbitration by any international institution to solve the territorial disputes. The negotiations between ASEAN countries and China on a binding code of conduct in South China Sea (COC) have also been prolonged.

The second set of disputes relates to maritime boundaries. Due to the close proximity of various countries and the islands under their sovereignty, there are several overlapping exclusive economic zones and the continental shelf areas in the region.[7] Most of them are being peacefully resolved by the countries concerned. The only big, unresolved problem is the nine-dash line which began in 2009, when China submitted a map to the United Nations, claiming 3 million square kilometres of the

South China Sea, equivalent to 85.7 per cent of the total area of 3.5 million square kilometres. The "nine-dash line" stretches hundreds of miles south from its most southerly province of Hainan. China now claims all the waters and islands within this nine-dash line as its historical territory.

The problem is that this nine-dash line overlaps largely with the Exclusive Economic Zones of Vietnam, the Philippines, Malaysia, Indonesia and Brunei.[8] The problem is becoming worse as China is trying to enforce its illegal "Nine-dash line". China has many times in the past imposed fishing bans. China has also warned its Southeast Asian neighbours against drilling for oil and gas in the contested region, disrupting other nations' oil exploration and seismic survey activities. In May 2014, China placed a huge oil rig inside Vietnam's Exclusive Economic Zone and continental shelf.

PCA Ruling on the South China Sea

Against this backdrop, in January 2013, the Philippines took China to a UN tribunal under the auspices of the United Nations Convention on the Laws of the Sea (UNCLOS), to challenge some of the Chinese contentions on the South China Sea, including the nine-dash line claims. The Permanent Court of Arbitration (PCA) in The Hague on 12 July 2016 made its final ruling rejecting the nine-dash line as illegal.[9] According to the PCA ruling, no article of the Convention expressly provides for or permits the continued existence of historic rights to the living or non-living resources of an exclusive economic zone and continental shelf on the high seas, or in the Area. It also stated that no structures in the South China Sea, including the artificial islands constructed by China, are entitled to island status, which can have an independent EEZ of their own. The PCA ruling also confirmed that its verdict was final and the non-participation by the People's Republic of China (PRC) did not constitute a bar to the proceedings.[10]

This ruling of PCA not only has implications for the Philippines and China, but also for the other disputants and parties concerned. The ruling can not only be the basis to solve the problems between the Philippines and China but also for the disputes among other claimants in the SCS. With the PCA verdict that declared the nine-dash line as illegal, the disputed areas in SCS have reduced significantly. The PCA ruling in fact also strengthens the UNCLOS itself. UNCLOS is only 34 years old and there remained differences amongst nations on how to interpret the convention. So, the ruling of PCA made a very clear with an unambiguous explanation: Regardless of how much nations claimed in the history for their EEZ, they are entitled only to a maximum of 200 nautical miles and if there is a continental shelf, a maximum of 350 miles from their sea shores. For UNCLOS, historical claims are invalid. The PCA ruling thus makes a huge contribution to the reestablishment of the order in the seas and oceans in general and to peace, stability and security as well as freedom of navigation, overflight and commerce in the South China Sea.

The Way Forward

The award by the PCA on 12 July 2016 was undoubtedly a significant step in the implementation of UNCLOS. However, the problem is that the PCA ruling has no mechanism to enforce it, whereas China refuses to comply with the PCA ruling. China continues to indulge in activities, which infringe on the sovereignty of Vietnam, the Philippines and other countries in the South China Sea, bullying smaller countries in their Exclusive Economic zones in the South China Sea. Chinese militarisation in the South China Sea has changed the balance of power in the region that causes the reaction of other powers and triggers an arm race that contributes to more tension and risk of conflict in the region. Chinese activities are threatening the freedom of navigation and overflight in the South China Sea.

It is therefore essential to look for ways to prevent the situation in the South China Sea from deteriorating and the steps needed to settle the disputes in SCS. Vietnam, as well as other nations in Southeast Asia, always wants to have peace and good relations with China. The way out of the current tension in the SCS depends mainly on China. First and foremost, the use of force or threat to use force and bullying acts should be strictly ruled out and excluded from a solution to the disputes in the SCS. The only answer to the problem in the SCS is a peaceful negotiation in accordance with international laws, especially UNCLOS-1982. As an international legal order for the seas and oceans, the UNCLOS regulates all aspects of the uses of the seas and oceans, including the settlement of disputes. As most of the States in the SCS region so far have ratified and become parties to the UNCLOS, they are required to interpret and apply the provisions of the Convention "in good faith in accordance with the ordinary meaning to be given to the terms of the treaty in their context and in the light of its object and purpose". Such obligation would have a great effect on the SCS dispute. Although the UNCLOS does not directly address sovereignty disputes over islands, many aspects of this dispute, such as the question of the entitlement of the islands, the delimitation of maritime boundary, etc., are governed by UNCLOS. The UNCLOS, therefore, can serve as the starting point for the states concerned and provide them with certain fundamental and internationally accepted legal approaches to guide them through the peaceful resolution of the SCS conflict.

With regards to the territorial issues, the Paracel Islands which related to only two parties could be solved through bilateral negotiations, but the issues related to many parties such as the dispute in the Spratly Islands, which are claimed by six parties (Vietnam, China, Taiwan, the Philippines, Brunei and Malaysia) must be solved through multilateral negotiations. Any diplomatic and legal solutions to the disputes should be welcome. International mediation and arbitration should not be ruled out, if direct negotiations are not possible. The successful settlement of the maritime dispute between India and Bangladesh through international arbitration is a good example for claimants in the SCS.

Pending a long-term solution acceptable to all parties concerned, the claimants should refrain from complicating the problems by not changing the status quo in SCS. The Declaration of Code of Conduct (DOC) that ASEAN and China signed in 2002 that requires parties to maintain the status quo in the SCS should be respected. In view of the worsening situation in the SCS, a binding Code of Conduct (COC) between ASEAN and China has become the need of the day.

The SCS is important not only to the littoral states but also to outside regional and global powers. The navigation, overflight, access to natural resources, trade, energy transport, stability and security in the SCS are essential not only to internal but also to external nations, especially the USA, Japan, South Korea, Australia, India, etc. The combined power of supportive political will and use of international legal institutions may provide a strong pull in the direction of stability through normative compliance. That is the reason why ASEAN in general and Vietnam in particular welcome all external powers to have a constructive engagement, thus contributing to peace, stability and security in the SCS. In fact, most of the important external powers are already members of regional mechanisms such as East Asia Summit (EAS), Asia-Europe Meeting (ASEM), Asia-Pacific Economic Cooperation (APEC), ASEAN Regional Forum (ARF), ASEAN Defence Ministers' Meeting Plus (ADMM-plus), etc., that discuss security issues in the region, including the SCS.

Southeast Asia in general and the SCS in particular are very important to India as 55 per cent of the total Indian trade crosses it. The Indian Ocean and the SCS are closely interconnected in terms of peace and security. India has been engaging with Southeast Asia for thousands of years. India has now very strong bilateral relations with many countries in Southeast Asia, including Vietnam. India now is not only an ASEAN dialogue partner but also a member of ARF, EAS, ASEM and ADMM-Plus. India's Look East policy has now become the Act East policy. India is a leading power and security provider in the Indo-Pacific region. India is in fact a very important factor in maintaining a balance of power in favour of peace and security in the region. Vietnam welcomes a more active role for India to play in South East Asia.

NOTES

1. Mostly export oriented and resources-deficient, Asia Pacific States depend heavily on seaborne trade. More than 41,000 ships—over half the world's shipping tonnage—sail through the sea each year and more than 80 per cent of the oil imported by Japan, South Korea, and Taiwan transits through the area. A total of $ 5 trillion goods pass through the area each year. The majority of the US$ 350 billion of Vietnam's annual trade is conducted by sea. India also has quite a big volume of trade with ASEAN, China, Japan and Korea. Most of this volume is transported across the South China Sea.
2. In Southeast Asia, the fishing industry remains an important economic activity since most of the States bordering the SCS are developing countries in which the agricultural economic sector still accounts for a considerable part of their national economies. It is estimated that roughly 70 per cent of the South East Asia population are coastal dwellers, representing approximately 270 million people, nearly 5 per cent of the world population. With respect to non-living resources, the SCS is widely known for its rich oil and gas reservoirs that have been discovered in most parts of the SCS.
3. The South China Sea is said to have a significant amount of oil and gas reserves: 11

billion barrels of oil and 190 trillion cubic feet of natural gas. In fact, 25 per cent of Vietnam's GDP comes from the oil and gas sector.

4. Vietnam has been controlling both these groups of islands in a peaceful and continuous manner since the 17th century. Historical evidence of Vietnam includes old maps and documents published by Vietnam and other countries. China has no evidence to prove its sovereignty over the Paracels and the Spratlys. In all the maps printed by China before 1947, Chinese territory stopped short at Hainan Island only. However, China used force to occupy the Paracels in 1974. In 1988, the Chinese again used force to occupy some islands in the Spratlys Group. The Chinese forceful occupation of territories of other nations is illegal as per Article 2, Paragraph 4 of the UN Charter.
5. China used force to occupy the entire Paracel Islands of Vietnam in 1974 and in 1988, occupied 7 rock islands in the Spratly Islands of Vietnam. Now, in the Spratly Islands, Vietnam controls 21 islands, China 7 reefs, the Philippines 9, Malaysia 5, Brunei 1 while Taiwan occupies the biggest island.
6. China turned the reefs, which are under water at high tide, into permanent artificial islands. Satellite pictures show nearly 3,000 acres of land have been reclaimed by China in the past two years, more than all the land reclaimed by all the others combined in the entire history of the region.
7. Brunei and Malaysia have overlapping claims to the exclusive economic zone and continental shelf areas off the coasts of Brunei and Sarawak. Vietnam's exclusive economic zone and continental shelf claim to the south and southeast of its coast overlaps Indonesia's continental shelf claims to the north of the Natuna Islands. Indonesia and Malaysia have overlapping claims to EEZ and continental shelf areas in a zone to the east of Peninsular Malaysia and to the west and north of Anambas Islands, as well as to the east-northeast of the Natuna Islands and to the northwest of Kalimantan (Indonesian part of Borneo) and to the west of Sarawak. Vietnam and Thailand, Vietnam and Malaysia and Vietnam, Malaysia and Thailand respectively have overlapping continental shelves and exclusive economic zones in the Gulf of Thailand. Another zone of overlapping claims to EEZ and continental shelf areas can be found to the southwest of Vietnam, to the east-northeast of the east coast of Peninsular Malaysia and to the southeast of the coast of Thailand. The claims of Malaysia, Thailand and Vietnam overlap in one area. In other areas, bilateral claims overlap between Malaysia and Thailand, Malaysia and Vietnam and between Thailand and Vietnam, respectively. There also existed a tripartite overlapping of continental shelf and EEZ among Vietnam, Thailand and Malaysia in this area. There are overlapping claims to EEZ and continental shelf areas in the Gulf of Thailand off the coasts of Cambodia, Thailand and Vietnam. Cambodia, Thailand and Vietnam overlap in one area. In other areas, bilateral claims overlap between Cambodia and Thailand, Cambodia and Vietnam and between Vietnam and Thailand, respectively.
8. This line caused disputed areas and often involves oil and gas resources such as: Indonesia's ownership of the gas-rich Natuna Island group was undisputed until China released an official map indicating that the Natunas were in Chinese-claimed waters. The Philippines' Malampaya and Camago natural gas and condensate fields are in Chinese-claimed waters. Many of Malaysia's natural gas fields located offshore Sarawak also fall under the Chinese claim. Vietnam and China have overlapping claims to undeveloped blocks off the Vietnamese coast. A block referred to by the Chinese as Wan' Bei-21 (WAB-21) west of the Spratly Islands is claimed by the Vietnamese in their blocks 133, 134, and 135. In addition, Vietnam's Dai Hung (Big Bear) oil field is

at the boundary of waters claimed by the Chinese.

9. The PCA ruling could be briefly summarised thus: (a) maritime entitlements of China may not extend beyond those expressly provided by the UNCLOS; (b) China's claims on "historic rights" based on the "nine-dash line" are contrary to UNCLOS and exceed the geographic and substantive limits of China's maritime entitlements expressly permitted by UNCLOS; (c) No entitlements to territorial sea, EEZ and Continental Shelf for the Scarborough Shoal, Mischief Reef, Second Thomas Shoal, Gaven and McKennan Reef, Johnson Reef and other construction activities in the some of these reefs and shoals; (d) China's failure to protect and preserve marine environment under UNCLOS; and (e) China's aggressive behaviour through its enforcement vessels in a dangerous manner causing serious risk of collision in the vicinity of some of the shoals and reefs.
10. Article 9 of Annex VII provides that "If one of the parties to the dispute does not appear before the arbitral tribunal or fails to defend its case, the other party may request the tribunal to continue the proceedings and to make its award. Absence of a party or failure of a party to defend its case shall not constitute a bar to the proceedings. Before making its award, the arbitral tribunal must satisfy itself not only that it has jurisdiction over the dispute but also that the claim is well founded in fact and law."

18

UNCLOS and the Relationships between Law & Power and Power & Principle:

Lessons (to be) Learned from the South China Sea Arbitration

Gudmundur Eiriksson

Introduction

This Chapter focuses on the relationships between law and power and between power and principle which have been referred to in other Chapters of this book.

What is said by Ambassador Karim in Chapter 11 on the politics of the delimitation disputes in the Bay of Bengal between Bangladesh and its neighbours recalls to mind the well-known adage by Professor Louis Henkin at Columbia Law School who wrote that "the distinction between law and politics is only a part-truth. In a larger, deeper sense, law *is* politics."[1]

This Chapter will present these relationships in the context of the *South China Sea Arbitration (Philippines* v. *China)* before an Arbitral Tribunal constituted under Annex VII to the United Nations Convention on the Law of the Sea (UNCLOS or the Convention).[2]

For reasons explained by Ambassador Ton Sinh Thanh in Chapter 17, the dispute between China and its neighbours about the legal status of the South China Sea can be regarded as an example *par excellence* of the Law/Power/Principle relationships. Even the casual observer of world affairs would readily recognise this continuing dispute as one of the most pressing concerns in the field of the law of the sea and beyond.

The importance of the Award of the Arbitral Tribunal cannot thus be overestimated, given the political interests involved and the complex legal situation. Commentators have written, "[t]he Arbitral Award . . . is undoubtedly one of the most anticipated decisions in recent memory"[3] and "surely the most important set of jurisprudential rulings in the modern history of the international law of the sea".[4] Laurence Boisson de Chazournes described 12 July 2016, the date of the Award, as "a date that will remain etched in the history of international adjudication".[5]

Given the high expectations and the inevitable criticisms to come, it was fortuitous that the Arbitral Tribunal should have been presided over by my dear friend and former colleague, Judge Thomas A. Mensah. Judge Mensah passed away on 7 April 2020 after a lifelong service to the cause of international law. I witnessed his integrity, legal acumen and drafting skills when I served under his Presidency on the first bench of the International Tribunal for the Law of the Sea. With his colleagues on the Arbitral Tribunal, all friends and esteemed colleagues of mine, it was no surprise that the Award turned out to be what I have on many occasions described as a masterpiece in our field.

Yet, having said this, I found myself in disagreement with certain important elements of the Award. This should not, however, be taken as detracting from the regard I have for members of the Arbitral Tribunal and the Registry for their professionalism in discharging their difficult task. Indeed, it is in the nature of our profession that there are many viewpoints on nearly every important question of international law.

I take issue with the Arbitral Tribunal on three counts:

(i) Firstly, I believe that it erred in its analysis of the provision on "rocks" found in article 121(3) of the Convention, as regards the questions of size and geological composition.
(ii) Secondly, I believe that the Arbitral Tribunal's treatment of "offshore" archipelagos was misguided.
(iii) My third and perhaps most important concern from a geopolitical point of view relates to China's claims as regards the so-called

Nine-dash Line. I believe that the Arbitral Tribunal erred in concluding when dealing with this claim that the Convention extinguished all pre-existing claims.

I have chosen to deal extensively below with the first of these concerns. From the legal (if not the "political") point of view, the Award will, I am sure, be recognised for its major contribution to the understanding of article 121(3) of the Convention which has been described as "laconic"[6] and as "one of the least understood provisions in UNCLOS".[7] The Arbitral Tribunal itself described its task in these circumstances as follows:[8]

> *Article 121 has not previously been the subject of significant consideration by courts or arbitral tribunals and has been accorded a wide range of different interpretations in scholarly literature. As has been apparent in the course of these proceedings, the scope of application of its paragraph (3) is not clearly established.* [Footnotes omitted]

Article 121 reads:

Article 121
Regime of Islands

1. An island is a naturally formed area of land, surrounded by water, which is above water at high tide.
2. Except as provided for in paragraph 3, the territorial sea, the contiguous zone, the exclusive economic zone and the continental shelf of an island are determined in accordance with the provisions of this Convention applicable to other land territory.
3. Rocks which cannot sustain human habitation or economic life of their own shall have no exclusive economic zone or continental shelf.

The difficulties faced by commentators in the interpretation of article 121(3) are a reflection of the negotiation methods at the Third United Nations Conference on the Law of the Sea (the Conference) where the Convention was adopted. In their authoritative description of the negotiating process of the conference,[9] Ambassadors Tommy Koh and Shanmugam Jayakumar highlighted a main feature of the proceedings, namely, that so much work was conducted without records, particularly in the work of the Second Committee of the Conference.[10] This has posed challenges for those wishing to have recourse to the preparatory work of the Convention in applying the rules on treaty interpretation laid down in the Vienna Convention on the Law of Treaties. In chapters which I contributed to works in honour of my late mentors, dear friends and close colleagues during the Conference, Judge Hugo Caminos and Ambassador Satya N. Nandan, I referred to the unique circumstances of the Conference negotiations and the implications on the application of the rules on treaty interpretation.[11]

In its pleadings before the Arbitral Tribunal, the Philippines acknowledged this, recognising that "only general—but still critical—insights can be gleaned from the [negotiating history]"[12] and quoting former Judge David Anderson:[13]

> *Paragraph 3 differs from the many proposals submitted to the LOS Conference that sought to qualify or reduce the effect of islands. The travaux préparatoires record disagreements which were not resolved by the main protagonists across the table. For this reason, the records are not a reliable guide to the provision's interpretation.*

The text of what is now article 121 was introduced at the third session of the Conference in 1975, in the Informal Single Negotiating Text (the ISNT). The then Chairman of the Second Committee of the Conference, Ambassador Reynaldo Galindo Pohl, had entrusted the task of preparing the ISNT on the matters within the mandate of the Committee to Satya Nandan, who had been elected as its Rapporteur.[14] The ISNT was the first of five "negotiating texts" presented at the Conference, followed by a Draft Convention (Informal Text) and a Draft Convention, eventually adopted as the Convention.

The positions of States on the article had become rigid when the text in the ISNT came to be considered at the next stages. The procedure followed in revising the texts required that only such changes would be made as were seen to improve the prospects of consensus. Since no proposed amendment had met in the text, the article remained unchanged in substance throughout the subsequent process. Thus, as it turned out, the only opportunity for delegations to have influenced the wording of the text was at the stage of the preparation of the ISNT.

Two groups of States, one loosely constituted by those seeking to reduce further the entitlements to generate an exclusive economic zone and a continental shelf and the other by those seeking to eliminate any such restriction, had continued to debate the article until the very end of the Conference. Some 50 States participated regularly in the debate, including States supporting the article unchanged. Three of the small number of formal amendments proposed in the final stages of the Conference related to this issue, but they had been withdrawn and not pressed to a vote.

The problems of understanding article 121(3) had been anticipated from the time the article first saw the light of day, in the ISNT. I have in my files an analysis of the provision as it emerged in the ISNT, prepared for a leading delegation in the Conference, identifying potential difficulties:[15]

> *The term "rock" is not defined in the Single Negotiating Text. While one may attempt to reconstruct a meaning for the term from the negotiating history of the developing Convention on the Law of the Sea, the results would, at best, be inconclusive.*
> *It is assumed that the proponent of the Paragraph really conceived of a very small island, the precise area of which is undetermined. The issue will immediately arise as to the competent authority for the determination of the areal requirement.*
> *[...]*
> *At best the Article may be interpreted by coastal states as they desire, since "rock" is undefined as are the other qualifications. Any State may declare an economic zone about its "rock".*

Non-appearance of China in the Proceedings before the Arbitral Tribunal

As is well known, China chose not to appear in the proceedings before the Arbitral Tribunal. Although the instances of non-appearance in international adjudication are too few to represent a pattern, it is noteworthy in the context of the theme of this Chapter that three other Permanent Members of the United Nations Security Council, France,[16] Russia[17] and the United States,[18] have also chosen not to participate in cases brought against them. China's and Russia's non-appearance in cases alleging breaches by them of the Convention have raised concerns about the erosion of respect for the dispute settlement mechanism of the Convention.[19]

The Legal Ramifications of Non-appearance

The formal answer addressing these concerns is that:

(i) Firstly, the Convention makes provision for the case when a party to a dispute does not appear before the International Tribunal for the Law of the Sea or an arbitral tribunal.[20]

(ii) Specifically, in such a case, the other party may request the Tribunal or arbitral tribunal to continue the proceedings and make its decision or award. The situation is not one of a default judgment as in some domestic jurisdictions. Absence of a party or the failure of a party to defend its case is not a bar to the proceedings.

(iii) Thirdly, the Tribunal or arbitral tribunal must, before making its decision or award, satisfy itself (i) not only that it has jurisdiction over the dispute, but also (ii) that the claim is well founded in fact and law.

(iv) Fourthly, despite the non-appearance of a party, the decision of the Tribunal or the award of an arbitral tribunal is final under the Convention and shall be complied with by the parties to the dispute.[21]

The Political Situation in Cases of Non-appearance

However, the political situation is far more complex and difficult to assess. It may well depend on the motivations behind the decision of a party to a dispute not to defend its case. For example, Iceland decided not to appear in the cases brought against it before the International Court of Justice with respect to the extension of its fisheries jurisdiction.[22] One of Iceland's motivations was certainly an appreciation that it would lose the case, despite a strong moral argument and a widely-held opinion that it was only a matter of time before the world community recognised extended coastal State fisheries jurisdiction. This was, of course, finally confirmed in the Convention, where, moreover, there was recognition, in article 71 of the Convention, of the special situation of a country (such as Iceland) whose economy is overwhelmingly dependent on the exploitation of the living resources in its exclusive economic zone.

Thus, given the legal situation set out above, it could be said that there is a general understanding that it is in a State's sovereign prerogative to decide whether or not to defend its case before international judicial bodies, with, however, the consequences of an adverse decision or award being nonetheless binding on it.

Yet it is quite clear that courts and tribunals are not pleased when a State does not appear before them. Indeed, it places an additional burden on them (and on the other party); they are obligated, in a sense, to present all possible arguments in favour of the party that has not appeared.[23]

Critique of the Arbitral Tribunal's Conclusions on the Interpretation of Article 121(3) of the Convention

As mentioned above, I take issue with two aspects of the Arbitral Tribunal's interpretation of article 121(3). In this, I find support in Sean Murphy's monumental work on international law in relation to islands. He wrote:[24]

> *Further, in asserting that the term "rock" conveys no geological or geomorphical meaning, and further that it conveys no meaning as to size, the tribunal seems to ascribe no significance whatsoever to the use of the word "rock" rather than "island" in paragraph 3. Given that the tribunal saw considerable significance in the precise wording of Article 121 in various other respects, the lack of attention to why the word "rock" was used in paragraph 3 is striking.*

The Arbitral Tribunal referred three times in its Award to the Judgment of the International Court of Justice in *Territorial and Maritime Dispute (Nicaragua* v. *Colombia),*[25] firstly in support of its conclusion that no geological or geomorphological criteria were intended in the term "rocks",[26] secondly in support of its conclusion that size cannot be dispositive of a feature's status[27] and thirdly in the application of article 121(3) to Scarborough Shoal, Johnson Reef, Cuarteron Reef and Fiery Cross Reef.[28]

The first reference was:[29]

> *This was also the conclusion reached by the International Court of Justice in* Territorial and Maritime Dispute (Nicaragua *v.* Colombia) *when it held Colombia's Quitasueño, a "minuscule" protrusion of coral, to be an Article 121(3) rock:*

> *International law defines an island by reference to whether it is 'naturally formed' and whether it is above water at high tide, not by reference to its geological composition . . . The fact that the feature is composed of coral is irrelevant.*

The second reference is preceded by the clause: "size cannot be dispositive of a feature's status as a fully entitled island or rock and is not, on its own, a relevant factor."[30]

The third reference stated that Rock No. 32 of Colombia's Quitasueño located in the area to be delimited was held by the Court to be a rock for the purposes of article 121(3).[31]

I cannot concur in the Arbitral Tribunal's reading of the Judgment. The Court did *not*, as claimed in the Award, determine in the quoted passage that QS 32 is a *rock*. Rather, it stated that it is an *island*, despite its very small size and despite being composed of coral debris. The Court, having pronounced the feature to be an island, introduced the "rock" element later in its Judgment, as a matter not in dispute between the parties, stating:[32]

> *It has not been suggested by either Party that QS 32 is anything other than a rock which is incapable of sustaining human habitation or economic life of its own under Article 121, paragraph 3, of UNCLOS, so this feature generates no entitlement to a continental shelf or exclusive economic zone.*[33]

I express my disagreement with the Arbitral Tribunal on this point with, however, the caveat that Judges Mensah and Cot, having been Judges *ad hoc* in *Territorial and Maritime Dispute (Nicaragua* v. *Colombia)*, may perhaps have had a better understanding of the Court's reasoning than has been reflected in the Award.

Geological or Geomorphological Criteria

I turn now to the first of my two objections to the interpretation by the Arbitral Tribunal of article 121(3), that is, the question of the geological or geomorphological criteria in the definition of "rocks". On this question, the Arbitral Tribunal concluded:[34]

> *[T]he use of the word "rock" does not limit the provision to features composed of solid rock. The geological and geomorphological characteristics of a high-tide feature are not relevant to its classification pursuant to Article 121(3).*

The Arbitral Tribunal supported this conclusion earlier in its Award:[35]

> *479. The use in Article 121(3) of the term "rocks" raises the question of whether any geological or geomorphological criteria were intended. In other words, was Article 121(3) intended to apply only to features that are composed of solid rock or that are otherwise rock-like in nature?*
> *480. In the Tribunal's view, no such restriction necessarily follows from the use of the term in Article 121(3). The dictionary meaning of "rock" does not confine the term so strictly, and rocks may "consist of aggregates of minerals . . . and occasionally also organic matter. . . . They vary in hardness, and include soft materials such as clays." This was also the conclusion reached by the International Court of Justice in* Territorial and Maritime Dispute (Nicaragua *v.* Colombia) *when it held Colombia's Quitasueño, a "minuscule" protrusion of coral, to be an Article 121(3) rock:*
>
> > *International law defines an island by reference to whether it is 'naturally formed' and whether it is above water at high tide, not by reference to its geological composition . . . The fact that the feature is composed of coral is irrelevant.*
>
> *481. Moreover, any contrary interpretation imposing a geological criterion on Article 121(3) would lead to an absurd result. Within Article 121, rocks are a category of island. An island is defined as a "naturally formed area of land," without any geological or geomorphological qualification. Introducing a geological qualification in paragraph (3) would mean that any high-tide features formed by sand, mud, gravel, or coral—irrespective of their other characteristics—would always generate extended maritime entitlements, even if they were incapable of sustaining human habitation or an economic life of their own. Such features are more ephemeral than a geological rock and may shift location or appear and disappear above high water as a result of conditions over time. A geological criterion would thus accord greater entitlements to less stable and less permanent features. This cannot have been the intent of the Article.*
>
> *482. The result of this interpretation is that "rocks" for the purposes of Article 121(3) will not necessarily be composed of rock.* [Footnotes omitted.]

The Arbitral Tribunal added, in a footnote to a passage on the diversity of islands:[36]

> *Attempts to include "geological configuration" or "geomorphological structure" as relevant factors in Article 121 all failed, confirming the Tribunal's interpretation of that portion of the text.*

I find fault with two points in the Arbitral Tribunal's conclusion on this aspect of the definition.

First, as for the reference to the Judgment of the Court in *Territorial and Maritime Dispute (Nicaragua* v. *Colombia)* in support of its conclusion that no geological or geomorphological criteria were intended in the term "rocks", I have already noted above that I disagree that the passage concerned provided authority for such a broad conclusion.

Secondly, the Arbitral Tribunal's statement that an interpretation imposing a geological criterion on article 121(3) would lead to an "absurd result" recalls the terms of article 32(b) of the Vienna Convention on the Law of Treaties.[37] The Arbitral Tribunal did not refer specifically to article 32(b) with its prerequisites but one should in any event be wary of characterising any result as "absurd". When preparing the text of the ISNT, Satya Nandan had before him two proposals which defined rocks, one as "a naturally formed rocky elevation of ground, surrounded by water, which is above water at high tide"[38] and another as "a naturally formed rocky elevation normally unfit for human habitation which is surrounded by water and is above water at high tide".[39]

In the early analysis referred to above of the provision as it emerged in the ISNT (as article 132(3)), potential difficulties had been identified:[40]

> *Situations are bound to occur where a State will claim that island 'X' falls under 132(3) while the administering State will counter that 'X' is not a "rock" but an "atoll". It is therefore entitled to an economic zone even if it is uninhabited.*

For these two reasons, I maintain, the conclusions of the Arbitral Tribunal are open to challenge. Individual delegates in the negotiations at the Conference would certainly have assessed the features in their country which might technically fall within the ambit of article 121(3) on the basis of their geological or geomorphological character. It would not be "absurd" for them to take a position on the provision accordingly.

Does Size Matter?

I turn now to the second of my reservations on the Arbitral Tribunal's conclusions on the interpretation of article 121(3), on the question of whether "size matters".

The Arbitral Tribunal stated:[41]

> *537. Third, the drafters accepted that there are diverse high-tide features: vast and tiny; barren and lush; rocky and sandy; isolated and proximate; densely and sparsely populated, or not populated at all. Many States considered that criteria such as surface area, population size, and proximity to other land might be useful in deciding whether a high-tide feature should be a fully entitled island. But the negotiating history clearly demonstrates the difficulty in setting, in the abstract, bright-line rules for all cases. Proposals to introduce specific criteria were considered, but consistently rejected. Against such attempts at precision, the drafters clearly favoured the language of the compromise reflected in Article 121(3).*
>
> *538. In particular, repeated attempts during the Conference to define or categorise islands or rocks by reference to size were all rejected. These included proposals to include "size" on a list of "relevant factors"; proposals to categorise islands and islets depending on whether they were "vast" or "smaller"; and proposals that made distinctions based on whether the surface area of a feature measured more or less than a particular figure, such as one square kilometre or ten square kilometres. In this respect, the representative of United Kingdom recalled that "there were large islands which were largely or completely uninhabited and small ones with dense populations which depend heavily upon the sea." Representatives of small island States, such as Micronesia, Fiji, Tonga, and Western Samoa, also argued that it was inequitable to deprive features of their maritime entitlements on the basis of size. The Tribunal considers that the* travaux *make clear that—although size may correlate to the availability of water, food, living space, and resources for an economic life—size cannot be dispositive of a feature's status as a fully entitled island or rock and is not, on its own, a relevant factor. As noted by the International Court of Justice in* Territorial and Maritime Dispute (Nicaragua *v.* Colombia), *"international law does not prescribe any minimum size which a feature must possess in order to be considered an island."* [Footnotes omitted.]

This conclusion is in my view astonishing and flies in the face of the ordinary meaning of "rock". Indeed, if anything was clear about the definition of "rock", it was that it was a very small, even tiny, feature. The Arbitral Tribunal itself referred to "tiny features" in explaining the rationale of article 121(3) and its relationship to the exclusive economic zone:[42]

> *It serves to disable tiny features from unfairly and inequitably generating enormous entitlements to maritime space that would serve not to benefit the local population, but to award a windfall to the (potentially distant) State to have maintained a claim to such a feature.*

The legislative history of the negotiations at the Conference after its third session, when the article which was to become article 121 was introduced into the ISNT, reveals a consistent effort by those proposing greater reductions in the entitlement to marine spaces than was set out in the prevailing text to amend paragraph 3 to include larger features, for example islets, within its ambit. In reaching its conclusions, the Arbitral Tribunal seems to have been labouring under some misconceptions about the legislative history. I refer again to my writings on the negotiating process at the Conference where I have attempted to set the record straight and thus be of service to future commentators.[43]

As for the specific language in the relevant passages of the Award, I would first address the assertions that "[p]roposals to introduce specific criteria were considered, but consistently rejected"[44] and that "repeated attempts during the Conference to define or categorise islands or rocks by reference to size were all rejected".[45] In fact, as I noted above, proposals could be said to have been "rejected" only at the stage of the elaboration of the ISNT. Any such "rejection" involved a choice by Satya Nandan among proposals then on the table. Subsequent proposals for amendment were not "rejected" *per se*; they were simply not incorporated in the text because they could not improve the prospects of consensus, given the divergent views of participants in the negotiations.

Secondly, the Arbitral Tribunal stated:[46]

> *Against such attempts at precision, the drafters clearly favoured the language of the compromise reflected in Article 121(3).*

As noted above, it is certainly true that Satya Nandan had fashioned article 121(3) from among various terms and phrases, rather from any one proposal, seeking a compromise among competing views, pleasing at that stage some delegates but displeasing others. In my commentary on the negotiating process leading to the preparation of the ISNT, I included the article on islands among those which "were not yet agreed but which reflected possible ways forward in the continuing negotiations".[47]

Finally, the Arbitral Tribunal introduced its major conclusion with "the *travaux* make clear". In this connection, I recall again Judge Anderson's caution that "the records are not a reliable guide to the ... interpretation [of article 121(3)]".[48]

Having said all this, I admit that we are no closer to an understanding of how small a feature must be in order to be considered to fall under article 121(3). It should, however, be clear that "size does matter".

Final Reflections

The foregoing discussion recalls to mind two features of multilateral treaty-making which call for special vigilance on the part of those seeking to apply the rules on the interpretation of international conventions found in the Vienna Convention on the Law of Treaties.

The first is the tendency for participants in negotiations to seek opportunities to place on record their views about a particular provision with the intent of using the record to buttress their position in any later dispute about its interpretation. This is particularly tempting when there is no opportunity for those delegations with a contrary interpretation to record their views. Examples of this abound in the case of the negotiations at the Conference.

A second feature of modern multilateral treaty-making is that, in efforts to reach consensus, proposals made by participants can be rejected, or not accepted, without explanation or public record of the reasons, unrelated to their merit. The sophisticated delegate exercises care in these circumstances so as not to have it used against his or her country, in a later dispute, that its position had been rejected during the negotiations and was therefore not a valid interpretation of a provision in dispute.[49]

Would the Award in the *South China Sea Arbitration* Have Been Different had China Participated?

Whether the Award in the *South China Sea Arbitration* would have been different had China participated is, of course, entirely in the realm of speculation. I have referred above to issues on which I had disagreed with the Arbitral Tribunal and have dealt extensively with one of them, its interpretation of article 121(3) of the Convention.

It can certainly be debated whether the Arbitral Tribunal would have benefitted from the arguments of China to reach other conclusions on these issues, amongst others.

Conclusion

When considering the Law/Power/Principle relationships in the context of what is said elsewhere in this book about the lack of an hierarchical structure in the regime of international law, I turn again to Professor Henkin and his postulations on parallel or horizontal enforcement of international law norms. He wrote:[50]

> *The international state system, we know, has never sought to develop an executive arm or a comprehensive judiciary to enforce international law and obligations. Instead, international law is maintained by "horizontal enforcement": states are induced to honor their obligations by various political forces, including the anticipated reaction of the state victim of a violation.*

Power relations are an inherently relative phenomenon. When applied to answer the questions posed above, I would argue that the jury is still out on whether the rule of law remains relevant in the disputes in the South China Sea.

The author is grateful to Sandrine De Herdt for her assistance in the preparation of this chapter.

NOTES

1. Louis Henkin, *International Law: Politics and Values* (Dordrecht: Martinus Nijhoff Publishers, 1995), pp. 4–5, as excerpted in Lori Fisler Damrosch et al. (eds.), *International Law: Cases and Materials* (St. Paul, Minnesota: West Group, 2001), 4th edition, pp. 1–2.
2. *The South China Sea Arbitration (Republic of the Philippines* v. *People's Republic of China), Award of 12 July 2016*, Permanent Court of Arbitration Case No. 2013-19 [Award].

3. Nilufer Oral, "'Rocks' or 'Islands'? Sailing Towards Legal Clarity in the Turbulent South China Sea," *AJIL Unbound*, Vol. 110 (2016), pp. 279-284, at p. 279.
4. Thomas J. Schoenbaum, "The South China Sea Arbitration Decision: The Need for Clarification," ibid., pp. 290-295, at p. 290.
5. Laurence Boisson de Chazournes, "Introduction to Symposium on the South China Sea Arbitration," ibid., pp. 263-265, at p. 263.
6. Jonathan I. Charney, "Rocks that Cannot Sustain Human Habitation," *American Journal of International Law*, Vol. 93, No. 4 (1999), pp. 863-878, at p. 863.
7. Nilufer Oral, op. cit., p. 283.
8. Award, op. cit., p. 204, para. 474.
9. Tommy T.B. Koh and Shanmugam Jayakumar, "The Negotiating Process of the Third United Nations Conference on the Law of the Sea," in Myron H. Nordquist (ed.), *United Nations Convention on the Law of the Sea 1982: A Commentary* (Dordrecht: Martinus Nijhoff Publishers, 1985), Vol. I, pp. 29-134.
10. Myron H. Nordquist (ed.), *United Nations Convention on the Law of the Sea 1982: A Commentary* (Dordrecht: Martinus Nijhoff Publishers, 1993), Vol. II, p. 18.
11. Gudmundur Eiriksson, "Satya N. Nandan's role in Drafting the Informal Single Negotiating Text: Aspects of the Preparatory Work for UNCLOS," in Michael W. Lodge and Myron H. Nordquist (eds.), *Peaceful Order in the World's Oceans: Essays in Honor of Satya N. Nandan* (Leiden: Brill Nijhoff, 2014), pp. 37-50; Gudmundur Eiriksson, "The Bay of Bengal Case before the International Tribunal for the Law of the Sea," in Lilian del Castillo (ed.), *Law of the Sea, From Grotius to the International Tribunal for the Law of the Sea: Liber Amicorum Judge Hugo Caminos* (Leiden: Brill Nijhoff, 2015), pp. 512-528.
12. *The South China Sea Arbitration (Republic of the Philippines* v. *People's Republic of China), Merits Hearings Transcript (Day 2)*, pp. 61-62.
13. David Anderson, "Islands and Rocks in the Modern Law of the Sea," in Myron H. Nordquist et al. (eds.), *The Law of the Sea Convention: U.S. Accession and Globalization* (Leiden & Boston: Martinus Nijhoff Publishers, 2012), pp. 307-340, at p. 313.
14. Gudmundur Eiriksson (2014), op. cit., p. 37.
15. Anon, "Article 132 of the Single Negotiating Text: An Analysis" [Paper Prepared for a delegation at the Third United Nations Conference on the Law of the Sea (on file with author)].
16. *Nuclear Tests (Australia* v. *France), Interim Protection, Order of 22 June 1973, I.C.J. Reports 1973*, p. 99; *Nuclear Tests (New Zealand* v. *France), Interim Protection, Order of 22 June 1973, I.C.J. Reports 1973*, p. 135.
17. *The "Arctic Sunrise" Case (Kingdom of the Netherlands* v. *Russian Federation), Provisional Measures, Order of 22 November 2013, ITLOS Reports 2013; Arctic Sunrise Arbitration (Kingdom of the Netherlands* v. *Russian Federation), Award on the Merits of 14 August 2015*, Permanent Court of Arbitration Case No. 2014-02.
18. *Military and Paramilitary Activities in and against Nicaragua (Nicaragua* v. *United States of America), Merits, Judgment, I.C.J. Reports 1986*, p. 14.
19. See *Joint Separate Opinion of Judge Wolfrum and Judge Kelly* in *the "Arctic Sunrise" Case*, op. cit., p. 258, para. 6.
20. Annex VI, article 28:

    Default

    When one of the parties does not appear before the Tribunal or fails to defend its case, the other party may request the Tribunal to continue the proceedings and make its decision. Absence of a party or failure of a party to defend its case shall not constitute a bar to the proceedings. Before making its decision, the Tribunal must satisfy itself not only that it has jurisdiction over the dispute, but also that the claim is well founded in fact and law.

Annex VII, article 9:

Default of appearance

If one of the parties to the dispute does not appear before the arbitral tribunal or fails to defend its case, the other party may request the tribunal to continue the proceedings and to make its award. Absence of a party or failure of a party to defend its case shall not constitute a bar to the proceedings. Before making its award, the arbitral tribunal must satisfy itself not only that it has jurisdiction over the dispute but also that the claim is well founded in fact and law.

21. Annex VI, article 33, paragraph 1:

    Finality and binding force of decisions

    1. The decision of the Tribunal is final and shall be complied with by all the parties to the dispute.

    Annex VII, article 11:

    Finality of award

    The award shall be final and without appeal, unless the parties to the dispute have agreed in advance to an appellate procedure. It shall be complied with by the parties to the dispute.
22. *Fisheries Jurisdiction (United Kingdom* v. *Iceland), Merits, Judgment, I.C.J. Reports 1974*, p. 3; *Fisheries Jurisdiction (Federal Republic of Germany* v. *Iceland), Merits, Judgment, I.C.J. Reports 1974*, p. 175.
23. Judge Sir Gerald Fitzmaurice, who served on the International Court of Justice in the cases against Iceland referred to above, wrote very colourfully on this. See Gerald Fitzmaurice, "The Problem of the 'Non-appearing' Defendant Government," *British Yearbook of International Law*, Vol. 51, No. 1 (1980), pp. 89-122.
24. Sean D. Murphy, *International Law relating to Islands* (Recueil des cours de l'Académie de Droit International de la Haye/Collected courses of the Hague Academy of International Law, Vol. 386, 2017), p. 74.
25. *Territorial and Maritime Dispute (Nicaragua* v. *Colombia), Judgment, I.C.J. Reports 2012*, p. 624, at p. 645, para. 37.
26. Award, op. cit., pp. 205-206, para. 480.
27. Ibid., p. 227, para. 538.
28. Ibid., p. 186, para. 423.
29. Ibid., pp. 205-206, para. 480.
30. Ibid., pp. 226-227, para. 538.
31. Ibid., p. 186, para. 423.
32. *Territorial and Maritime Dispute*, op. cit., p. 693, para. 183.
33. Freestone and Schofield wrote:

    As neither party to the dispute had characterized QS32 as 'anything other than a rock which is incapable of human habitation or an economic life of its own, under Article 121, paragraph 3, of UNCLOS', this issue did not need to be addressed.

    David Freestone and Clive Schofield, "The Caribbean Sea and the Gulf of Mexico," in Donald R. Rothwell et al. (eds.), *The Oxford Handbook of the Law of the Sea* (Oxford: Oxford University Press, 2015), pp. 672-700, at p. 697, fn 131.
34. Award, op. cit., p. 227, para. 540.
35. Ibid., pp. 205-206, paras. 479-482.

36. Ibid., p. 225, fn. 578.
37. Vienna Convention on the Law of Treaties (Vienna, 23 May 1969, in force 27 January 1980), 1155 UNTS 331, Article 32 reads:
    Supplementary means of interpretation
    Recourse may be had to supplementary means of interpretation, including the preparatory work of the treaty and the circumstances of its conclusion, in order to confirm the meaning resulting from the application of article 31, or to determine the meaning when the interpretation according to article 31:
    (a) leaves the meaning ambiguous or obscure; or
    (b) leads to a result which is manifestly absurd or unreasonable.
38. "Main Trends Working Paper," UN document A/CONF.62/L.8/Rev.1 (1974), provision 239, formula B, para. 3.
39. "Articles submitted to the informal consultative group on islands, dated 28 April 1975," article I, para. 3 (on file with author).
40. Anon, op. cit.
41. Award, op. cit., pp. 225-227, paras. 537-538.
42. Ibid., p. 217, para. 516.
43. Gudmundur Eiriksson (2014), op. cit.; Gudmundur Eiriksson (2015), op. cit.
44. Award, op. cit., p. 225, para. 537.
45. Ibid., p. 226, para. 538.
46. Ibid., p. 225, para. 537.
47. Gudmundur Eiriksson (2014), op. cit., pp. 42 and 46.
48. David Anderson, op. cit., p. 313.
49. Ambassador Hayes of the Irish delegation to the Conference wrote of two instances in point. At the ninth session of the Conference, the group to which Ireland belonged feared "that a failed attempt at amendment could detrimentally affect the interpretation of a provision that was actually lacking only in specificity" (Mahon Hayes, *The Law of the Sea: The Role of the Irish Delegation at the Third UN Conference* (Dublin: Royal Irish Academy, 2011), pp. 182-183). At the tenth session, "the Irish delegation . . . was aware that only a very small number of delegations would support either amendment [to article 121(3)], and that defeat could detrimentally affect interpretation of the provision" (ibid., p. 213).

50 Louis Henkin, "Human Rights and State 'Sovereignty'," *Georgia Journal of International and Comparative Law*, Vol. 25 (1995/96), pp. 31-45, at p. 41.

Maritime Security Architecture in the Indo-Pacific

19

Freedom of Navigation in the Indo-Pacific:
A View from the Indian Ocean

Gurpreet S. Khurana

> *"As responsible stewards in the Indo-Pacific region, President Trump and Prime Minister Modi agreed that a close partnership between the United States and India is central to peace and stability in the region.... To this end, the leaders: reiterate the importance of respecting freedom of navigation, overflight, and commerce throughout the region...."*
>
> **U.S.-India Joint Statement Washington, D.C. (June 27, 2017)[1]**

Increasingly over the past few years, the articulations that political leaders have been making *ad nauseum* on "freedom of navigation (FON)"[2] *bring to mind the quintessentially American belief* of 'motherhood and apple pie' representing something virtuous and important. Today, FON has become a catchword among regional countries and stakeholders in the Indo-Pacific region; interestingly, being used by both those who wield the power to interpret FON for the others in their own favour, and those who may be at the receiving end of the 'stick'. Whereas political leaders may adopt such a 'broad-brush' approach to foster diplomatic goodwill, there is much variance at the functional level on what precisely is FON.

The political statements on FON are often conjoined with the phrase 'in accordance with international law'. But as Sam Bateman observes, "...adding (such) caveats makes little difference as there is no agreement on key points of international law related to particular freedoms".[3] If no law, state practice or any established norm provides a conclusive answer on what precisely is meant by FON, the Indo-Pacific region may be headed for stormy weather, given the 'shadow-boxing' between China and its potential adversaries in the waters of Pacific-Asia (western Pacific Ocean), including over the outstanding maritime-territorial disputes. The western part of the Indo-Pacific—the Indian Ocean Region (IOR)—is unlikely to remain insulated from the geopolitical insecurities in the East, particularly considering the rise of China as a 'non-status quo' maritime power in Asia and beyond. After all, the genesis of the contemporary 'Indo-Pacific' concept in 2006-07 was indeed premised on the emerging security linkage between the Indian and Pacific oceans.[4]

Pacific-Asia is a region that has achieved remarkable economic progress through emphasis on manufacturing industries and export-led development. This translates into the growing salience of maritime communications. The IOR countries like India seek an economic integration with their extended eastern neighbours to benefit from the success of Pacific-Asia. This was the rationale of India's 'Look-East' Policy of the early 1990s, and its reinvigorated 'Act East' Policy launched in 2014. Currently, about 30 per cent of India's total seaborne trade transits east of the Malacca Straits, and this proportion is increasing. Added to this, India's resource-related engagements with the littorals of Pacific-Asia dictate its interest in a benign and conducive maritime environment in the western Pacific. As for the IOR, this region has always been critical for India, not only for its economic development, but also for its national security.

In the geopolitical context, Pacific-Asia and IOR are lately being seen as an integrated 'Indo-Pacific' maritime supra-region. However, one cannot ignore the fact that the security environment in the two regions are vastly dissimilar. Hence, the emergent issues relating to FON would also differ. Accordingly, whereas this paper examines FON in the entire Indo-Pacific, it seeks to provide a prognosis and policy prescriptions specific to the IOR.

FON and International Law

As the Constitution of the oceans, the United Nations Convention on the Law of the Sea, 1982 (UNCLOS) stipulates the provisions for FON in very broad terms. It is premised upon the consensual trade-off between the historical tenet of *Mare Liberum* (Free Sea) on the one hand, and on the other, the need for nations to assert sovereign rights over their adjoining maritime spaces to meet their legitimate economic and security objectives, as derived from the erstwhile concept of *Mare Clausum* (Closed Sea).

Article 87 of UNCLOS says that the freedoms of the high seas—subject to some qualifications—are available to all states. UNCLOS does not address all scenarios, but then, it was only meant to be an umbrella convention to provide overarching guidance, and its interpretation to specific circumstances must be found by countries based on their specific conditions, and eventually, a consensus on its interpretation be evolved from state practice.

An analysis of the varied interpretations of the Law on FON yields interesting results. The core deduction is the divergent emphases on the specific objectives of FON, viz., maritime economics including sea-borne commerce and harnessing of marine resources versus maritime-military mobility. This difference flows from the security concerns of the erstwhile 'developing' coastal states, pitted against the interests of the traditional maritime powers that have held military-mobility very close to their hearts.

Question of Emphasis: Ends or Means?

Although UNCLOS does not explicitly address the aspect of military operations, evidently, FON is necessary for both non-military and military purposes. However, the variance of emphasis is palpable. For most countries—such as the IOR littorals—FON for non-military economic and commercial activity would suffice, since therein lies the essence of maritime communications for the societal and economic well-being of the people, which is the ultimate national objective of most countries. It is in consonance with this spirit that the Indian 'Maritime Security Strategy' document of 2015 contextualises FON. It says,

> *"India's trade and energy security, development of its deep-sea mining areas, and supporting its scientific research stations in Antarctica, are all dependent on its Sea Lines of Communication (SLOCs). This*

has lent a pivotal role to the security of India's SLOCs and increased the importance of the sea routes, international shipping and freedom of navigation to India's national interests."[5]

It is in this context that China asserts that its position on FON is similar to that of India, and Beijing is not threatening FON in the South China Sea (SCS). There is no evidence that China has denied the right of navigational freedom to any foreign merchant ship in the SCS, including within China's own waters—its 12 nautical-mile (NM) territorial sea and the 200 NM exclusive economic zone (EEZ). It is important to note that China would be among the worst affected if FON of commercial shipping in the SCS were to be impeded. It is an export-led manufacturing economy, and has major stakes in unimpeded maritime commerce. It also imports nearly 80 per cent of its hydrocarbon-based energy resources via the sea. Navigational freedom for commercial vessels is thus germane to China's own economic prosperity, which it will disrupt at its own peril.[6] However, China's assertion of being a proponent of FON is weakened by its other actions in the SCS, as we shall see.

All would have been well today if the global order was benchmarked to the United Nations' vision of sovereign equality of countries, but which remains merely an ideation. In practice, the world is driven by a hierarchical order, wherein powerful states seek to enhance their power and preserve their superior status in the order. This leads to the major naval powers laying greater emphasis on military mobility, even though such mobility is merely a 'means' to attain the economic 'ends'. The United States (U.S.) 'Asia-Pacific Maritime Security Strategy' of 2015 says,

"The United States has, throughout its history, advocated for the freedom of the seas for economic and security reasons... Freedom of the seas, however, includes more than the mere freedom of commercial vessels to transit through international waterways. While not a defined term under international law, the Department (of Defence) uses 'freedom of the seas' to mean all of the rights, freedoms, and lawful uses of the sea and airspace, including for military ships and aircraft, recognized under international law."[7]

In this context, China's actions also impinge on FON owing to its expansive maritime-territorial claims and reclamation/militarisation activities in the South China Sea. Beijing's approach goes even further to blur the military-commercial (means-ends) distinction. It is increasingly using its 'maritime militia' (fishing boats under State control) to engage in fishing in the maritime zones of its neighbours within its claimed "nine-dash line" in the SCS. In March 2016, these fishing boats—supported by the Chinese Coast Guard—clashed with Indonesia's law-enforcement agencies in the Indonesian waters off the Natuna Islands, which happen to lie within the 'nine-dash line'.[8] In October 2015, the international arbitration tribunal had ruled that:

> *"China's claims to sovereign rights and jurisdiction, and to "historic rights", with respect to the maritime areas of the South China Sea encompassed by the so-called "nine-dash line" are contrary to the Convention and without lawful effect to the extent that they exceed the geographic and substantive limits of China's maritime entitlements under UNCLOS".*[9]

In the light of this verdict, China's use of maritime militia to enforce its fishing rights in the Indonesian EEZ amounts to interference with Jakarta's sovereign rights, and thereby also impeding FON for 'commercial' ends.

This is also leading to a dangerous trend for other countries, who may emulate China in retaliation, thereby lowering the threshold of conflict in the SCS. Vietnam is particularly threatened by fishing by Chinese fishermen in its EEZ.[10] In 2018, it formulated a national plan to curb illegal fishing by 2025.[11] It was in this context that the Vietnamese researcher, Nguyen Giang, suggests how his country should prevent foreign fishing in its waters. He writes about the 2009 Vietnamese domestic law that permits the operations of a "fishing militia", and how it assisted Vietnam's coast-guard in its 2014 standoff with the Chinese oil rig HD-981.[12]

The Philippines may also respond in a similar manner. Rafael M. Alunan III—an eminent Filipino political figure who served in the cabinets of two former Presidents—writes in his June 2019 opinion piece,

> *"Because China uses a three-ring offensive to occupy, deny access and eventually conquer an area through its CMM (Chinese Maritime Militia), CCG (China Coast Guard), and PLAN (PLA Navy), we too must apply a layered defence in the West Philippine Sea (SCS)... the local governments should contribute to a common fund to build 200-*

foot steel-hulled fishing trawlers or acquire reconditioned ones from abroad—at least 100 vessels with armed maritime CAFGUs (Citizen Armed Force Geographical Units) aboard and placed under the Philippine Coast Guard's operational control...".[13]

Military Mobility versus Security of Coastal State

Since the days of UNCLOS negotiations (1973-82), the developing countries and major naval powers have held divergent positions on FON, based on differing interpretations of the Law. UNCLOS Article 87 merely says that freedoms of the high seas are available to all states subject to some qualifications *inter alia* "due regard for the interests of other States". The divergence of positions flow from the subjectivity of this statement, which leads to interpretation by countries in many different ways, based on their specific circumstances.

The U.S. has been among the foremost of the military powers that interpret the Law[14] to bestow holistic navigational freedoms, including for its naval units in territorial seas and EEZ of the coastal states. Clearly, such an approach is not considerate of the security concerns of the coastal states, though realists may justify its legitimacy in context of international relations theory. Accordingly, since 1979, the U.S. Navy has been undertaking regular Freedom of Navigation Operations (FONOPS) worldwide to prevent any norm-building that is not favourable to US interests as a major global maritime power.

On the other hand, due to their overwhelming national security concerns, most developing states have placed certain restrictions for the innocent passage of foreign warships through their territorial seas. Article 4 of India's Maritime Zones of India (MZI) Act of 1976 says,

> *"All foreign warships may enter or pass through the territorial waters after giving* prior notice *to the Central Government...(which) may if satisfied that it is necessary so to do in the interests of the peace, good order or security of India... suspend... (their) entry...".*[15]

Therefore, India seeks only 'prior notification', whereas all its maritime neighbours place a more restrictive requirement of 'prior consent' for the innocent passage of foreign warships through their territorial seas.

The coastal states also expect prior notification of foreign military activities in their EEZ. For instance, India's declaration while ratifying UNCLOS in June 1995 said,

> *"The Government of the Republic of India understands that the provisions of the Convention do not authorize other States to carry out in the exclusive economic zone and on the continental shelf military exercises or manoeuvres, in particular those involving the use of weapons or explosives without the consent of the coastal State."*[16]

Accordingly, in 2002-03, India protested against the activities of the U.S. surveillance ship USNS *Bowditch* in the Bay of Bengal. The ship was undertaking an underwater survey within India's EEZ.[17] The USA asserted it was a lawful survey being undertaken for the navigational safety of warships. India believed that it was 'intelligence gathering'.

While the UNCLOS—meant to be merely an umbrella Convention—cannot be faulted, the fact remains that it does not even define 'military activity', much less explicitly prohibiting it, which complicates the interpretation of Law on FON. This also leads to the debate on whether the 'sui generis' EEZ can be regarded as 'international waters' with unqualified FON, as the U.S. interprets it. Notably, the contrarian views of India and most other regional countries—including regional powers like Australia—seem to be aligned on this aspect.[18]

Between India and the U.S., who is more accurate in the interpretation of the Law remains a moot issue. However, in substance, the U.S. does not acknowledge India's position on any of the aforementioned activities relating to FON.[19] This has led to the US Navy conducting annual FONOPS against India as well, since as early as in 1992 (if not earlier), as recorded in the U.S. Department of Defence (DoD) Annual Freedom of Navigation Reports.[20] As these reports indicate, the U.S. contention against India is premised on three key issues:[21]

- Prior notice for foreign warships to undertake Innocent Passage in Indian Territorial Sea (based on Section 4(2) of India's MZI Act, 1976, as mentioned above).
- Authorisation required for foreign military exercises or manoeuvres in Indian EEZ (based on India's 1995 declaration, as mentioned above), and

- Security jurisdiction claimed in Indian contiguous zone (based on Section 5(4)(a) of India's MZI Act, 1976)

In contrast, the divergence between the USA and China on FON has lately magnified to an adversarial level, which is not without good reason. China presents an interesting case of duplicity, which is possibly a result of a shifting position as it emerges as a major global naval power. During the UNCLOS negotiations in the 1970s, Beijing had shared the position held by the other developing countries. It continues to maintain this position with regard to its maritime periphery in the East and South China Seas, owing to its insecurities that stem from US military activities. However, in more distant seas, China seems to be emulating the position of a major naval power like the U.S. In 2013, Chinese warships were involved in intelligence gathering within the U.S. EEZ off Guam,[22] and later in 2017, off Australia's Queensland coast.[23]

Even on the issue of innocent passage of foreign warships in the territorial sea, China has traditionally maintained a highly restrictive provision. Article 6 of its Law on the Territorial Sea and the Contiguous Zone, 1992 states that

> *"To enter the territorial sea of the People's Republic of China, foreign military ships must obtain permission from the Government of the People's Republic of China."*[24]

However, in February 2019, Chinese warships transited the territorial seas of the Philippines without even notifying Manila, and with their onboard Automatic Identification Systems (AIS) switched off.[25] Though a major naval power today, China is yet to demonstrate that it is a 'responsible power' that upholds the international maritime order established by UNCLOS. Beijing seems to be developing a new narrative on the premise is that the UNCLOS is based on the erstwhile 'western' legal system—and is, therefore, an unfair imposition upon "Asian values". This was the essence of the talk by a Chinese speaker at the 6th International Maritime Security Conference held in May 2019 at Singapore. As a Conference participant, the author interjected: "India too represents "Asian values", but upholds the Law (UNCLOS). Unlike China that rejected the verdict of the Permanent Court of Arbitration (PCA) in the case initiated by the Philippines,[26] India accepted the adverse verdict of the international court against Bangladesh.[27,28] In all likelihood, therefore, China's growing naval footprint in the IOR may be accompanied with adverse ramifications for the regional countries.

Primal Role of Indian Ocean Rim Association (IORA)

The maritime-configured Indo-Pacific being a superset of the IOR, its vision *ipso facto* applies to the IOR. The region seeks socio-economic prosperity of the citizens of the countries through their use of the sea, unimpeded by disruptive forces of all kinds, state, non-state or natural.

Accordingly, in the early years of the current decade, the Indian Ocean Rim Association (IORA) designated maritime safety and security (MSS) as a "top priority area of focus".[29] This was largely enabled by India and Australia, as chairs of IORA in those years. Having been first proposed by India at the 11th IORA Council of Ministers Meeting (COMM) held in Bengaluru in 2011, the inclusion of MSS in the IORA's Charter was given effect by Australia during the 2014 Perth meeting. The IORA's MSS agenda is now being taken forward by Sri Lanka as the coordinator of the MSS working group.

It is important to revisit the rationale of incorporating MSS in IORA's agenda. It was driven by two pressing imperatives: human safety and response to non-traditional threats. The former was needed to respond to humanitarian disasters ranging from the 2004 tsunami to the 2014 disappearance of the Malaysian airliner MH-370, against the backdrop of growing maritime activities (trade, fishing, air travel, etc.). The latter emanated from the increasing menace of piracy and maritime terrorism in the IOR since 2005.

The IORA's focus on MSS may also have been driven by other reasons, albeit implicitly.[30] One possibility was the growing concerns of China's increasing naval presence in the IOR beginning with its counter-piracy mission in the Gulf of Aden in December 2008, combined with its growing politico-military assertiveness in the SCS since 2009-10.

Another possible reason was that the *hitherto* dormant maritime disputes in the IOR were becoming active. Three such cases had come up for international arbitration in those years, viz., Bangladesh-India (2009), Bangladesh-Myanmar (2009) and Mauritius-United Kingdom (U.K.) on "Chagos archipelago as a marine protected area" (2010-11). It was necessary for the IOR to avoid a repetition of the insecurities in the SCS. Since then, the Bangladesh-Myanmar and Bangladesh-India disputes have been amicably settled through international arbitration in 2012[31] and 2014[32] respectively; and in 2015, the arbitral tribunal decided in favour of Mauritius on the UK's attempt to declare Chagos as a marine protected area.[33]

Nonetheless, in recent years the wisdom of the IORA's focus on MSS has begun to unfold. The disruptive potential of the overlapping maritime claims in the IOR is just beginning to be realised. Notable among these are the vestiges of the decolonisation process. The 2019 judgement by the International Court of Justice (ICJ) in the Mauritius-U.K. dispute over Chagos is a case in point.[34] As the IOR develops economically in the coming years, the regional countries will develop both the national will and capacity to assert their maritime claims, which would need to be managed amicably.

Also, the attacks on tankers in the Persian Gulf since May 2019 in the wake of the geopolitical stand-off between Iran and the USA—plus its West Asian allies—is the latest exemplification of the vulnerability of the IOR to conflicting legal positions, with both sides blaming each other for impeding FON in the Gulf.[35] The most notable case is Iran's July 2019 seizure of the British tanker MV *Stena Impero* in the Strait of Hormuz, arguably in retaliation against the British Marines' seizure of Iranian tanker *Adrian Darya* (a.k.a. *Grace One*) off Gibraltar three weeks earlier, allegedly for breaking EU sanctions against Syria.[36] This is clearly violative of the UNCLOS provision on the "right of transit passage" across the "Straits used for International Navigation".[37] The fact that 15 countries like Iran have not yet ratified UNCLOS, and another 15 have not signed the Convention further enhances the risks to the established maritime order.

Also, today, the PLA Navy has established a permanent military presence in the IOR with at least six warships deployed at any given time. Its submarines are also making regular forays into the Indian Ocean since 2014, purportedly on counter-piracy mission. Since this is a sub-optimal employment of a high-value naval asset and thus defies the basic tenet of naval operations.[38] China's likely objective is to prepare for a sub-surface military campaign, but with attendant peace-time risks and curtailment of FON for the others. Also, the need for basing these submarines in the IOR during hostilities bears profound legal complexities relating to the neutrality of the states providing such basing.

Lately, China has also begun to deploy in the IOR its intelligence-gathering ships. One such vessel was detected in the Indian EEZ in September 2019.[39] Very soon, the IOR may witness a replay of China's assertiveness in the western Pacific involving the maritime militia, possibly in the form of its distant fishing fleet.

Furthermore, there exists a high probability of unintentional naval encounters at sea involving the PLA Navy and the other navies operating in the IOR, which could advertently escalate due to miscalculations, with attendant adverse ramifications for regional security. Notably, the number of submarines operating in the Indian Ocean is likely to increase significantly in the coming years. Apart from China, the regional countries themselves will contribute to this trend, particularly the new submarine-operating navies like Bangladesh, Myanmar and Thailand. With stealth being the essential attribute of submarine operations, de-conflicting such undersea encounters will be a major challenge in the years to come, besides the issues of water-space management and submarine safety.

Towards a Regional Consensus on FON

The emerging maritime security environment in the IOR relates closely to FON, which can only be addressed by a pan-regional multilateral organisation like the IORA. Fortuitously, the imperative has been appropriately acknowledged by the IORA, for the first time ever, during its March 2017 Leaders' Summit held in Jakarta, Indonesia. Consequently, the *Jakarta Concord* carries a seminal intent and commitment of the IORA members towards FON, besides for preventing and managing accidents and incidents at sea.[40]

To achieve this, it would be essential for the Indo-Pacific countries—and the IOR countries in particular—to agree upon a common inter-pretation of international law—particularly the UNCLOS—pertaining to FON and related issues. It would also be necessary to take on board the extra-regional stakeholders in the IOR. This will not be easy. The process is likely to be as complex as the protracted negotiations over nine years that led to UNCLOS. However, there seems to be no alternative option. Fortuitously, it may be possible to achieve a sort of regional solidarity considering the magnitude of the FON challenge, and also the fact the IOR countries have a similar 'DNA' in terms of their common historical narratives as coastal developing countries vis-à-vis the Western maritime powers. These are strong reasons that may usher an IOR convergence with regard to the presently divergent national positions.

The consensus-building on FON may be based on the following four-phase deliberation approach, spearheaded by the IORA's Working Group on MSS (WGMSS) and involving legal experts:

- Achieve a common understanding among the members of the IORA MSS Working Group at the initial workshop on FON.
- Expand the understanding to all IORA members, and achieve an 'IORA Consensus'.
- Make 'IORA Consensus' more representative by incorporating the views of IOR countries not represented at IORA, thereby arriving at 'IOR Consensus' based on the outcome of deliberations.
- Convey 'IOR Consensus' to the IORA dialogue partners, seeking their views, but without any obligation to amend it.

To make the objectives attainable, at the outset, the WGMSS may neither expect, nor seek to achieve a complete consensus on a uniform regional position on FON. If the sharing of mutual national perspectives and the ensuing debates in successive meetings could lead to identifying a near-common denominator, it would be a valuable contribution to the IORA's endeavour. Also, the IORA deliberations need not seek a legally binding agreement. The 'IOR Consensus' could fruitfully build norms of conduct in the IOR over a period of time, before a more uniform state practice is established, and even codified later in legal terms.

Indian Ocean Naval Symposium as a Supplement

The Indian Ocean Naval Symposium (IONS) was established in 2008 following an initiative of the Indian Navy to achieve synergy among maritime security forces of the IOR countries. So far, three IONS Working Groups (IWG) have been instituted, viz., the HADR (Humanitarian Assistance and Disaster Relief) IWG, currently chaired by India; the

Maritime Security IWG, co-chaired by Iran and the U.K.; and the Information Sharing and Interoperability IWG, co-chaired by India and Australia.

The IONS is a valuable supplement to IORA's MSS agenda at the functional level. Accordingly, during the establishment of the IORA Working Group on MSS (WGMSS) at Colombo in September 2018, it was decided to incorporate the IONS as a sub-group of the WGMSS.[41] The 35-member IONS is a highly representative forum, with the navies—or alternatively, the primal maritime security forces—of all IOR countries represented in it, either as members or observers. The key regional stakeholders like China are also represented in the IONS as observers. The USA is not currently represented in the IONS, which is a major void that needs to be addressed.

FON is closely linked with the geopolitical and strategic objectives of countries, but it manifests at sea. It is, therefore, as much of a functional issue, as a geopolitical one. Accordingly, the FON endeavours of IORA need to be synergised with the activities of the IONS, particularly in terms of sharing maritime domain awareness (MDA) and de-conflicting unintended naval encounters at sea.

Whereas much progress has already been achieved on MDA, the IONS may need more emphasis on de-confliction of incidents at sea among warships and other vessels operated by governments for non-commercial purposes, including unmanned surface and submersible craft. The IONS may consider establishing an IWG on FON, on the lines of the existing IWGs. The IWG could be tasked to emulate the Code for Unplanned Encounters at Sea (CUES)—instituted by the Western Pacific Naval Symposium (WPNS)—that comprises a set of non-binding rules to manage such incidents amongst the navies operating in the western Pacific The IWG will need to iron out the existing voids in CUES in terms of its non-applicability to other government vessels including the coast guards and maritime militia.

Conclusion

FON is the key to realising the Indo-Pacific vision of the two-ocean regional prosperity through inter-connected security, and conforms to the Indian vision of "Security and Growth for All in Region" (SAGAR).

The future security environment in the IOR will be shaped by how well the regional countries achieve a consensus on FON. The IORA—albeit with its fledging maritime security architecture—will need to drive this endeavour, enabled by the major regional players like India, Australia and South Africa, and supported by the stakeholders in the IOR.

Considering the high functional content of FON, and the fact that maritime security 'culture' in the IOR is still in its infancy, the IORA would need to be 'shored-up' by the IONS. The immense value of the IONS should not be frittered away due to inter-departmental biases within the governments of IORA member-states.

A concerted endeavour on FON must be initiated now, since it will take many years for a uniform practice to evolve through norm building. Regional consensus-building on FON, therefore, must be initiated without delay, before the memory of the UN Conference on the Law of the Sea (UNCLOS III) 1973-82 fades further, and while some eminent personalities that participated in the discussions are still around to provide their expert guidance. A successful consensus within the IOR could be an apt model for emulation across the entire Indo-Pacific region, and may even be proposed as an addendum to the UNCLOS itself.

NOTES

1. "United States and India: Prosperity Through Partnership", Joint Statement, Ministry of External Affairs (Government of India) Press Release, 27 June 2017, available at https://mea.gov.in/bilateral-documents.htm?dtl/28560/United_States_and_India_Prosperity_Through_Partnership (Accessed on 04 June 2019).
2. In this writing, the term 'freedom of navigation' refers to the broader concept of 'navigational freedoms', including the freedom of over-flight.
3. Sam Bateman, "Freedom of navigation is in the eye of the beholder", *East Asia Forum*, 24 August 2017, available at http://www.eastasiaforum.org/2017/08/24/freedom-of-navigation-is-in-the-eye-of-the-beholder/(Accessed on 15 June 2019).
4. Gurpreet S. Khurana, "What is the Indo-Pacific? The New Geopolitics of the Asia-Centred Rim Land", in Axel Berkofski and Sergio Miracola (eds.) *Geopolitics by Other Means. The Indo-Pacific Reality* (Milan, Italy, ISPI, Ledizioni Ledi Publishing, February 2019), pp. 13-32, available at https://www.ispionline.it/sites/default/files/pubblicazioni/indo-pacific_web.def_.pdf#page=13 (Accessed on 04 June 2019).
5. "Ensuring Secure Seas: Indian Maritime Security Strategy", Naval Strategic Publication (NSP) 1.2, Indian Navy, Integrated Headquarters, Ministry of Defence (Navy), October 2015, pp. 5-6.
6. Gurpreet S. Khurana, "China and Freedom of Navigation in South China Sea: The Context of International Tribunal's Verdict", *National Maritime Foundation* (NMF), New

Delhi, 19 July 2016, available at http://www.maritimeindia.org/View%20Profile/636044789090304939.pdf (Accessed on 21 June 2019).
7. "The Asia-Pacific Maritime Security Strategy: Achieving U.S. National Security Objectives in a Changing Environment", US Department of Defence (DoD), 2015, p. 2, available at http://www.defense.gov/Portals/1/Documents/pubs/NDAA%20A-P_Mari time_SecuritY_Strategy-08142015-1300-FINALFORMAT.PDF (Accessed on 07 June 2019).
8. Haeril Halim, Anggi M. Lubis and Stefani Ribka, "RI confronts China on fishing", *The Jakarta Post*, 21 March 2016, available at https://www.thejakartapost.com/news/2016/03/ 21/ri-confronts-china-fishing.html (Accessed on 07 June 2019).
9. Arbitration between the Republic of The Philippines and the People's Republic of China, Permanent Court of Arbitration (PCA), *The Hague*, 29 October 2015, available at https://www.pcacases.com/web/sendAttach/1503 (Accessed on 13 June 2019).
10. Giang Chinh, "Vietnam repels Chinese-flagged vessels for illegally fishing in its waters", *VN Express*, 09 April 2019, available at https://e.vnexpress.net/news/news/vietnam-repels-chinese-flagged-vessels-for-illegally-fishing-in-its-waters-3906574.html(Accessed on 15 June 2019).
11. "National action plan on illegal fishing approved", *Vietnam News*, 25 January 2018, available at https://vietnamnews.vn/society/education/421808/national-action-plan-on-illegal-fishing-approved.html#roV717dHbXYRCr4A.97 (Accessed on 07 June 2019).
12. Nguyen Khac Giang, "Vietnam's response to China's militarised fishing fleet", *East Asia Forum*, 04 August 2018, available at https://www.eastasiaforum.org/2018/08/04/ vietnams-response-to-chinas-militarised-fishing-fleet/ (Accessed on 21 June 2019).
13. Rafael M. Alunan III, "The Chinese Maritime Militia: To Take A Stand", *Business World*, 17 June 2019, available at https://www.bworldonline.com/the-chinese-maritime-militia/ (Accessed on 15 June 2019).
14. The USA has not ratified UNCLOS, but claims to stand by its provisions that are reflective of customary international law.
15. The Territorial Waters, Continental Shelf, Exclusive Economic Zone and Other Maritime Zones Act, 1976, Act No. 80 of 1976, 25 August 1976, available at http://www.un.org/depts/los/LEGISLATIONANDTREATIES/PDFFILES/IND_1976_Act.pdf (Accessed on 21 August 2020).
16. United Nations Treaty Collection, Chapter XXI, Law of the Sea, United Nations Convention on the Law of the Sea 1982, available at https://treaties.un.org/doc/Publication/ MTDSG/Volume%20II/Chapter%20XXI/XXI-6.en.pdf (Accessed on 07 June 2019).
17. Ranjit Bhushan, "Port Hole: An American Warship Is 'Caught' Spying in the Indian Waters under the Pretext of Research", *Outlook*, 07 June 2007, available at http://www.outlookindia.com/magazine/story/port-hole/224131 (Accessed on 02 June 2019).
18. Sam Bateman, "Chinese spy ships: The devil in the detail", *The Interpreter*, 31 July 2017, available at https://www.lowyinstitute.org/the-interpreter/chinese-spy-ships-devil-detail (Accessed on 29 May 2019).
19. "Limits in the Seas: US Responses to Excessive Maritime Claims", US Department of State (Bureau of Oceans and International Environmental and Scientific Affairs), No. 112, 09 March 1992, p. 52.
20. DoD Annual Freedom of Navigation (FON) Reports, Under Secretary of Defence for

Policy, US Department of Defence, available at https://policy.defense.gov/OUSDP-Offices/FON/ (Accessed on 21 August 2020).

21. Ibid.
22. Kathrin Hille, "Chinese Navy begins US Economic Zone Patrols", *Financial Times*, 02 June 2013, available at https://www.ft.com/content/02ce257e-cb4a-11e2-8ff3-00144feab7de (Accessed on 07 June 2019).
23. Jamie Seidel, "A Chinese spy ship has been watching Australia's Talisman Sabre war games", *News.com.au*, 22 July 2017, available at http://www.news.com.au/world/a-chinese-spy-ship-has-been-watching-australias-talisman-sabre-war-games/news-story/41db16b1e9f27a55f3c9dfd1ac672bd0 (Accessed on 15 June 2019).
24. "Law on the Territorial Sea and the Contiguous Zone", People's Republic of China, 25 February 1992, available at https://www.un.org/Depts/los/LEGISLATIONANDTREATIES/PDFFILES/CHN_1992_Law.pdf (Accessed on 07 June 2019).
25. Roel Pareño, Pia Lee-Brago, Alexis Romero and Jaime Laude, "China warships trespassing in Philippine waters – DND, AFP", *The Philippine Star*, 16 August 2019, available at https://www.philstar.com/headlines/2019/08/16/1943878/china-warships-trespassing-philippine-waters-dnd-afp (Accessed on 10 September 2019).
26. PCA Press Release: The South China Sea Arbitration (The Republic of the Philippines vs. The People's Republic of China)", Permanent Court of Arbitration, 12 July 2016, available at https://pca-cpa.org/en/news/pca-press-release-the-south-china-sea-arbitration-the-republic-of-the-philippines-v-the-peoples-republic-of-china/ (Accessed on 13 June 2019).
27. Bay of Bengal Maritime Boundary Arbitration between Bangladesh and India (Bangladesh vs. India) under Annex VII to the UNCLOS, Permanent Court of Arbitration, 08 July 2014, available at https://pca-cpa.org/en/news/bay-of-bengal-maritime-boundary-arbitration-between-bangladesh-and-india-bangladesh-v-india/
28. The Chinese speaker was Tian Shichen, a retired Captain of PLA Navy, presently Research Fellow, Collaborative Innovation Center of South China Sea Studies, Nanjing University. The International Maritime Security Conference, 2019 (IMSC-2019), Singapore was co-organised by S. Rajaratnam School of International Studies (RSIS), and Republic of Singapore Navy (RSN) at Singapore. The Conference theme was "Safe and Secure Seas: Fostering Mutual Security in Our Maritime Commons". See, 6th IMSC Session 1: Panel Discussion, available at https://www.youtube.com/watch?v=hTESVrQMGFc&feature=youtu.be
29. "Indian Ocean Rim Association (IORA)", IORA website, available at https://www.iora.int/en/priorities-focus-areas/maritime-safety-and-security (Accessed on 07 June 2019).
30. This assertion is based on the author's close association with IORA activities, *inter alia* the 1st Indian Ocean Dialogue (IOD) at Kochi (2014), the 4th IOD at Abu Dhabi (UAE, 2017), and the Initial Conference for establishing the IORA Working Group on MSS (WGMSS) at Colombo (September 2018).
31. Dispute Concerning Delimitation of the Maritime Boundary between Bangladesh and Myanmar in the Bay of Bengal, International Tribunal for the Law of the Sea (ITLOS), Hamburg, Case No. 16, Judgement of 14 March 2012, available at https://www.itlos.org/fileadmin/itlos/documents/cases/case_no_16/published/C16-J-14_mar_12.pdf (Accessed on 05 June 2019).
32. "Bay of Bengal Maritime Boundary Arbitration (Bangladesh vs. India) Award, Permanent Court of Arbitration," *The Hague*, 07 July 2014, available at http://

www.pca-cpa.org/showpage.asp?pag_id=1376 (Accessed on 05 June 2019).

33. "Chagos Marine Protected Area Arbitration (Mauritius vs. United Kingdom), Case No. 2011-03, Permanent Court of Arbitration (PCA)", *The Hague*, 18 March 2015, available at https://files.pca-cpa.org/pcadocs/MU-UK%2020150318%20Award.pdf (Accessed on 10 May 2019).
34. Legal Consequences of the Separation of the Chagos Archipelago from Mauritius in 1965, International Court of Justice, General List No. 169, 25 February 2019, available at https://www.icj-cij.org/files/case-related/169/169-20190225-01-00-EN.pdf (Accessed on 12 March 2019).
35. "Freedom of navigation must be safeguarded", *The National*, 11 July 2019, available at https://www.thenational.ae/opinion/editorial/freedom-of-navigation-must-be-safeguarded-1.885064 and "Iran calls for freedom of navigation in Strait of Hormuz", *Sputnik/ ANI*, 07 August 2019, available at https://www.aninews.in/news/world/middle-east/iran-calls-for-freedom-of-navigation-in-strait-of-hormuz20190807064834/ (both accessed on 05 September 2019).
36. "Seized British tanker Stena Impero still in Iran: Stena Bulk CEO", *Reuters*, 24 September 2019, available at https://www.reuters.com/article/us-mideast-iran-tanker/seized-british-tanker-stena-impero-still-in-iran-stena-bulk-ceo-idUSKBN1W90W9 (Accessed on 21 August 2020)
37. United Nations Convention on the Law of the Sea (UNCLOS), 1982. UNCLOS Article 38 on 'Right of Transit Passage' across 'Straits used for International Navigation'.
38. "Odd that China has submarines in Indian Ocean for anti-piracy ops: Navy chief", *Hindustan Times*, 01 December 2017, available at https://www.hindustantimes.com/india-news/odd-that-china-has-submarines-in-indian-ocean-for-anti-piracy-ops-navy-chief/story-eUwmKlcyYOWIGrZckvyoHJ.html. Also see, Gurpreet S. Khurana, "PLA Navy's Submarine Arm Stretches its Sea-legs to the Indian Ocean", *NMF Commentary*, National Maritime Foundation (NMF), New Delhi, 21 November 2014, available at http://www.maritimeindia.org/CommentryView.aspx?NMFCID=2347 (both accessed 07 June 2019).
39. "Alarm Bells for India as China sends Spy Ship near Andaman and Nicobar in Indian Ocean: Report", *News Nation*, 02 September 2019, available at https://www.newsnation. in/india/news/alarm-bells-for-india-as-china-sends-spy-ship-near-andaman-and-nicobar-in-indian-ocean-report-236240.html (Accessed on 03 September 2019).
40. "Jakarta Concord: The Indian Ocean Rim Association: Promoting Regional Cooperation for a Peaceful, Stable and Prosperous Indian Ocean", Adopted by the First IORA Summit held in Jakarta, Indonesia on 07 March 2017, para 16, available at http://www.dirco.gov.za/docs/2017/iora0309a.pdf (Accessed on 07 June 2019).
41. This refers to the initial Conference for Formulation of the Terms of Reference (ToR) for the WGMSS, held in Colombo (Sri Lanka) on 05 September 2018. The author represented the Ministry of External Affairs (MEA), Government of India, at the Conference as a maritime expert.

20

Maritime Security Architecture in Indo-Pacific under UNCLOS:

A Sri Lankan Perspective

Jayantha Perera

Introduction

India's first Prime Minister Mr. Jawaharlal Nehru had emphasised that "To be secure on land we must be Supreme at Sea."[1] It is no longer just a text book quote; it has become a geo-strategic reality. Every big power has realised the importance of their dominance in Indo-Pacific region due to various reasons. The developments that are taking place in the Indo-Pacific region and matters related to maritime security are extremely important for Sri Lanka in the present context due to various reasons. Ever since, it won the three-decade old conflict in 2009, Sri Lanka has been known as the only country to emerge victorious by defeating a terrorist outfit that was considered as invincible at a given point of time. The huge role played by the Sri Lanka Navy, especially in defeating the LTTE maritime capabilities in the vicinity of sea shores as well as in the deep seas made an enormous impact and eventually resulted in the victory achieved on land. It was the Sri Lanka Navy that took the initiative in turning the tide in Sri Lanka's favour and regained the total sea control.

As an Island nation, Ocean affairs are extremely crucial for Sri Lanka. Consequently, Sri Lanka has taken far too many international regional initiatives related to Ocean affairs. Sri Lanka was closely involved with the UNCLOS, right from its outset, which resulted in the development of a new legal regime for the oceans.

Former Sri Lankan Prime Minister Ranil Wickremesinghe had emphasised at the Indian Ocean Conference 2017 that the traditional and modern security concerns are yet to be addressed internationally. Articles 34 to 56 of UNCLOS are insufficient to deal with the concerns that are related to Freedom of Navigation. Therefore, Sri Lanka intended to work with all parterres in creating shared vision for economic and secured engagement. Sri Lanka is convinced that the Code of Conduct will ensure the freedom of Navigation in our oceans. Indian Prime Minister Narendra Modi had said that "respecting freedom of navigation and adhering to international norms are essential for peace and economic growth in the interlinked geography of the Indo-Pacific."[2] More importantly, the example is being set here in the Indian Ocean by actions as well as words.

The Indo-Pacific Emerges as a "Region of Opportunities"

Within the shifting global geo-economics and geopolitical landscape of the 21st century, the Indo-Pacific region has been identified as a new expanded theatre of power competition. Development within the Indo-Pacific region and its surrounding waters has subsequently held the attention of policy makers and strategic analysts.

The Indo-Pacific region is central to the issue of energy security. Its Sea Lines of Communication (SLOCs) are critically located as conduit for the transit energy supplies from Gulf States to the economic power houses in South Asia and East Asia with China projected to become the world's largest oil importing country and India to be the largest importer of Coal in next few years. A reorientation of energy trade from the Atlantic basin to the Indo-Pacific is imminent with implication for cooperative effort to ensure energy Security.

The Indo-Pacific region is witnessing a global power shift from the west to the east. The emergence of traditional and non-traditional maritime security challenges is posing a challenge to the countries in the Indo-Pacific region. This maritime region has always been of immediate relevance to the resident stake-holders, but has now gained greater eminence during an era of major global churn[3].

Since the end of the 1960s and the 1970s, the Indo-Pacific region and resident countries in the region have been growing economically and their geopolitical significance is also growing in the world geopolitics. It is a region of great diversity and contrasts in terms of politics, population, economy and environment, as well as being a complex geopolitical framework where foreign powers and local states' interests deeply intermingle.[4] Taking into account the significance of its strategic energy resources, the importance of its strategic shipping lanes, the 'rise of China and India' as a dominant economic power houses and regional and global military powers, the turbulences of the Islamic world, East and South China sea territorial claims and disputes, the deep and broad involvement of the United States (and its allies) in the region, as well as China's increasing presence with ambitious Belt and Road Initiative (BRI) project in Indo-Pacific ocean region with aggressive Chinese funded maritime infrastructure in number of Indian Ocean Countries has increased the geo-strategic competition in the region.

The Indo-Pacific Ocean Region has become one of the major spotlights in international security in recent times. With the importance of SLOCs and the increasing appetite for energy resources for the booming Asian economy, security in the Indian and Pacific Oceans are a matter of concern for all stake holders. With the US pivot to Asia policy and China's maritime silk route ambitions, India's maritime activities has also heated up in the maritime domain of Indian Ocean in particular.

In the Western Indian Ocean and Arabian Sea, the Somali pirates had paralyzed the sea trade and freedom of Navigation in and around Horn of Africa and Gulf of Eden where majority of energy transportation takes place. The piracy of this region impacted hugely to the world trade as a whole and incurred heavy cost since many nations are committed for UN mandated anti-piracy patrol in the region and insurance companies started to impose the insurance surcharge to the shipping. The piracy hindered freedom of navigation significantly and disturbed the energy exports and imports through this vital sea area.

In this context, the Eastern Indian Ocean has set a good example in terms of effective management and cooperation among various nations for anti-piracy operations. The Strait of Malacca Patrols, cooperatively undertaken by Indonesia, Malaysia, Singapore, and Thailand have helped to dramatically reduce the number of piracy incidents along that choke point since its inception.[5]

What UNCLOS says about Freedom of Navigation?

International Customary Law and United Nations Convention on the Law of the Sea (UNCLOS) emphasise freedom of Navigation in oceans as long as ships ensure innocent passage irrespective of territorial sea, Contiguous waters, Exclusive Economic Zones (EEZ) as well as international waters. In the modern law of the sea, freedom of navigation was perceived as equally important, and this status was reflected in the now superseded Geneva Conventions on the Law of the Sea. Article 14 of the Convention on the Territorial Sea and Contiguous Zone 1958 guaranteed a right of innocent passage to vessels, non-suspendable for waters in international straits, and article 23 indicated explicitly that such rights were available to warships.[6]

Freedom of navigation on the high seas was guaranteed in Article 2 of the Convention on the High Seas 1958, with Article 3 of the Convention of the Continental Shelf Convention 1958 ensuring that the status of waters above a State's continental shelf remained as high seas, and therefore enjoying freedom of navigation.[7] These efforts had been prefaced by the International Court of Justice in 1949, in the Corfu Channel Case, which confirmed the right of innocent passage, available even to warships, passing through 'straits used for international navigation'. The Court was also prepared to state that foreign vessels, including warships, during peace-time had a right of innocent passage through all international straits.[8]

Need for a Strong Maritime Security Architecture in the Indo-Pacific Region

It is a reality that Indo-Pacific region is life-line of world trade thus ensuring unimpeded sea passage is imperative for any vessel for any country under the obligation of international law need to be preserved and safe guarded. Due to complexity of many different issues in the ocean region from nation states involving East and South China issues to Western Indian Ocean piracy that involve both state and non-state actors are clear impediment and interruption to the freedom of Navigation. There is a necessity of collective security architecture in place which covers entire Indo-Pacific region with the involvement of all stake holder states.

There are some issues where the Indo-Pacific region lacks a credible Maritime Security Architecture initiative to enhance maritime security which are mentioned below:

(a) No collective regional organisation with maritime domain awareness which is urgently required for tackling the current situation.

(b) No reliable and dominant leadership who can muster and partner with regional stakeholder nations to initiate the organisation responsible for maritime security and lead to collectively identify initiatives for architecture development in the Indo-Pacific region.

(c) Absence of proper analysis of the current security status and views on maritime security issues and disputes ranging from East and South China Seas to piracy in Horn of Africa region by central authority to find the course of action against the existing and potential threats for freedom of Navigation from state and non-state actors.

(d) Lack of initiative in resolving maritime disputes through discussion and consultation based on international law in a multilateral environment among state actors.

Framework for Proposed Maritime Security Architecture and Infrastructure in Indo-Pacific Region

All stakeholder countries should be part of the maritime security architecture of the Indo-Pacific Ocean region countries. US, China, India, Japan and Australia can play a major and dominant role while other nations in the maritime region should also play a significant role. All regional organisation like ASEAN, BIMSTEC, SAARC and IORA should be a part of it. Integrated maritime strategy should be adopted by the regional and stakeholder states. Each maritime zone needs to be equipped with monitoring and enforcement mechanism and should be staffed with representatives of countries of that zone. Regional maritime coordinating centre should be responsible for the strategic coordination of the zones. It should also serve as an information collection and dissemination point and liaise with Maritime Inter-regional coordination Centre (ICC) East, South and West Indian maritime domain. The purpose of implementing and strengthening maritime security Architecture and Infrastructure in Indo-Pacific Ocean is as follows:

(a) To ensure freedom of navigation to all stakeholder nations who abide by the international law in particular UNCLOS
(b) To deter/counter increasing piracy activities in the Horn of Africa region
(c) Large scale drugs and transportation through Indian ocean region
(d) Human Smuggling
(e) Marine Pollution

There is also a need for Multinational Maritime Coordinating Centre (MMCC) towards the strengthening of the regional maritime security architecture in the Indo Pacific region which can be jointly coordinated by regional organisation and stakeholder countries of Indo-Pacific region. The Regional Navies should strategically support in partnership with governments, regional and international organisation in the region for effective policing of the Indo-Pacific waters in order to avoid the spill-over effect of nefarious maritime activities, ranging from Piracy, Sea robbery, Human smuggling, Drug trafficking, IUU (Illicit Unreported Unregulated) fishing, Illegal migration, Illicit toxic dumping etc.

The operationalisation of the Indo-Pacific region maritime zone is part of the implementation of the broader scope of the Indo-Pacific regional maritime security management mechanism which seeks to achieve among others, enhanced information/intelligence exchange, training and capacity building including basic and improved specialised training for staff dealing with maritime security and establishment and expansion of operational networks among law enforcement entities operating at all sea routes.

Conclusion

In the strategic context, all countries need to be mindful and understand the evolving security partnerships that are centric to the Indian Ocean region. The maritime cooperation between India and US is of great importance. Both countries have a large presence and foothold in the Indian Ocean Region and the commitment shown by both nations for increased cooperation and partnership and for a rule based maritime order is encouraging and such corporation would bring greater stability to the region. In this backdrop of building a Maritime Security architecture, there has been nevermore opportune and necessary time. A new architecture should allow cooperation and partnership, promote rule base maritime activity, allow bilateral and multilateral cooperation, create space for assistance of needy nations to be supported by advanced nations for capacity building in a transparent approach, enhance Maritime Domain Awareness and most importantly should have voluntary consensus on refraining of planning or carrying out actions that hinders the security balance of the Indo-Pacific Region.

NOTES

1. Indian Navy, Naval Strategic Publication 1.1, *Indian Maritime Doctrine 2009*, Chapter 10 (2009), p. 155.
2. James S Hartsell, "Major General James S Hartsell's Speech at the Indian Ocean Conference 2017 in Colombo", available at https://lk.usembassy.gov/major-general-james-s-hartsells-speech-indian-ocean-conference-2017-colombo/ (Accessed on 21 July 2020).
3. "India has a major stake in Indo-Pacific region: Navy chief", available at https://www.rediff.com/news/report/indo-pacific-region-emerging-as-power-centre-navy-chief/20170214.htm (Accessed on 21 July 2020).
4. Christian Bouchard and William Crumplin, "Neglected no longer: the Indian Ocean at the forefront of world geopolitics and global geostrategy", *Journal of the Indian Ocean Region*, Vol 6, No. 1 ((2010), p. 26 (Accessed on 21 September 2020).
5. James S Hartsell, "Major General James S Hartsell's Speech at the Indian Ocean Conference 2017 in Colombo", available at https://lk.usembassy.gov/major-general-james-s-hartsells-speech-indian-ocean-conference-2017-colombo/ (Accessed on 21 July 2020).
6. A R Thomas & James C Duncan (ed.), Annotated Supplement to The Commander's Handbook on the Law of Naval Operations, *US Naval War College International Law Studies*, Vol. 73 (1999), pp. 119-125 (Accessed on 21 July 2020)
7. Ibid, pp. 131-132.
8. Corfu Channel case, Judgment of 09 April 1949: I.C.J. Reports 1949, pp. 29-31 (Accessed on 21 July 2020).

21

Maritime Security Architecture in the Indo-Pacific Region to Maintain Freedom of Navigation under UNCLOS

Sidharto Reza Suryodipuro

At no other point in human history have people and their economic activities gone to sea in greater numbers than today. Consequently, people, different types of vessels and activities on the surface and below the surface of water, as well as on the seabed and beneath it, are growing and will continue to grow in future. As a result of these increased activities, the need for laws and norms to govern them will acquire greater salience. The United Nations Convention on the Law of the Sea (UNCLOS) will, therefore, only grow in relevance and importance to govern these human activities. The Indo-Pacific region is going to be the focus of human activities in the maritime arena in 21st Century and even within this geo-economically and geo-strategically significant maritime region, Southeast Asia and especially Indonesia lie at the very centre.

Indonesia is an archipelagic state under UNCLOS, and with it come specific legal rights and obligations.[1] Being the largest archipelago state in the world comprising 17,480 islands, possessing second largest coastline in the world and with almost eight million square kilometres of sea area, it is undoubtedly one of the most significant maritime countries in the globe. Its key location between the major trading routes of Indian and

Pacific Oceans results in almost half of the world's cargo and oil transiting through Indonesian waters, which include the Straits of Malacca, the Strait of Sunda and the Strait of Lombok.[2] Indonesia's efforts to maintain freedom of navigation in the archipelago in accordance with UNCLOS and therefore vitally important and form a part of its contribution to the maritime security architecture of the region and the world. Indonesia therefore has to make sure that not only are its waters open to all, but that all countries have an interest in its efforts and support them.

It is all the more important from this perspective, to understand the contours of the region's maritime security architecture and how should it look like in the next five years. However, the future of maritime architecture of the Indo-Pacific cannot be determined without looking at its evolution over a period of last fifteen years and Indonesia's place in it.

Association of South East Asian Nations (ASEAN) had no overarching maritime agenda till 2002, which was a peculiar state of affairs for a region that is by and large maritime in nature. It also did not have any maritime organising concept or institution, even though many of its bodies included a maritime element in their agenda. Even more significantly, Cambodia, Laos, Myanmar and Vietnam had just joined ASEAN and for the first time in history, the organisation had all the ten Southeast Asian countries under its umbrella.[3] It was a development that was welcomed by all stakeholders and observers alike. At the same time, this enhanced membership also expanded its geographical frontiers of ASEAN. Its geographic features also underwent a metamorphosis. From being a predominantly maritime entity, it transformed into a region that included maritime, continental, and peninsular Southeast Asia. It emerged as a region with differing levels of development, and one that now shared land boundaries with China, besides the existing maritime boundaries and therefore had greater proximity to the Chinese centre of gravity of China.

As a response, the ASEAN Maritime Forum (AMF) and ASEAN Community were established during the ASEAN Summit of 2003.[4] The move was aimed at strengthening the region's cohesion and integration, as well as to respond to the new international and regional realities. Since 2002, the region's maritime security architecture has progressively been strengthened by the establishment of regional institutions. They included the establishment of the ASEAN Maritime Forum and the Expanded AMF, ASEAN Regional Forum's (ARF) Inter-sessional Meeting on Maritime Security, the ASEAN Defence Ministers' Meeting (ADMM) and ADMM's maritime agenda, and ASEAN Pacific Economic Cooperation's (APEC) focussing on ocean and fisheries issues and the Blue Economy agenda.

Indonesia's own maritime outlook has also evolved in significant ways. A multifaceted foreign policy in accordance with the realities of a complex neighbourhood was devised. Maritime and community agenda were pro-actively promoted in South East Asia. In the West and South Pacific, Indonesia in collaboration with other countries of the region established the Southwest Pacific Dialogue[5] and the Coral Triangle Initiative.[6] Engagements were also initiated with the Pacific Islands Forum and the Melanesian Spearhead Group, along with establishment of bilateral ties with almost all Pacific Island Countries. Indonesia translated its emerging consciousness of its Indian Ocean heritage into a more active role in the Indian Ocean Rim Association (IORA), such as by chairing IORA in 2015-17 and hosting the first ever IORA Summit in 2017.[7]

Indonesia intensified its maritime border diplomacy and negotiated delimitation of its maritime boundaries with all ten of its neighbours: India, Thailand, Malaysia, Singapore, Vietnam, Philippines, Palau, Papua New Guinea, Timor Leste, and Australia. In 2014, Indonesia concluded maritime boundary treaties with Philippines and Singapore. Talks were initiated with India on delimitation of overlapping EEZs, trilateral agreement with Thailand on continental shelf boundaries.

Indonesia holds military exercises and cooperation with various countries, such as with India in the form of the India-Indonesia Coordinated Patrol (IND-INDO Corpat). The latest edition of IND-INDO Coordinated Patrol (CORPAT) along the International Maritime Boundary Line (IMBL) was carried out on 15 and 16 June 2020. The coordinated patrols, which started in 2002, have completed more than 34 coordinated patrols in last 18 years.[8] Indonesia also participates in Malacca Strait Patrol with Malaysia, Singapore and Thailand. It also carries out naval exercises with Brunei, Australia, Philippines and the US, besides Thailand, Malaysia and Singapore. Three of the seven Indian Ocean choke points, namely, the Strait of Malacca, Sunda Strait and the Lombok Strait lie within Indonesia's sphere of responsibility.[9]

The exercise of Indonesia's rights and obligations as archipelagic state under UNCLOS will in effect provide public goods for the international community by ensuring that its waters are safe, secure, and open to all for lawful navigation. Indonesia can strengthen its free and active foreign policy only by fulfilling these obligations. In this context, President Joko Widodo in 2014 introduced the concept of Indonesia as a Global Maritime Fulcrum, with the five pillars of maritime culture, marine resources, infrastructure development and maritime connectivity, maritime diplomacy; and maritime defence forces.[10]

Consequently, maritime security architecture based on these facts and developments, in the Indo-Pacific region in the next five years should have the following contours.

First, the maritime regional architecture should continue to ensure open and free maritime Southeast Asia for lawful international navigation. Throughout history, and modern history in particular, Southeast Asian waters and sea lanes of communications have been a source of tension and competition. New developments, such as the melting of the Arctic and advent of super ships (super tankers, super container ships, super LNG ships), will make these waters even more crucial for the economic and national well-being and even survival of many countries in the Indo-Pacific region.

Countries of the first island chain should guarantee that their waters remain open and safe for freedom of navigation, in accordance with UNCLOS, so that everybody can lawfully sail through these waters. Other countries, on their part, have to respect this status and continue to support peaceful and legitimate use of these waters.

Second, the regional architecture has to be inclusive and not directed towards any country. At the same time, the regional architecture should not be governed by an agreement of a limited number of large states. The security of one should be the security of all, based on dynamic equilibrium. Maritime Southeast Asia will remain an arena of geopolitics, but these waters should be open to all states and that all states parties to UNCLOS should have a concern in the application of the UNCLOS regime in the region's waters.

Third, the regional architecture should take into account cross cutting and new issues that impact the seas. The issues that result from population growth, global warming, shortages of fresh water, disasters, cross-border diseases and pandemics, as well as illegal and overfishing, will become even more significant in days to come and none of these can be resolved within the borders of any single state.

Furthermore, as the countries continue to build armaments, and the trajectory of the current trends in this regard seems certain, the region would need to have a more robust arms registry and may need to start thinking about the possibility of some form of arms limitation talks in the future.

Fourth, the institutional setup should be allowed to evolve in line with the shaping of the maritime regional architecture. The parallel universe of ASEAN-based institutions, including the East Asia Summit, and the Asia Pacific Economic Cooperation (APEC) should end and their complementarities should be brought into play through stronger institutional linkages.

APEC has the most advance sectoral cooperation, as well as capacity for community building in the Indo-Pacific region. Had there been no APEC, one would need to be created. APEC's deliberations and cooperation on maritime issues will benefit East Asia Summit's (EAS) deliberations and cooperation. India was the first membership applicant, who is still not in APEC, but support for its membership has been growing and several APEC economies have expressed open support for its membership, such as Russia, Australia, and Japan. When (or before) APEC decides on its post-2020 vision, the question of membership would have to be addressed.[11]

Fifth, the maritime regional architecture should be based on laws and norms. They include existing ones, such as the UN Charter, UNCLOS, the Treaty of Amity and Cooperation in Southeast Asia, as well as the development of new ones, such as a treaty that would cover the Indo-Pacific region. There is a need for development of Indo-Pacific—wide rules and norms. These rules and norms should be based on the evolving needs for more robust norms to govern the relations and interactions between and among states. They should incorporate renunciation of the use of coercive measures and functioning dispute settlement architecture with a compliance mechanism. There is also a strong need for a more robust security dialogue for the purpose of conflict prevention and the implementation of confidence-building measures.

The strength of laws and norms within the UNCLOS regime cannot be taken for granted. The region must be vigilant against efforts to weaken these laws and norms. For example, in the past, the United Nations Security Council (UNSC) had presumably inadvertently, considered measures under Chapter VII that would have definitely weakened UNCLOS. Fortunately the UNSC did not proceed with it. The United States, in spite of the decision by its executive branch to accept and comply with all of UNCLOS provisions, has still not ratified it. Meanwhile, China's actions in the South China Sea have also weakened the UNCLOS regime.

There will always be efforts to build upon or change UNCLOS and, therefore, an agreement must be made on the elements to be strengthened. As the world moves forward, ASEAN and Indonesia must seek to ensure the support and interest of others in making South East Asian maritime region open for all, in accordance with the provisions of UNCLOS. They must strive that other countries engage constructively in Southeast Asia because they have a common interest in the stability and security of this crucial maritime region.

NOTES

1. An archipelagic state is an island country that comprises of an archipelago and has been defined in UNCLOS. Archipelagic states comprise of groups of islands, which form a state and are considered as a single unit. For an archipelagic state, the islands and the waters within the baselines are deemed as internal waters with exclusive sovereignty, irrespective of their breadth and dimensions. The ratio of enclosed water to land within the baselines enclosing the main islands of the archipelago must be "between 1:1 and 9:1". The Bahamas, Fiji, Indonesia, Papua New Guinea and Philippines are the five states originally accorded the status of archipelagic states by UNCLOS on 10 December 1982. At present 17 other states, besides the five originally accorded, have sought to claim the status of archipelagic states. Indonesia is the largest archipelagic state in the world.
2. Lyle J. Morris and Giacomo Persi Paoli, *A Preliminary Assessment of Indonesia's Maritime Security Threats and Capabilities* (Santa Monica: Rand Corporation, 2018), p. 15. Also see Senia Febrica, *Maritime Security and Indonesia: Cooperation, Interests and Strategies* (London: Routledge, 2017).
3. ASEAN was initially conceived as a common bulwark against Communism in 1967.

However, after the end of Cold War, Vietnam joined ASEAN on 28 July 1995. It was followed by Laos and Myanmar, who joined it on 23 July 1997. Cambodia was the last country to join ASEAN on 30 April 1999.

4. Press Statement by the Chairperson of the 9th ASEAN Summit and 7th ASEAN+3 Summit in Bali, Indonesia on 07 October 2003, available at https://asean.org/?static_post=press-statement-by-the-chairperson-of-the-9th-asean-summit-and-the-7th-asean-3-summit-bali-indonesia-7-october-2003 (Accessed on 28 July 2020).
5. Joeffe B Santaria, "Southwest Pacific Dialogue: Indonesia's Newest Leverage in the Asia Pacific", Asian Studies, Volume 38 Number 2 2002, pp. 124-125. Southwest Pacific Dialogue (SwPD) has emerged as a forum for Australia, the Philippines, Indonesia, Papua New Guinea, New Zealand, and Timor Leste to exchange views and information on important issues concerning the region. The inaugural Ministerial meeting of the South West Pacific Dialogue (SWDP) was held in Yogyakarta in Indonesia on 04-05 October 2002. For more details see Ministry of Foreign Affairs of the Republic of Indonesia Website, available at https://kemlu.go.id/portal/en/read/138/halaman_list_lainnya/south-west-pacific-dialogue-swpd (Accessed on 28 August 2020).
6. The Coral Triangle Initiative on Coral Reefs, Fisheries, and Food Security (CTI-CFF), also shortly known as the Coral Triangle Initiative (CTI), includes Indonesia, Malaysia, Philippines, Papua New Guinea, Solomon Islands and Timor-Leste. It works towards sustaining the unique marine and coastal resources by addressing crucial issues such as food security, climate change, and marine biodiversity. The regional Secretariat was established in Bali in December 2007, during the First CTI-CFF Meeting. For more details see Ministry of Foreign Affairs of the Republic of Indonesia Website, available at https://kemlu.go.id/portal/en/read/136/halaman_list_lainnya/coral-triangle-initiative-on-coral-reefs-fisheries-and-food-security-cti-cff (Accessed on 28 August 2020).
7. The Indian Ocean Rim Association, earlier known as the Indian Ocean Rim Initiative and the Indian Ocean Rim Association for Regional Cooperation (IOR-ARC), is an organisation comprising of 22 states bordering the Indian Ocean and 10 dialogue partners with stakes in the region.
8. Press Brief on IND-INDO CORPAT 2020 from Embassy of India, Jakarta Website, available at https://www.indianembassyjakarta.gov.in/whats_new?id=eyJpdiI6Im05 MzRWMmxqMU Z5a VM5TFdMMFdvVHc9PSIsInZ hbHVlIjoic1lkaE9kNUdQbm 1Jaz I0dml CM 0E3QT09I iwibWFjIjoiYjE0MTRkMWMzNmU3OWRhNTI2Zm Q2N2U5ZDZjNTg4Z mY1NDM1MWVlNWJlNDVhNDJiNzcxYmI2ZmVkNTYz OTBiZiJ9 (Accessed on 28 August 2020).
9. Other four choke points of India Ocean are the Cape of Good Hope, Strait of Bab-el Mandeb, the Suez Canal, and the Strait of Hormuz.
10. Text of Speech by the President of Indonesia Joko Widodo at the East Asia Summit in 2014 at Nay Pyi Taw, Myanmar last accessed at https://setkab.go.id/en/pidato-presiden-ri-joko-widodo-pada-ktt-ke-9-asia-timur-di-nay-pyi-taw-myanmar-13-november-2014/ (Accessed on 28 July 2020).
11. The Asia-Pacific Economic Cooperation (APEC) is an inter-governmental forum for 21 member economies in the Pacific Rim that promotes free trade throughout the Asia-Pacific region. It was established in 1989 with 12 countries. The term economies has been used to facilitate both Taiwan (Republic of China) and Hong Kong to participate alongside People's Republic of China (PRC).

22

Law and Power:
Enforcing UNCLOS in the Indo-Pacific

Dhruva Jaishankar

Introduction: The Chatham Island Rule

Two centuries ago, the remote Chatham Islands in the South Pacific was inhabited by a tribe known as the Moriori. They were a proud, strong people, who appreciated feats of strength and hunting prowess. However, they lived by a code of justice which mandated the resolution of disputes through ritual fighting and conciliation. This helped ensure that the Moriori did not grievously hurt or kill each other. While this system was subsequently (and misleadingly) described as a form of pacifism, it did prove successful in resolving disputes and preserving peace.

However, in 1835, around 900 Maori arrived from New Zealand on a British vessel. The Maori were fearsome warriors, and they practised cannibalism. They also engaged in a practice of claiming land by walking it and this is what they did in Chatham Islands. The Moriori faced with this existential challenge from the invading Maori tribesmen held a council, where some of them, especially those who were younger, said that their longstanding code of conduct was only a survival strategy. It could therefore be amended or discarded should the situation arise. Others however said that they had a moral imperative to maintain it at all costs. While they were deciding upon which course to follow, the

Maori attacked them. The Maori were fewer in number and were outnumbered two-to-one. But they believed in striking first and striking hardest, which they did, slaughtering, raping, and cannibalizing the Moriori. Those who survived were enslaved. Today there are no longer any full-blooded Moriori people, although there are a handful of descendants of mixed marriages.[1]

This grisly incident occurred on a remote Pacific island almost two centuries ago, but it carries important lessons today for international law. Many people may now be familiar with the Chatham House Rule, which dictates that the proceedings of a conference can be recounted but without divulging the identity of the speakers to preserve a sense of candour. But when considering matters of international law and agreements, perhaps it would be appropriate to invoke a Chatham Island Rule. Order and norms are important, and are valuable. But they matter little when confronted with determined force. The act of preserving international order requires not just the ability but also the willingness to defend it, including through military means. It also requires flexibility of interpretation rather than dogmatism, as well as moral clarity. Implementation using military means may well remain a last resort, but there are additional measures that can stop short of military force.

The Importance of UNCLOS

The importance of the UN Convention on the Law of the Sea (UNCLOS) cannot be underestimated. Over a series of lengthy and detailed negotiations, an almost universally recognised system was established to grant authority and exploitation privileges to sovereign states over the oceans, which cover over two-thirds of the Earth's surface. While infractions and disputes continued, they were minimised, and until recently, the greatest challenge to UNCLOS came from non-state actors. Piracy off the coast of Somalia and in the Gulf of Aden at the end of the first decade of the 21st century required intervention by actors as diverse as the USA, China, India, Japan, the European Union, and NATO.[2]

However, UNCLOS also suffered from the absence of firm support from the world's two leading powers. The USA signed but never ratified UNCLOS, owing largely to concerns about the costs it would bear as a consequence. While this undercut the United States' moral authority,

U.S. officials argued that they respected and defended the spirit of UNCLOS, including by using the Navy as a tool to enforce freedom of navigation.

In some sense, a bigger challenge arrived in the form of the People's Republic of China, which remains a signatory of UNCLOS even now. Following a series of aggressive claims in the South China Sea—using artificial islands to claim large portions of that important waterway as territorial waters—China was taken to international arbitration by the Philippines. Territorial control of the South China Sea would give it a monopoly over valuable mineral and fishing resources and would also deny warships the right to traverse waters through which a significant amount of the world's trade passes. The issue therefore directly involves not just the claimant states, but also all the major economies, particularly those in Asia such as India.

This importance has repeatedly been highlighted by Indian officials, including former Defence Minister Manohar Parrikar.[3] Most of India's trade transits through the maritime route and consequently, the principle of freedom of navigation and overflight are absolutely crucial, particularly in important maritime trade routes. Moreover, China's handling of the South China Sea dispute also serves as an indicator of how Beijing might approach other disputes, including its territorial disputes with India and Bhutan. The 2017 and 2020 stand-offs between India and China in Doklam and in Ladakh indicated that China's refusal to recognise past agreements were not limited to the maritime domain. Furthermore, when it comes to arbitration under international law, India had set a positive precedent, having accepted international arbitration on the Indus Waters Treaty and in its maritime dispute with Bangladesh, and respecting the result of the latter even though it went largely against India.

A New Precedent: The Philippines vs. China

In July 2016, the Permanent Court of Arbitration in The Hague released its much-awaited ruling on the Philippines' case against China.[4] It was at that time the most high-profile development concerning the overlapping and intensifying territorial disputes in the South China Sea, which involved not only the People's Republic of China and the Philippines, but also Vietnam, Malaysia, Brunei, Indonesia, and Taiwan.

Lobbying in the run-up to the ruling had reached fever pitch, with China going on a global public affairs blitz to make its case heard, including briefing academic experts and journalists and taking out full-page advertisements in newspapers in India, the USA, Europe, and elsewhere.

Despite these immense efforts, the Philippines had constructed a clever legal case, invoking international law not for a judgement on the legality of China's territorial control, but instead to assess the status of the islands claimed by China. Around islands, countries can claim territorial sea and an exclusive economic zone (EEZ), where they can exercise sole fishing, drilling, and resource rights. But that does not apply if the feature is an uninhabitable rock or submerged during high tide. It was on this simple, yet technical, issue that the legal case against China rested.

The Court's verdict has proved a resounding rebuttal to China, essentially on four grounds.[5] First, the Court determined that almost all of the Philippines' complaints fell within its jurisdiction, despite Chinese arguments that the South China Sea was a matter of territorial sovereignty, that Beijing had not agreed to such international arbitration, and that military matters fell outside the Court's purview. Second, the Court rubbished China's claims to the South China Sea on historical grounds, deeming them contrary to UNCLOS, the bedrock of international maritime law.

Third, it ruled that the islands claimed by China were, in some cases, low-tide elevations, and thus within the Philippines' EEZ, and in other cases were rocks, incapable of "sustaining human habitation or economic life" under natural circumstances. Despite China's reclamation and construction efforts, these were not islands under the legal definition of the term. China was thus in violation of the Philippines' EEZ, and not the other way around. Finally, and in conclusion, the Court ruled clearly that China had violated UNCLOS and other elements of international law by denying the Philippines access to fishing and other maritime resources, by constructing artificial islands, by disregarding environmental concerns, and by aggravating and expanding the dispute while resolution proceedings were underway.

For the first time since its rise as a global power, the People's Republic of China found itself in flagrant violation of international law on an issue that it deems to be a "core national interest," and thus non-negotiable. This has naturally led to concerns that China would respond by further aggravating tensions with the Philippines, its backer, the USA, or other regional actors directly or indirectly involved in the South China Sea disputes. This would in turn contribute to the fracturing of the uneasy consensus in Asia, forcing various countries to take sides, either with China or against it. The broader political implications would therefore have indirect consequences for others, including India.

Indian officials in 2015 and 2016, including Prime Minister Narendra Modi, External Affairs Minister Sushma Swaraj, and Defence Minister Manohar Parrikar, all made statements on the South China Sea issue in the run-up to the South China Sea ruling. They all indicated their firm belief that maritime disputes should be resolved in accordance with UNCLOS. Absent that, in the words of Parrikar, "all of us will suffer, irrespective of whether we are big or small states."[6]

New Partnerships: The Military Implications of Non-compliance

In the context of the ruling in The Hague, which the Filipino government of Rodrigo Duterte ultimately sought not to pursue whole-heartedly, as he reset relations with Beijing, there are evidently ways to strengthen the legal regime that governs the law of the sea. These include implementation agreements, changes in interpretation, and adaptations of the rules of reference. There are also ways of strengthening the moral element, including through precedents. For example, valuable precedents were set between India and Bangladesh, and between Bangladesh and Myanmar in the Bay of Bengal. In recent years, the foreign ministers of both Vietnam and Australia have drawn attention to India's exemplary behaviour in resolving its maritime dispute with Bangladesh.

By comparison, less thought has traditionally been given to the military implications of non-compliance. One outcome of violations of freedom of navigation by state and non-state actors is deepening military partnerships among those countries that seek to uphold international norms.

What does that mean in practice? One is improving communication, cooperation and coordination. It Is about monitoring developments, summits, dialogues, and meetings, where relevant stakeholders from different countries can candidly share perspectives. The second is helping countries build each other's capacity to monitor and enforce maritime infractions. Such efforts are ongoing. India is both a beneficiary of capacity building assistance from the USA, Europe, Russia, and possibly, soon Japan, but it is also a provider to Vietnam, Myanmar, Bangladesh, Mauritius, Mozambique, Seychelles, Sri Lanka, the Maldives, and possibly soon Indonesia. Cooperation is also increasing two-way, as with Australia. The third is operations. Joint operations may still be a step too far for many countries, with implications for their political relationships, command structures, and comfort levels. But perhaps a deeper discussion is required about the impediments, including political impediments, costs, and risks associated with joint operations to enforce the law of the sea.

New Dynamics: Maritime Contests in the Indo-Pacific

Nonetheless, the important question remains: Who enforces violations of international law? In an anarchic international system, even one with well-defined laws, rules, norms, standards, and agreements, it is up to nation states to implement them, to impose them if necessary. Since 1945, the bedrock has been the U.S alliance structure. These alliances remain (as with Japan, Australia, and the Philippines), but are legacies. It is unlikely that such alliances in their current forms would be created today. Instead, a growing nexus of military partnerships is evolving. This transition, from a clear but contested order to a looser one with ambiguous leadership, is what raises concerns and questions.

Military partnerships will be crucial to the Indo-Pacific. If one were to draw an arc from Karachi to Bali and up to Sapporo, and circle back around, you encompass over half of humanity. Within this space, you have at least three major dynamics of maritime competition: One in the East China Sea, a second is the South China Sea, and a third is the Indian Ocean.

In the East China Sea, the disputes are territorial, but there is still a normative basis and no shortage of willing implementers of a rule-based order, including the USA, Japan, and South Korea. One challenge, related but not directly to freedom of navigation, relates to overflight, and there are overlapping Air Defence Identification Zones (ADIZ) between China, Japan, and South Korea.

The South China Sea is more problematic. The challenge is of one party claiming the territorial sea through a unilateral "Nine-Dash Line", while changing the facts on the ground through island building. Furthermore, there are serious questions about enforcement. Everyone is interested in freedom of navigation in principle, and a handful of countries are directly involved in contesting such unilateralism. But these countries may not have the ability or willingness to enforce non-compliance with international law, as recent examples involving the Philippines and Malaysia make clear.

A New Arena: The Indian Ocean

The Indian Ocean may represent the biggest challenge of the future. India wants to play a greater burden-sharing role in the Indian Ocean. Prime Minister Modi, along with President Trump, led their joint statement at their inaugural summit by highlighting India and the USA as "responsible stewards in the Indian Ocean".[7] This formulation is both interesting and important. While assuming responsibility, it is not exclusive. It is not just India's ocean, although India has obligations, vital national interests, and a nascent capability to play its role as a security provider. Naturally, India cannot do it all on its own, and needs cooperation to build capacity, get information, and improve operability with others. This necessitates deeper cooperation with the USA, Japan, Australia, Indonesia, Vietnam, Singapore, Bangladesh, Sri Lanka, Myanmar, and others.

The Indian Ocean is important for India and for the world.[8] It remains a major conduit for international trade, particularly energy trade, as well as the exchange of people and ideas. These reflect historical antecedents, including ancient and medieval trading networks that once linked Zanzibar to Muscat, Basra to Gujarat, the Coromandel coast to Aceh, and eastwards to Indochina, China's Pearl River Delta, and Nagasaki. But in more recent years, regional linkages have assumed modern characteristics as the global economy has developed. The Indian Ocean littoral is now home to some of the fastest-growing regions of the world, from South and Southeast Asia to East Africa and the Gulf.

At the same time, the Indian Ocean is under-governed. It remains vulnerable to natural disasters such as cyclones and tsunamis. It has several weak and fragile states along its coast. It still witnesses dangerous activities by non-state actors, from smugglers and traffickers to terrorists and pirates. And the region's institutional architecture, while much improved, is less well-developed than other maritime regions of the world.

It is amid this backdrop that the security of the Indian Ocean is undergoing significant changes in its security. The most significant change is the permanent entry into the Indian Ocean of the China's People's Liberation Army Navy (PLAN). As India's previous Navy Chief Sunil Lanba said in 2018:

> *Since 2008, there has been a permanent presence of the Chinese Navy in the Indian Ocean region in the form of an anti-piracy escort force. The 31st anti-piracy escort force is presently in the Gulf of Aden. So at any given time there are 6 to 8 Chinese navy ships in the northern part of the Indian Ocean. Also, two years ago they commissioned their first overseas facility, or base, in Djibouti.*
>
> *The stated aim of this deployment is to protect their trade, which is flowing through this area, from piracy. That included deployed submarines for anti-piracy operations, which is the most unlikely platform to be used for this role. There is no doubt they are spending a huge sum of money in developing their military capability. They are modernising their forces; they are modernising the command structure. And in my opinion, no navy has grown so rapidly in the last 200 years as the Chinese navy. They've added 80 new ships in the last five years. So, the Chinese navy is a force, and it is a force which is here to stay.*[9]

China's Navy is not the only one to have increased its footprints in the region. Japan's Maritime Self Defence Force is also operating regularly in the Indian Ocean, as is the case with the U.S. Navy, the maritime forces of several European powers, and Russia. The Indian Ocean is no longer just under-governed, it is increasingly contested. This presents new kinds of challenges for the regional navies, including the Indian Navy.

A New Role: India in the Indian Ocean

In response to these changes, the Indian Navy, – the Indian Ocean's most capable resident maritime force, has stepped up its operations, especially since 2017. It has been assisted by other elements of India's defence establishment, including the Coast Guard, Army, Air Force, space and cyber assets, military diplomacy, defence industry, and civilian agencies. Moreover, it has benefited tremendously from partnerships with other countries: both resident Indian Ocean states and partners among the major powers. There are at least five ways in which India—led by the Navy—is attempting to better manage security in the Indian Ocean.

The first is that since 2017, the Indian Navy has stepped up its patrols in the Indian Ocean. Seven zones were identified for permanent patrols by armed surface vessels, submarines, or aircraft: the Straits of Malacca, the Andaman and Nicobar Islands, the northern Bay of Bengal, the Lakshadweep Islands and the Maldives, the northern Arabian Sea, the Gulf of Aden, and the exclusive economic zones of Mauritius and the Seychelles. These mission-based deployments are a departure from the past, when the Navy participated in flag waving, port calls, or periodic visits for surveillance or other missions. The current efforts include coordinated patrols with local forces, whether with Myanmar, Thailand, Malaysia, or Indonesia, or other patrolling and security efforts in conjunction with Sri Lanka, the Maldives, Mauritius, and Seychelles. Such operations have also been bolstered by Indian humanitarian assistance and disaster relief (HADR), search and rescue, and evacuation operations. Over the past decade, India has executed or assisted in such operations in Myanmar, Sri Lanka, Bangladesh, Mozambique, and Yemen, among other places. The operational reach of the Indian Navy has also improved considerably with a host of bilateral agreements signed over the last few years, including with the USA, France, Singapore, and others. From Sabang in Indonesia to Salalah in Oman, the Indian armed forces today have unprecedented access across the Indian Ocean region.

The second area has involved improvements in maritime domain awareness (MDA). India has signed white shipping agreements—for sharing information about known commercial shipping—with over thirty countries. It recently established an information fusion centre, the Information Management and Analysis Centre (IMAC), in Gurugram, to link with similar centres in both Singapore and Madagascar. This would give a real-time and all-encompassing picture of the presence of vessels and other developments across the Indian Ocean. MDA coordination mechanisms with other countries—the Maldives, Mauritius, and the Seychelles—continue, and India has benefited from the acquisition of new platforms, such as P-8i maritime reconnaissance aircraft, which brings down the cost and efficiency of MDA activities.

A third major development has involved a host of new strategic coordination mechanisms, as well as the gradual development of new institutions for governing the Indian Ocean region. The evolution of the Indian Ocean Rim Association (IORA) and the Indian Ocean Naval Symposium (IONS) are well-known. But these are being buttressed by a network of bilateral and trilateral dialogues. These include configurations such as India-U.S.-Japan, India-Japan-Australia, and India-Indonesia-Australia, as well as quadrilateral conversations. Such coordination mechanisms extend to strategic assessments, working level information sharing, and infrastructure coordination activities.

A fourth development has been the growing interoperability between the Indian military and others. This is reflected in a large and growing number of military exercises involving armies, air forces, and navies. Today, India holds regular exercises of different scales and frequencies with almost every Indian Ocean littoral state, as well as the USA, Russia, Japan, China, France, and the United Kingdom. Breakthrough exercises with Indonesia, Vietnam, Singapore, and Australia are but some of the new changes reflected in this area. Such exercises have moved beyond basic passing exercises (PASSEX) to more sophisticated anti-submarine warfare and mid-air refuelling.

The final element of India's step-up in the Indian Ocean involves capacity building. This is reflected even in an area such as equipment, despite India's poor capabilities in that department. India has provided coastal radar systems, transport aircraft, and offshore patrol vessels (OPVs) to a number of smaller countries around the Indian Ocean basin. Training too has increased, particularly for South Asian and African countries; in Southeast Asia this extends to combat aircraft pilots and submarine sailors. And there is also the development of military and civilian infrastructure. Among other projects, India has helped develop a container port in Chabahar in Iran as well as a port in Sittwe in Myanmar, to linking them to the north-south connectivity infrastructure.

Additional infrastructure projects are being negotiated with other countries in the region, including island nations.

Taken together, all these developments reflect a significant change in India's presence and activities in the Indian Ocean, which are driven by both the traditional and non-traditional security dynamics that are changing the region's landscape. These efforts are largely cooperative in nature, based on transparency, sustainability, and consent. They are part of a broader effort to preserve the Indian Ocean as a free, open, and inclusive zone, one that witnesses dampened, rather than heightened, security competition.

Conclusion: A Distribution of Labour

India's evolving maritime posture in the Indian Ocean has wider implications for the region. It is in line with its role as a net security provider, and one that upholds international law in the maritime domain and not undermines it. The challenge is resources. India's potential to extend this role into other zones of the Indo-Pacific will be limited. But if it can do its share of burden-sharing, New Delhi will help free up resources for others to improve their enforcement capabilities in other contested regions, including in the East China Sea and South China Sea. Coordinating this distribution of labour ought to be a major focus of strategic consultations across the Indo-Pacific, including the various trilateral forums, and especially the quadrilateral security dialogue involving the USA, India, Japan, and Australia.

It is still possible for the international community, and particularly like-minded and democratic governments that believe in the rule of law, to successfully take a few important and outstanding steps. These include strengthening the legal basis for UNCLOS, improving the moral standing by highlighting successful precedents, better coordinating and sharing information, and helping each other build capacities to implement UNCLOS by military and non-military means. But even if these steps are taken, especially gradually, a continuing question will be whether these steps will be sufficient to preserve a notion of cooperation and justice in international maritime law.

NOTES

1. A semi-fictionalised version of these events is recounted in David Mitchell, *Cloud Atlas* (London: Hodder & Stoughton, 2004).
2. Pradeep Kaushiva and Abhijit Singh (eds), *Indian Ocean Challenges: A Quest for Cooperative Solutions* (New Delhi: KW Publishers, 2013).
3. Manohar Parrikar, "Speech of the Defence Minister Shri Manohar Parrikar at the Shangri-La Dialogue", 04 June 2016, available at https://idsa.in/resources/speech/defence-minister-manohar-parrikar-shangri-la-dialogue
4. Adapted from Dhruva Jaishankar, "China's South China Sea Setback," *ABP Live*, 12 July 2016, available at https://www.abplive.in/blog/chinas-south-china-sea-setback
5. "PCA Case No. 2013-19 Award: South China Sea Arbitration (The Republic of the Philippines vs. the People's Republic of China)," *Permanent Court of Arbitration (PCA)*, 12 July 2016, available at https://pca-cpa.org/en/news/pca-press-release-the-south-china-sea-arbitration-the-republic-of-the-philippines-v-the-peoples-republic-of-china/
6. Manohar Parrikar, "Speech of the Defence Minister Shri Manohar Parrikar at the Shangri-La Dialogue", 04 June 2016, available at https://idsa.in/resources/speech/defence-minister-manohar-parrikar-shangri-la-dialogue
7. Fact Sheets, "The United States and India: Prosperity Through Partnership," *The White House, U.S. Government*, 26 June 2017, available at https://www.whitehouse.gov/briefings-statements/united-states-india-prosperity-partnership/
8. Adapted from Dhruva Jaishankar, "India Steps Up: Securing the Indian Ocean Region," *Indian Ocean Conference, India Foundation*, 03 September 2019.
9. Press Trust of India, "Chinese navy a force which is here to stay: Navy Chief Lanba," *Economic Times*, 10 January 2019.

Index

*